THE URBAN CRISIS: PROBLEMS & PROSPECTS IN AMERICA

GOODYEAR SERIES IN AMERICAN SOCIETY
Jonathan H. Turner, Editor

INEQUALITY: PRIVILEGE & POVERTY IN AMERICA
Jonathan H. Turner and Charles E. Starnes

WOMEN IN AMERICA: THE OPPRESSED MAJORITY
Carol A. Whitehurst

THE URBAN CRISIS:
PROBLEMS & PROSPECTS IN AMERICA
Edgar W. Butler

Forthcoming volumes will include perspectives on:

Crime in America
Social Stratification in America
Marriage and the Family in America

THE URBAN CRISIS: PROBLEMS & PROSPECTS IN AMERICA

Edgar W. Butler
University of California

Goodyear Publishing Company, Inc. Santa Monica, California

Library of Congress Cataloging in Publication Data

Butler, Edgar W.
    The urban crisis.

    (Goodyear series in American Society)
    1. Cities and towns—United States.
I. Title.
HT123.B87   301.36′3′0973   76-21540
ISBN 0-87620-933-9
ISBN 0-87620-932-0 pbk.

Y-9320-6 (paper)
Y-9339-6 (case)

Current printing (last digit):
10 9 8 7 6 5 4 3 2 1

Printed in the United States of America

Designed by Don McQuiston

To Pattie, Brian, and Tracey Butler

CONTENTS

PREFACE

The Urban Crisis: Problems & Prospects in America was developed to provide a systematic approach to the study of urban problems in the United States. It shows how a variety of diverse phenomena are interrelated within the urban complex to urban problems. It demonstrates that the variety of areas within the city and the differences among cities are systematically related to urban problems. While the heaviest emphasis is placed on sociological research endeavors, research from other disciplines is utilized when appropriate. Whenever possible, tentative statements are made about future prospects in relation to the urban problems examined in this book. The presentation brings together a great diversity of urban problems and the research necessary to describe and to evaluate urban prospects in regards to these problems.

This book brings a vast array of research into a systematic framework that emphasizes how urbanization, variation among urban complexes in cities, and variation within urban places and cities are associated with urban problems. It emphasizes population composition, environment, technology, social organization in regards to cultural values, behavior, and attitudes—especially their spatial elements. The material in this book has been successfully used in urban problems courses at the University of North Carolina, Chapel Hill, and more recently at the University of California, Riverside.

My appreciation is extended to students who have helped me in examining my ideas about urban problems. I appreciate the contributions of Maurice D. Van Arsdol, Jr., Georges Sabagh, F. Stuart

Chapin, Jr., J. Richard Udry, Amos H. Hawley, Gerard J. Hunt, and John H. Freeman to my intellectual growth. I want to thank S. John Dackawich, who read an earlier draft and made valuable suggestions. I owe my very special appreciation to Patricia Newcomb and Alma Heyse; they have gone through the manuscript in meticulous detail and probably know it better than I do. Also, my thanks to Susan Steiner and Derek Gallagher at Goodyear Publishing Company for their invaluable assistance. Finally, I would like to express grateful appreciation to all those researchers and writers who granted permission to me to quote from their work; similarly, many other research endeavors were drawn upon in all sections of this book and I hope that I have done justice to them in appropriately citing them. Obviously, all of these people really made this book possible.

Edgar W. Butler
Idyllwild and Riverside, California
September, 1976

THE URBAN CRISIS: PROBLEMS & PROSPECTS IN AMERICA

PART I
INTRODUCTION

1
SOCIOLOGICAL APPROACHES TO URBAN PROBLEMS

INTRODUCTION

The study of social problems requires an understanding of the conditions that create those problems. Two approaches have dominated sociological approaches to social problems. One perspective stresses "objective conditions" (Merton and Nisbet, 1971). This view focuses on the distributions of a variety of phenomena, such as drug abuse, pollution, and mental illness. Another approach views problems from a "value-conflict" perspective.[1] Within this frame of reference, urban problems are what people think they are. Thus, only conditions defined by people as problems are problems.

Consistent with this latter perspective is the fact that not everyone in the United States agrees as to what is and is not an urban problem. In this book we will examine a variety of phenomena and conditions that have been considered as urban problems—mass society, alienation, population growth and differentiation within urban areas, urban segregation, population density and land use, social power and its use, government and services, slums, poverty, housing, mortality and illnesses, crime, suicide, riots and racial violence, environmental hazards, transportation, planning, and social policy.

These are what I believe to be the important problems facing cities and metropolitan areas in the United States. Some urban sociologists and many citizens would disagree with the view that some or all of these conditions are problems in cities or metropolitan areas of the United States. The point is that what conditions constitute a problem is socially determined and not a universal given.

To determine what constitutes an urban problem we must ask: "To whom are the conditions undesirable and by what values?" Some observers believe that drug and alcohol use are the major social problems; others believe that the breakdown of the nuclear family and divorce are the major problems facing the United States. Still others are most concerned about war, segregation in cities, or urban sprawl. The seriousness of each of these problems is a function of the values of the observer.

Problems are evaluated human behavior phenomena or conditions, and different people have different values. Although you and I may agree that some condition or behavior is a problem, it is only a meaningful problem if influentials and a large number of others consider it a problem. Most social scientists and many citizens believe that segregation of minorities in cities *is* a problem. However, many other citizens feel that the *real* problem is the tinkering of social scientists and militants who are trying to change a social system that has been devised to keep minorities "in their place."

After a decision has been made that a particular urban social problem does exist, those who have made that decision must decide whether to do anything about the problem. *If* the decision is to do something, they must decide what to do. Countless alternatives can be considered as viable solutions to any particular social problem. Here, too, values play an important part in determining what any particular individual will consider acceptable solutions to any given urban problem.

There does appear to be substantial agreement among social scientists that some types of problems are characteristic of cities and metropolitan areas in the United States. Many of these problems are the product of basic conditions in our society and so are found in virtually every large urban or metropolitan region in the United States. When patterns of undesirable conditions do not appear to be characteristic of any one metropolitan area but are widespread, probably something is wrong with the system. Types of problems that are broadly characteristic of contemporary metropolitan areas in the United States include: (1) indebtedness of local governments, (2) blight and slums, (3) inadequate housing, (4) economic dependence of a large segment of the population, (5) poorly financed and staffed schools—especially in the inner cities, (6) high delinquency and crime rates, (7) inadequate provisions for the mentally and physically ill, (8) the aged, (9) high unemployment, (10) bureaucratic competition for funds, (11) transportation and traffic congestion, (12) air pollution, (13) water pollution, and (14) inadequate waste disposal.

Recently Spector and Kitsuse (1973) examined an array of case studies concerned with urban problems in an attempt to delineate the process whereby some conditions come to be defined as a problem. As a result of their analysis, they proposed "a simple four-stage natural history model for the analysis of urban problems." These four stages are as follows:[2]

> *Stage 1: The attempts by some group(s) to assert the existence of some condition, define it as offensive, harmful, and otherwise undesirable, to publicize the assertions and stimulate controversy and to create a public or political issue over the matter.*
> *Stage 2: The recognition by some official organization, agency, or institution of the group(s) legitimate standing. This may lead to an official investigation of the matter, proposals for reform, and the establishment of an agency to respond to those claims and demands.*
> *Stage 3: The re-emergence of claims and demands by the group(s), expressing dissatisfaction with the established procedures for dealing with the imputed conditions, the bureaucratic handling of complaints, and the failure to generate a condition of trust and confidence in the procedures as sympathetic to the complaints, etc.*
> *Stage 4: The rejection by complainant group(s) of the response or lack of response of the agency or institution to their claims and demands, and the development of activities to create alternative, parallel, or counter-institutions as responses to the established procedures (p. 147).*

Stage one assumes that some group perceives and judges some condition(s) to be undesirable. Thus, initial activities related to a specific perceived condition are "to transform private troubles into public issues" (p. 148). Obviously, not all such attempts are successful. Spector and Kitsuse argue that the "objective seriousness" of the condition is not necessarily related to the relative success or failure of efforts to make these private troubles public issues. The process of making such claims into public issues is influenced by the social power of the group doing the complaining and, in some situations, by the interest of some powerful group or organization in the problem. In some instances, when it is not directly apparent who should redress the problem, the media may be of particular importance in transforming the private complaint into a public issue. If the private complaint does become a public issue, controversy usually results. Spector and Kitsuse assume that problems that become controversial public issues then move on to the next stage. However, it is possible, when a group is not successful in turning the private complaint into a public issue, that the process will move directly to stage four.

When an issue does become controversial, the process has entered stage two—"governmental agencies or other official and influential institutions to which claims might be put respond to the complaints of some group" (Spector and Kitsuse, 1973, pp. 151–152). Now the activity related to the social problem undergoes a considerable transformation. Recognition may range from passive acknowledgement of the claim to active attempts to control, regulate, or otherwise influence the problem. Of course, at this stage a problem may die or disappear. If it is to continue as a public issue, generally some mechanism is established whereby the condition can be dealt with. Stage two is complete when the routine for dealing with the condition has been institutionalized in the form of a bureaucracy or agency that is concerned with doing something about complaints, "though not necessarily dealing with the conditions the complaints are presumably about" (p. 154).

Stage three of this process may result in an amelioration of the original conditions. The problem may have been solved. However, the structure created in stage two may have been an unsuccessful attempt to solve the problem, or it may have been a cynical maneuver to define the complaint activity without solving the problem. Edelman (1967, p. 39) calls this "dissemination of symbolic satisfactions." This is a public relations approach, which tries to convince the original petitioners that their problem has been solved but does not actually deal with it. Spector and Kitsuse argue that there has been a transfer of complaints at this stage, with complaints now typically directed not against the original condition but against organizations and agencies institutionalized to overcome the original complaints. That is, the complaints are now directed against the ineffectual means being used by the organization to deal with the original problem. For example, Spector and Kitsuse note the following:

> Thus, the establishment of procedures in Stage Two provides for the routinization of claims; complaints about pollution are directed to the environmental control agency; claims about unfair business practices might be referred to the Better Business Bureau; complaints about suspected phone taps might be taken to the phone company or police. But Stage Three claims are generated when the environmental control agency itself is accused of licensing polluters of the environment, the Better Business Bureau is said to be in league with the local businessmen against consumers, or the phone taps asserted to be monitored by the phone company or police. That is, the complaints are against the very agencies that have been established to process the complaints in question. Stage Three activities may be intensified when responsibility for handling such claims are distributed among several agencies, creating a system of passing such claimants from one office to another, each of them denying responsibility for "that kind of problem" (pp. 155–156).

Almost invariably this process leads to a general distrust of institutional means of dealing with complaints about problems.

Finally, stage four is reached when mistrust and lack of action result in the feeling that there is no way to solve the problem within the current system. There are two approaches to going outside of the system. One is based upon the value orientations of those involved and of those who go outside of the system, attempting to construct alternatives and restructure society so that it can effectively deal with the problem. A second approach in stage four is to go outside of the system only in an attempt to structure alternatives that will appeal to those originally interested in solving the problem. Thus, this approach attempts to influence a more limited number of people and does not require the restructuring of society.

It should be apparent that limiting an analysis of urban social problems to conditions that already have become issues results in a limited world view. Currently, some conditions are ignored by social scientists and citizens alike, even though those conditions may be adversely affecting the population and the environment. In addition, there probably are other current conditions that virtually everyone is unaware of that in the future will become vital urban problem issues. It does appear that there are points in time when a condition becomes an issue or urban problem, yet these conditions may have existed prior to that time and adversely affected the population and/or environment. Thus, it is likely that at some future time conditions now present will be recognized by the public as urban problems. The current concern with the environment is one such example; another is with a specific segment of the environment—the air we breathe. Air pollution is a Johnny-come-lately issue that only emerged as a primary concern in the late 1960s and 1970s. Yet the literature going back several decades prior to that time attempted to alert the public about the condition and its adverse affect. Similarly, the use of tobacco, presumably since its first manufacture into cigarettes, has had potentially dire health consequences for heavy users. In England (as an example) extensive public warnings of such potential dire consequences has been mandatory for several decades; however, in the United States such precautionary warnings have been mandatory only for several years and exist only on the product or in advertising. Thus, the concern varies between the two countries and apparently is unrelated to the actual health hazard, which has remained constant.

So it appears that any really meaningful appraisal of what constitutes an urban problem must consider (1) the actual conditions (when we are aware of them), (2) how people differentially evaluate the seriousness of those conditions (if they are aware of them), and (3) what people believe should be done about those conditions—if anything. After all, one could be aware of air pollution, be aware of its health consequences, and yet believe that nothing should be done about it!

Urban problems can be considered as part of a dynamic society. Or each problem can be taken out of its situational context and treated in isolation from the basic societal conditions that produced it. So far, the latter approach has been used. Many contemporary urban problems in the United States probably are not solvable at the local level or on an individual problem basis. In dealing with these problems, local effort has made little headway against the tide of the larger society. Some urban problems have developed as a result of the loss of local autonomy to the larger society—including corporations, state government, and the federal government. When resources and interest are sufficient, this second group of problems can be handled at the local level. Factors working against the mediation of many urban problems are: lack of identification with the local community, apathy, residential mobility, and alienation or anomia.

In the contemporary United States, there is disagreement about whether some problems exist and about what society can and should do about them. Clearly, in some instances, the proposed solutions to a problem—busing and school racial segregation—have created additional problems that need to be solved. Often such solutions create more difficulties than they eliminate. It should be noted that some people believe that most contemporary urban problems in the United States are too large and complex to be solved. Others believe that, since human nature cannot be changed, we should leave the conditions alone.

Finally, it should be noted that despite the voluminous literature concerned with urban problems, the public is unaware of the extent of current urban problems in the United States and unaware of alternative solutions for them. Further, it appears that there is a lack of willingness to undergo social change to solve urban problems. Accordingly, we can expect most of these urban problems to be with us well into the future. *Perhaps apathy is human nature and a problem in itself!*

FRAME OF REFERENCE

Throughout the remainder of this book, the two orientations discussed will be used to facilitate understanding of urban problems in the United States.[3] Both of these orientations sensitize us to observe certain conditions that are considered urban problems in our society. Neither of them fit or help describe urban problems in their entirety. The systematic approach used in this book allows the utilization of each of these two approaches when each is appropriate to the urban problem under discussion.

Although, at first glance, the systematic framework used in this book may appear to be rather simple, that appearance is deceiving. It is deceptive mainly because it is possible, in any given theory or research effort oriented toward a specific condition of urban society, to utilize more specifically generated propositions (although even in these more limited approaches this is not often accomplished), hypotheses, and a specific research method. However, in a textbook of this nature, a broader frame of reference is necessary so that several orientations and research methods can be drawn upon. The orientation of this volume is, as far as possible, to fit systematically, in each topical area under discussion, the following: (1) the objective conditions that exist, including variations *among* urban complexes and cities and variations *within* urban places and cities; and (2) perceptions of the problem, proposed solutions, and citizen views of them.

Emphasis is placed on the *spatial distributions* of urban problems. The focus on spatial distributions is not necessarily one that requires "geographical determinism" or attributing "cause" to such distributions. However, there can be no denial of two factors related to spatial distributions. First, virtually all phenomena associated with urbanization, urbanism among and within cities, and urban places are differentially distributed in space. Thus, space becomes one organizing element along which phenomena can be viewed. Second, any adequate theoretical explanation of human behavior in urban environments has to account for the differential spatial distribution of phenomena (Butler, 1976).

Many also will detect an emphasis on the *temporal* facets of urban problems. The temporal receives less emphasis and is less discernable at points only because the theoretical and research effort by social scientists to date is not as substantial or as advanced and thus there is less material to draw upon. Future work in the temporal aspects of urban problems will add substantially to the knowledge base utilized in this book and will allow expanded discussion and analysis.

In summary, this volume fits a vast array of studies into a systematic framework that primarily, but not exclusively, emphasizes objective evaluation and perceptual observation of urban problems as well as their impact, variation among urban complexes and cities and within urban places and cities. In addition, factors such as population composition, social organization, environment, technology, cultural values, behavior, and attitudes—especially the spatial element—will be considered. Similarly, there is an emphasis on the temporal aspects of urban problems as they are affected by and affect these other factors.

A NOTE ON RESEARCH METHODS

In carrying out analyses of urban problems, a variety of research methods and techniques have been used. Research methods have included: participant observation, such as the Liebow (1967) and Hannerz (1969) studies of segregated black life in Washington, D.C.; surveys of various populations, such as the Middletown Study of Mental Health in the Metropolis (Srole et al., 1962); and the use of secondary sources of data in poverty and housing (Duncan and Reiss, 1956). These research endeavors range from descriptions of urban problems in one area within an urban complex to very sophisticated statistical analyses of places all over the United States. In other words, the use of methods and techniques is highly variable. Anyone concerned with urban problems must be at least aware of a large number of research methods.

One of the most basic problems in urban research is the definition and delineation of adequate and meaningful geographic units of analysis (Eldridge, 1956). Urban problems has been varied with research analysis in the United States focusing on states, counties, standard metropolitan statistical areas, cities, census tracts,[4] enumeration districts, block groups in which there are subdivisions of census tracts, and other kinds of units. Some authors have argued that these are artificial units and the units of analysis should be "natural areas" (Hatt, 1946).

The major source of statistical data to date has been the U.S. census, which is conducted every ten years. A variety of other kinds of data is gathered by various agencies of the federal government, and these also are made available on a systematic basis. There are many administrative statistics available for some jurisdictions, including political administrative units, educational districts, and vital statistic areas. Survey data are available for certain samples of the population through private and governmental facilities. Another major source of urban problems data are locally conducted surveys of agencies.

Currently, there is a need for persons concerned with urban problems to be more acutely aware of the time dimension, that is, to carry out longitudinal as opposed to cross-sectional studies. Although some current statistical techniques appear to be highly sophisticated, they are hardly developed in the areas of measuring change- or time-related statistics (Duncan et al., 1961). In longitudinal studies, the time dimension is important also because they involve the conflict between studying natural areas vs. comparable areas over time as defined by the census of other political bodies.

There is a need to go beyond case studies and focus on comparative studies. For example, rather than studying air pollution or crime in one urban place, it would be useful to know how these conditions differ (if indeed they do) according to some structural urban base such as the division of labor or income level. Related to all of the comments made so far, there is a parochial focus on the United States, with a neglect of cross-cultural studies. How useful is an urban problems perspective based on the experience of the United States? As an example, in most cities in the United States, the poor tend to live in transitional zones near the central business district (CBD) whereas in other contemporary cities—for example, Raleigh, North Carolina and Riverside, California—they live to some degree in the outer city or on the periphery. How do we account for these empirical differences? Our concern here, then, is a theoretical and methodological one: Can one legitimately generalize from localized (United States based) case studies to other nations? In other words, is there any *external validity* in generalizations based on the United States experience? Here we face head on the problem of proper units of analysis, the time dimension, and generality of findings.

Little work has been accomplished to date dealing with the ecological context or situations of persons holding different attitudes about urban problems. Contextual studies are concerned with a central controversy in the social sciences, that is, how can we separate *individual* from *structural* or *contextual* effects on attitudes and behavior? This is a level of analysis problem. In this book I utilize studies of individuals and census tracts, through larger units such as cities and larger urban complexes. Robinson (1950, but also see a rebuttal by Menzel, 1950) has argued that the social sciences can advance only on the basis of concepts and empirical observations based on descriptive properties of individuals, such as height, income, color, or race. In this book, I am concerned with the individuals as well as their contexts—cities, urban complexes, and census tracts. This may seem to be a minor problem, but it actually gets at the very basis of many differences that currently divide social scientists. Are organizations, cities, census tracts, groups, and so on, useful units of analysis in analyzing urban problems, or can we deal only with individuals? In this book, I assume that all of these aspects of urban problems are useful and utilize all of them. There also is the problem of how to interrelate various data sets—for example, data obtained in a survey with census data and with other kinds of information, such as citizen perception of a problem (for a good example related to air pollution see Van Arsdol et al., 1964).

The above perspectives are highly varied. As a result, different research methods and techniques and different theoretical and conceptual approaches to phenomena are used. This, of course, is the problem of all sciences: What are we studying and what approach will we take? Are we going to study objective conditions or attitudes and perceptions related to specific conditions? In this volume we are going to do both, and we will draw on a variety of studies from all of the methodological perspectives noted above.

NOTES

1. For early references from this perspective, see Fuller and Myers (1941) and Becker (1966). For more recent expositions, see Kitsuse and Spector (1973) and Spector and Kitsuse (1973).

2. Quotations from Spector and Kitsuse (1973) are reprinted with the permission of the authors and The Society for the Study of Social Problems. Copyright © 1973 by *Social Problems*.

3. Some may criticize this book because it substantially ignores other societies. This is a deliberate omission. In my opinion, there is so little material available on urban problems in the United States that it is premature to carry out a cross-cultural urban problems analysis. However, this book lays the groundwork for cross-cultural comparisons of urban problems, and I urge students to examine cross-cultural studies when they are available.

4. *Census tracts.* For statistical purposes, large cities and metropolitan areas have been divided into small areas, called census tracts. Tract boundaries generally were established cooperatively by a local committee and the Bureau of the Census. They were designed to achieve uniformity of population characteristics, economic status, and living conditions. Initially, an average tract had about 4,000 residents. Officials

intended that tract boundaries would be maintained over a long time so that comparisons could be made from census to census.

REFERENCES

Becker, Howard S. "Introduction." In *Social Problems: A Modern Approach*. New York: Wiley, 1966.

Butler, Edgar W. *Urban Sociology: A Systematic Approach*. New York: Harper and Row, 1976.

Duncan, Otis Dudley, and Albert J. Reiss, Jr. *Social Characteristics of Urban and Rural Communities, 1950*. New York: Wiley, 1956.

Duncan, Otis Dudley, Ray P. Cuzzort, and Beverly Duncan. *Statistical Geography: Problems in Analyzing Areal Data*. Glencoe: Free Press, 1961.

Edelman, Murray. *The Symbolic Use of Politics*. Urbana: University of Illinois Press, 1967.

Eldridge, Hope Tisdale. "The Process of Urbanization." In *Demographic Analysis*, edited by J. J. Spengler and Otis Dudley Duncan. Glencoe: Free Press, 1956, pp. 338–343.

Fuller, Richard, and Richard Myers. "The Natural History of a Social Problem." *American Sociological Review* 3 (1941):24–32.

Hannerz, Ulf. *Soulside: Inquiries into Ghetto Culture and Community*. New York: Columbia University Press, 1969.

Hatt, Paul. "The Concept of Natural Area." *American Sociological Review* 11 (August 1946):423–427.

Kitsuse, John I., and Malcolm Spector. "Toward a Sociology of Social Problems: Social Conditions, Value-Judgments, and Social Problems." *Social Problems* 20 (Spring 1973): 407–419.

Liebow, Elliot. *Tally's Corner*. Boston: Little, Brown, 1967.

Menzel, Herbert. "Comments on Robinson's Ecological Correlations and the Behavior of Individuals." *American Sociological Review* 15 (October 1950):674.

Merton, Robert K., and Robert A. Nisbet. *Social Problems*. 3rd ed. New York: Harcourt, Brace and World, 1971.

Robinson, William S. "Ecological Correlations and the Behavior of Individuals." *American Sociological Review* 15 (June 1950):351–357.

Spector, Malcolm, and John I. Kitsuse. "Social Problems: A Re-Formulation." *Social Problems* 21 (Fall 1973):145–159.

Srole, Leo, Thomas S. Langner, Stanley T. Michael, Marvin K. Opler, and Thomas A. C. Rennie. *Mental Health in the Metropolis: The Midtown Manhattan Study*. New York: McGraw-Hill, 1962.

Van Arsdol, Jr., Maurice D., Georges Sabagh, and Francesca Alexander. "Reality and the Perceptions of Environmental Hazards." *Journal of Health and Human Behavior* 4 (Winter 1964):144–153.

2
MASS SOCIETY
AND ALIENATION

INTRODUCTION[1]

Prevalent today is the notion of alienation[2] of man from society. Many social scientists believe that alienation is exacerbated by life in the contemporary urbanized United States. This perspective assumes that urban life creates solitary souls, uproots individuals from their customs, results in a social void, and weakens traditional restraints on personal behavior. Personal existence and social solidarity in urban society hang together by a slender thread. There is a feeling that relations between people are based on economics. Relations between people are thought of as being disturbed by a multitude of forces over which individuals have little or no control. This has led to a sense of individual helplessness and a feeling of despair and estrangement from society—to what many call alienation (Josephson and Josephson, 1962).

The alienated person is unstable, inadequate, and insecure because he is cut off from the channels of social membership and clear beliefs. Further, rapid change and dislocation in society are followed by an increasing scale of personal disorganization. These dislocations and changes are in conflict with the desire for cultural participation, social belonging, and personal status. Very clearly in existence here is a postulated conflict between what has been called community—the family, the religious association, and local neighborhood, and the intimate relationships generally found there—and the release of the individual from the boundaries of community and the extensive freedom gained by this release. A concomitant of this release from community is the isolation of the individual from his cultural heritage, the isolation of individuals from others, and the creation of an alienated, sprawling, faceless mass—the mass society.

Nisbet (1953) suggests that "increasingly, individuals seek escape from the freedom of impersonality, secularism, and individualism." They look for community in marriage, they look for it in attachment rather than commitment to religion, they look for it on the psychiatrist's couch, in cults, and in pseudointimacies with others. A question of utmost importance, then, is "Where are people going to find status and security?" Some find status and community in the primary associations of family, neighborhood, and church. Others find status and community in large-scale organizations. Still others may have economic security and ultimate freedom from constraints but few intimate, personal relationships.

The major element of alienation in the view of mass society outlined above is the isolation of individuals from meaningful social participation. The isolation of individuals from meaningful social contacts is presumed to be related to alienation of individuals from society. Let us look first at the advantages and disadvantages of mass society.

MASS SOCIETY

Most social scientists associate the increase in alienation with the development of industrialization and mass society. Mass society is characterized by the evaporation of moral bonds, the shriveling of kinship and traditional institutions and beliefs, and the isolation of the individual from his fellows. This characterization describes modern Western society, including the United States (Shils, 1960). Further, a mass society is territorially extensive, has a large population, and is highly urbanized and industrialized. Social power is highly concentrated, and the mass media exercise much of that power in their manipulation of the population. Civic spirit is poor, local loyalties are few, and basic social solidarity is nonexistent. There is no individuality, only egotism, and the isolation of individuals in mass society results in extremist responses (Gusfield, 1962). Some of the characteristics of mass society have led to conditions that some people believe are responsible for the urban problems that exist in the United States.

Shils (1960) has pointed out another relatively neglected perspective on mass society. This view brings together the mass society and the neighborhood or community (Wilensky, 1964) and evaluates both the negative and positive aspects of mass society. According to this perspective, a mass society has a nationwide market economy dominated by large nationwide (and multinational) corporations and by central governmental regulations, or it has a socialist planned economy. In either situation the results include a higher level of educational attainment, a higher degree of literacy, and a greater availability of cultural products (such as newspapers, television, and records) than in smaller societies. In mass societies, culture, which used to be available only to a small elite, is available to almost everyone. Mass society and the spread of mass culture have facilitated common citizenship extending over a vast territory, such as the United States. Thus, the confines of kinship, caste, religious belief, and feudal boundaries have been broken down. Alienation is one of the negative results of this breakdown.

A mass society, in contrast to traditional society, requires a substantial consensus about the central institutions of society. Despite internal conflicts in the mass society there is more sense of attachment to the society, more sense of affinity with one's fellows, more openness to understanding, and more reaching out of understanding among people than at any point in earlier history. While mass society is not the most peaceful or orderly society that has ever existed, it is the most consensual. Even today, of course, the elite and the masses do not have identical life styles, tastes, or outlooks, but the mass has more influence now than it did previously.

As a result of the growth of mass society, especially between World Wars I and II, authority structures have changed markedly. Formerly, the authority hierarchy had direct traditional control over citizens. Traditions continue to exert influence but they are less important now than formerly, more ambiguous, and more open to divergent interpretations. For example, more alternative life styles now exist. They are both the product of mass society and part of the problems that have arisen out of mass society. In any case, in earlier society, such divergent life styles were not tolerated and had to be participated in covertly. The increased freedom and awareness of rights by the working classes, women, youth, and ethnic groups are products of mass society and creators of special and unique problems. The dispersion of mass culture to a whole variety of ethnic groups and peoples was made possible by the increased stress on individual dignity and rights in mass society. Obviously, inequalities remain, but the inequalities are much less severe in mass society than in traditional society. Individuality, meaningful personal relationships, and love, while not discovered by mass society, have come to be regarded as part of the rights of every individual.

Some believe that mass society has resulted in a loss of individuality by creating dull acceptance of what is readily available. Since what is readily available is widespread, the result is mass mediocrity. However, mass society presents more choices than existed previously and the individual's choices are not determined only by tradition, authority, and scarcity.

Mass society is a welfare society. This means that the society is concerned with its members' well-being. This attitude is not necessarily related to industrialization or poverty. It is only in mass society that poverty can be considered as needing redress because there is concern for the well-being of others.

To some extent the alienation that is believed to exist in mass society is related to the nature of industrialized work. In earlier societies people did not have time to be alienated. The individual's survival was dependent upon how successfully he worked at hunting, farming, and so on. Without industrialization, mass society would not be possible and the elaborate networks of communication and transportation would not be possible. The communication and transportation networks allow heightened mutual awareness of well-being. Concern for others in mass society has enlarged the internal population that individuals consider themselves part of, for example, national and international. By-products of industrialization are the intellectual professions and the educational system. Although deficiencies exist in the educational system, mass society opened up the educational system to virtually the entire population and has made people more aware of the experiences of their fellow human beings.

This view of mass society differs from the view that presents mass society as characterized by alienation, lack of faith, atomization, amorality, conformity, rootless homogeneity, moral emptiness, facelessness, egotism, and the lack of loyalty. All of these characteristics do exist in mass society, but there are also many others. Mass society arose out of a society that was inegalitarian, against a background of puritanical authority, local allegiance, traditional authority and social control, and unbelievable poverty and drudgery. Thus, modern urban life is very different from earlier societies.

Early sociologists pictured the megalopolis—the mass city—as culturally heterogeneous, dominated by bureaucratic structures and mass media, and destructive of the smaller units of society. More recently, however, the importance of organizations and social interaction in mediating the relationship of isolated individuals to the mass society has been stressed (Nisbet, 1953). Current literature emphasizes that the contemporary metropolis consists of a variety of geographic areas that are variable in the extent to which they have organizations and social interaction patterns that mediate between the individual and mass society. Mediating relationships consist of informal social groups (such as sewing circles, peer groups, neighbors, friends, and relatives) and formal organizations (such as service organizations, child-oriented organizations, and church groups).

URBANIZATION AND THE MASS SOCIETY
The trend toward a mass society began with the Industrial Revolution. Changing technology created more efficient forms of transportation. The movement of vast numbers of people from one country to another and from the rural areas to cities made it more difficult to form and maintain the highly integrated forms of social existence that

are possible in isolated areas and small villages. Similarly, changes in traditional institutions, such as the family and church, reduced some of their impact and influence and increased the influence of the larger, impersonal community.

Improvements in transportation and production resulted in loss of the basic economic security associated with ownership of a plot of land. As a result of industrialization, labor became just another cog in the production of goods, and workers felt a loss of individuality. Social aspects of the change from a folk society to a mass society are evident in the great migrations from the countryside to cities, the separation of workplace and residence, the formation of increasingly large and complex settlements, the changing functions of the family, the changing functions of the church and other institutions of society (Rose, 1967, pp. 181–212), and the loss of community.

COMMUNITY AND THE NEIGHBORHOOD

Community is as widely used as any term in the professional vocabulary of sociologists. Yet no one knows as well as sociologists how ill-defined and imprecise the concept really is. Hillery (1955) measured the depths of confusion over this concept by examining a wide variety of definitions. Out of his work comes the conclusion that definitions of community are almost as varied as the number of persons dealing with the concept. Nevertheless, its extensive use shows that it describes something that many people see as important. "Neighborhoods, suburban municipalities, and central cities, as well as the monastery and beehive, are spoken of as communities" (Bollens and Schmandt, 1965, p. 44). Hawley's (1950, pp. 157–258) definition of community as that area in which the resident population is interrelated and integrated with reference to its daily requirements, whether contacts be direct or indirect, is closely allied to another concept extensively employed—that of the neighborhood.

Neighborhood is the most frequently identified meaningful social unit in mass society (Thomlinson, 1969, p. 181). Neighborhoods in mass society are important because (1) they are persistent forces affecting the personality and behavior of residents and (2) the character of a neighborhood is determined by its inhabitants.[3] Not all areas within a metropolis or urban region qualify as neighborhoods. Definitions of neighborhood usually involve at least three elements: (1) spatial proximity to some focus of attention, (2) physical or cultural differentiation from surrounding areas, and (3) intimacy of association among inhabitants of an area.[4]

Some believe that the traditional neighborhood is disappearing; others believe that neighborhoods and neighboring are merely developing into different forms. Where neighborhoods exist, they affect the personality and behavior of residents (Thomlinson, 1969, p. 181). Also, it has been noted that the reverse is true: The character of a neighborhood is determined by its inhabitants. To be a neighborhood, an area must have a commonly accepted name and must be known by the residents of the area as well as by many people residing elsewhere in the metropolis. Generally there is some discrepancy as to actual boundaries of the neighborhood, except when such boundaries are formed by barriers such as parks, rivers, and large streets. Names of neighborhoods generally have class and ethnic connotations. Most sections of cities—and large portions of many cities—do not have neighborhoods in the standard sense (Thomlinson, 1969, p. 182). Rather, they are areas with an aggregation of individuals.

SOCIAL AND ORGANIZATIONAL PARTICIPATION
According to many early ecologists and sociologists, heterogeneity, specialization, anonymity, formality, and impermanence characterize urban life. More recently it has been recognized that there are many relatively stable, enduring, and highly structured relationships in all sections of the urban complex. Urban people have primary as well as impersonal and segmental social relations. Among primary relations, kin, neighbors, and friends are the most important. Each of these also may form a mutual aid network, although kin are the most likely to be systematically included in such a network. The social networks of urban dwellers are highly complex and include relations both within and outside the neighborhood and community of residence.

In addition to kin, neighbors, and friends, voluntary association participation is important to many individuals. Such participation may act effectively as a mediator between the individual and society. However, there is general agreement that informal social participation with relatives, friends, neighbors, peer groups, and so on is more important for most individuals. It has been argued that if an individual participates in informal groups, it does not matter if that person does not belong to voluntary associations. However, a number of studies report that many individuals participate extensively in both informal groups and in organizations.

Kinship Networks
Kinship networks are the web of relationships that exist among familial statuses. Generally, they are characterized by long-term, relatively permanent ties, and by mutual aid; they play an important role in shaping the value systems and behavior patterns of individual members. Kinship networks ordinarily are bound by affectional ties, although certainly the influence of habits established in early childhood years are important.

The relationship between urbanization and family structure ordinarily assumes that pressures of urban living discourage traditional extended family systems and encourage the modern conjugal or nuclear family—that is, the father, mother, and their children. The contemporary United States family kinship system has been called by some the "modified extended family," because a number of nuclear families—even though not living with either the wife's or husband's kin—are able to maintain social ties, mutual aid, contact by telephone and letter, and visits by automobile and airplane, despite long distances.

Studies concerned with the prevalence of kinship patterns among urban families consistently report that visits with relatives substantially exceed visits to friends or neighbors, and this extensive visiting with relatives occurs at all social-class levels (Axelrod, 1956). Because of less long-distance migration, working-class kin networks are generally less scattered geographically and kin, therefore, are more available for frequent interaction (Young and Willmott, 1957). Nevertheless, there remains a controversy over which social class visits relatives most often. Dotson (1951) reports that in New Haven, Connecticut, working-class families visit most members of their larger kinship group—brothers, sisters, cousins, and in-laws, both in the immediate neighborhood and in other areas of the metropolitan complex. Further, he reports that the total participation pattern for almost a third of his sample consisted exclusively of kinship. In well over half, kinship relationships represented the major feature of their social life.

Another study suggests that among white Protestant, middle-class families, strong affectional and economic ties continue to exist between middle-aged parents and their children. Mutual aid assistance such as gifts, loans, baby-sitting, and nursing care during illnesses or childbirth are exchanged by a vast majority of families; further, sons are given opportunities in the family business (Sussman, 1953; Litwak and Szelenyi, 1969). Middle-class parents have widespread involvement in activities, such as PTAs, music lessons, Boy and Girl Scouts, and so on, that they believe are related to the status and welfare of their children. Finally, Warner and Lunt (1941), in a study of Newburyport, Massachusetts, report that upper-class families maintain close ties to their extended family.

Social participation with relatives in the inner city black ghetto (Winston Street, District of Columbia) is rather extensive (Hannerz, 1969). Similarly, well over half of the adults and teen-agers in another black ghetto (Near Northeast, District of Columbia) have three or more households of relatives living in the District and visit them often (Chapin, et al., forthcoming). Feagin (1968) reported that 84 percent of Boston inner city blacks had relatives in the metropolitan area. Similar percentages of inner city blacks having relatives nearby were reported in Philadelphia (Blumberg and Bell, 1959) and Highland Park, Michigan (Meadow, 1965).

Scanzoni (1971, p. 135) notes that aid received by black relatives from kin is primarily financial (60 percent) and the remainder is advice and counsel. On the other hand, Feagin (1968, p. 663) reports that 24 percent of Boston blacks received aid such as financial assistance, business advice, and help when someone was ill in the family; 22 percent reported giving such mutual aid. He further noted that 48 percent of families had received aid from their kinsmen in moving into their current places of residence. Generally, women's kinship ties exceed men's, and women report more interaction and feel closer to their kin than do men (Booth, 1972).

In summary, kinship networks are of particular significance for working-class families, ethnic populations who continue to identify as ethnic, women, and upper-class families. All of the evidence suggests that most people in contemporary urban United States continue to have strong kinship ties.

Neighboring and Friendship Patterns

Prevailing urban folklore is that little neighboring and informal visiting takes place in metropolitan centers. Nevertheless, there is ample evidence that substantial neighboring and friend-visiting takes place in contemporary metropolitan centers. Neighborhood and friend interaction are influenced by a variety of factors. Ecological position and neighborhood character, demographic composition and structural characteristics of people in the neighborhood, and social psychological factors all have some impact upon neighboring and friendship patterns. Friends, who may not necessarily live in the local neighborhood, are typically similar in sex, age, social class, ethnic background, and religion. Church affiliation, particularly among blacks and middle-class whites, is an important factor in generating close ties among some people. For some adults, work or profession is important in forming friendship ties, and, in other instances, neighbors and friends are the same.

In general, contacts with neighbors, friends, and co-workers tend to increase with social class. Dotson (1951) reported that most working-class families in New Haven rarely visit outside of their kinship network, although a few have strong neighborhood ties. In Detroit, only one-third of lower-class persons visit with friends at least a few times a month, whereas three-fifths of upper-class people visit at least that often (Axelrod, 1956). In Lansing, Michigan, friends are about equally divided between neighbors and nonneighbors, with close neighborhood friendship patterns more prevalent in middle and higher social-class areas than in lower social-class areas. Similarly, lower-class individuals in Evanston, Illinois, had fewer intimate friends and engaged in less visiting among friends than middle- and upper-class persons in that city (Reissman, 1954). Further, lower-class persons in Evanston tended to limit their social interaction more to immediate kin and the local neighborhood.

Black friendship patterns have been reported to vary by life styles, as well as by neighborhood (Hannerz, 1969). In the black Near Northeast neighborhood of the District of Columbia (Chapin, et al., forthcoming) there are some persons who are virtually complete social isolates, and others have friends only outside of the neighborhood. In the Near Northeast, about two-thirds of teenagers' best friends live in the neighborhood. On the other hand, only about 30 percent of adults' best friends live in the neighborhood. Adults have a wider geographical range than teenagers—adults have friends throughout the entire Washington metropolitan area. From this study, it appears that adults have a greater choice than teenagers for friends, because many of them have been freed from spatial limitations. There is some indication that more recent inmovers have a higher interaction rate with friends than persons who have lived in the neighborhood for a longer period of time (Feagin, 1970, p. 307). In St. Louis it appears that black neighborhoods high in familism also have greater neighborliness (Nohara, 1968).

Ethnic populations other than blacks have been studied. For example, second-generation, lower-class, Italian-Americans living in an ethnic neighborhood of New York City have more friends and more close friends than first-generation persons. Second-generation Italian-Americans have a wider range of social contacts with people at work and in other formal situations, and that increases the chances of learning urban values and of having the opportunity to develop friendships. In addition, most second-generation Italian-Americans have a better command of the English language and an orientation toward activities outside of the family setting (Palisi, 1966). On the other hand, when ethnic heritage of friends was examined by generation, friends of different generations did not vary by ethnicity, since virtually all of them were Italian. This is probably accounted for by the ethnic homogeneity of the neighborhood and the fact that residential proximity is related to the development of close and intimate friendship ties.

Similarly, Gans (1962) has shown how the social life of West End Boston Italians revolves around peer groups. Peer groups consist primarily of compatible kinsmen and friends of similar age, social class, and specific interest. They meet in homes, and most interaction consists of discussing celebrations, weddings, neighborhood activities, child-rearing practices, housekeeping, and gossip. Peer groups serve as an important integrating mechanism for the people in this community, and while they take away some privacy, individuals prefer these peer groups and do not like being alone.

More females than males visit with neighbors on a daily basis (Berado, 1966, p. 301). Also, it appears that white-collar husbands are more likely than wives to initiate and maintain mutual friendships and to have more close friends (Booth, 1972). Children in Lakewood, a suburb of Los Angeles, neighbor more than their parents, and men in this particular suburb tend to neighbor where their wives neighbored previously (Riemer, 1959, p. 440). Nevertheless, women—even when employed—see friends more often than men. Also, women do more visiting outside the neighborhood than do men (Butler, et al., 1973, p. 222). In addition, female friendships are richer in spontaneity and confidences, and women do more things together on the spur of the moment. On the other hand, men have more friends of the opposite sex than do women.

Especially for females, there are competitive factors for neighboring and friends, such as working status. The working female typically has less time available than the nonworking female, and the time she does have is more likely to be devoted to her family than in establishing friendships or visiting with neighbors (Meadow, 1965, p. 180; also see Greer and Kube, 1959). As with kin, there appears to be a wide variety of neighboring and friendship patterns, and most people visit with neighbors and friends.

Voluntary Organization Participation

Voluntary associations are highly specialized and explicitly organized groups composed of persons with a common interest that is not satisfied by individual behavior or by already existing forms of social interaction. In most instances, membership is voluntary and entrance and withdrawal are dependent upon personal decisions of interest.

Formal organizations have several functions: (1) to confer social status on individual members, (2) to give security and mutual support, and (3) to provide a link that connects the individual with the larger society, thus facilitating his adjustment to the social milieu. Formal organizations represent a wide range of human activities, including professional, veterans, social, civic-service, cultural, and of course, religious and political. Every major study of formal organization participation in the United States reports a large number of organizations available to the population, and the extent and variety of these organizations has led to the characterization of the United States as a nation of joiners.

Voluntary organizations have developed and attracted members for a variety of reasons. Some urbanites join voluntary associations because of interests in literature, taxes, the poor, personal status, and to enhance the opportunity for social mobility. Others do not have personal contacts elsewhere and they use voluntary associations to interact with others who have similar interests. Available literature shows that some people belong to many organizations while others do not belong at all. Only a few members of each organization attend every meeting and become intimately involved. This core of active participants tends to be made up of longer-term members.

Formal organizations have been classified into two major types, the expressive and instrumental (Rose, 1953, pp. 55–66). *Expressive* organizations provide opportunities for self-expression, creativity, and exchange of ideas, and are directed toward limited fields of interest. They include hobby clubs, literary societies, fraternal lodges, veterans' organizations, and book clubs. *Instrumental* organizations are concerned with influencing other persons and organizations. They include political organizations, lobbying groups, taxpayers' associations, educational, professional, and medical organizations, and social action organizations (also see Bell and Force, 1956).

One major factor in differential voluntary association participation is status or social class. Middle and upper social classes have much greater involvement in associations than lower social class individuals. These differences by social class persist no matter which indicator is selected to measure it—salary (Freeman, et al., 1957), income, education, occupation, subjective identification with a social class, or social rank of neighborhood. Many studies report that people in middle and upper social classes are more likely than people in lower classes to belong to multiple organizations. Further, there are differences in types of associations belonged to by social class (see Boskoff, 1970, pp. 180–181; and Barber, 1957).

One reaches different conclusions about the prevalence of black and white memberships in voluntary associations, depending on the sources consulted. A number of years ago Mydral (1944) argued that blacks are "exaggerated" Americans because they belong to a larger number of associations than whites. This associational pattern was considered by Mydral and his associates to be "pathological," because blacks are a generation behind white patterns of associational membership and because black associations achieve little of what their members set out to achieve in them. Further, these associations are primarily expressive and nonutilitarian in nature—birthday clubs, Northside Squires, etcetera, as opposed to more instrumental organizations such as the NAACP (Babchuck and Thompson, 1962, p. 653; and Dackawich, 1966, p. 74). On the other hand, several national surveys indicate that a larger proportion of whites than blacks are members of voluntary associations (Hausknecht, 1962; and Wright and Hyman, 1958). Organizations may mean much more to blacks who belong to them, because they offer a congenial environment for collective social activity. This is in contrast to whites, who view organizations as a mechanism for the enhancement of their prestige when they choose to belong to the right kinds of organizations.

Ethnographic studies typically reveal little voluntary association participation by blacks in urban areas. Hannerz (1969) describes four ideal type life styles for adult ghetto residents and identifies and describes differential social interaction patterns for each of them. For the most part, "Mainstreamers" (those who ascribe to and succeed in achieving dominant cultural goals, values, and goods) comprise the membership in such voluntary organizations that exist in the black inner city (PTA, church, community improvement projects, and so on). "Swingers" (young single or married adults) tend toward cosmopolitanism rather than localism, finding friends and acquaintances and participating in informal social events and parties throughout the city. "Streetcorner men" and "street families" center informal interaction patterns in the local community and, with the exception of church attendance, avoid formally organized activities. Hannerz' data corresponds closely with other social anthropological studies of ethnic ghetto life, such as those of Boston (Gans, 1962), Chicago (Suttles, 1968), and Washington, D.C. (Liebow, 1967; Chapin, et al., forthcoming).

Immigrants from other nations developed networks of ethnic-specific voluntary associations. In addition, rural to urban migrants developed voluntary associations and used them to help throw off their old rural ways of life. Voluntary associations, then, may function as mediators between the old ways of doing things, whether in the old country or rural areas, and they may help migrants adjust to the complexity of urban life. However, it also should be noted that if organizations are oriented toward maintaining the old ways of doing things, it is doubtful if they help migrants in adapting to urban life (Hunt and Butler, 1972, pp. 449–450). This is especially so if ethnic voluntary association participation is coupled only with intensive relative and ethnic friend interaction.

The proportion of males that belong to voluntary associations varies over time and evidently varies by metropolitan place, as well as by district within the metropolitan complex. In Detroit, Axelrod (1956) reported that 63 percent of males belonged to voluntary associations while in San Francisco, 77 percent belonged (Bell and Force, 1956). On the other hand, Komarovsky's study (1946) conducted in New York City found that only around half of the males belonged to voluntary associations other than church. Generally, women are less likely to belong to organizations than are men. Men belong to a greater variety of volunteer associations and are more likely to hold multiple memberships than are women, although men are less stable in their membership. Males typically belong to instrumental type organizations, whereas women are more likely to belong to expressive organizations, especially recreational and church-oriented groups. Women are less likely to belong to organizations while they have young children in the household, but when the youngest child enters school, they once more begin to join organizations (Booth, 1972).

All available research tends to show that there are substantial numbers of people who do not belong to voluntary associations; however, most of these people do associate with kin, friends, and neighbors, and thus they have ties with others. Many people belong to multiple associations. Interestingly, those with associational memberships still maintain kin ties and visit with friends and neighbors.

ALIENATION

A major focus in mass society is alienation. The assumption that alienation is universal in mass society has not been tested, and there remains a lack of consensus on a definition of what alienation is (Taviss, 1969). Particularly evident in various definitions of alienation is the distinction between alienation from self and alienation from society. Alienation from society exists when an individual believes that the social system is oppressive or incompatible with his or her desires. Self-alienation means that the individual manipulates the self in accordance with apparent social demands and feels incapable of controlling his or her actions. "The socially alienated maintain distance from society, while the self-alienated engage in self-manipulatory behavior so as to eliminate this distance" (Taviss, 1969, p. 47).

A study of alienation themes in magazine stories at two different time periods (1900s and 1950s) found a higher proportion of stories that contained alienation themes during the latter period than the earlier period. However, during this time span, social alienation themes decreased slightly. Self-alienation showed a large overall increase *and* a heightened intensity. "Contributing most heavily to this increase are the sense of lack of control over one's own behavior and the deliberate development of a particular style of response in order to influence or manipulate others" (Taviss, 1969, p. 51).

In further refinement, Faia (1967, p. 399) argues that alienation may be from society at large or from a specific milieu within society. The consequences of these two types of alienation are assumed to be quite different. Thus, alienation has come to mean many things. It has been defined as the feeling people have when they cannot relate to the world around them. This takes the form of (1) estrangement from work, (2) powerlessness in political affairs, (3) social isolation, (4) cultural or value estrangement as a result of the breakdown of societal values (Seeman, 1971), and (5) generalized despair and distrust (anomia). One measure consistently used to measure *anomia*, alienation, is Srole's (1956) scale.[5] The items in this scale presumably measure the extent of *normlessness* felt by an individual, as originally conceived by Durkheim (1951).

One strain of research focuses on mass society, with its emphasis on access to large-scale industrial bureaucratic structures. Another focuses on social class oriented economic influences and opportunity structures. These and other approaches suggest somewhat different possibilities in regard to alienation. The mass society approach assumes generalized alienation for workers, a social class (economic) approach assumes that those who are deprived economically, whether they are workers or managers, are likely to be alienated. For example, in a study of twenty-eight Minnesota communities, owners were more likely to be anomic than managers. This was attributed to the managers' greater commitment to social and geographical mobility and higher economic status (Nelson, 1968, p. 191). Deprived owners become antagonistic toward and reject the larger society, whereas anomia for managers is more related to their economic level. In general, this study showed that anomia was related more to economic deprivation than to access to bureaucratic structures.

Some argue that many workers in modern urban, industrialized societies are alienated from their jobs and employers, and that this alienation from work is particularly evident for workers whose jobs are monotonous, unrewarding, and involve hard labor. However, Seeman (1971, p. 137) stresses that when propositions about alienation from work are tested, the supposed consequences generally do not materialize. He found that urbanites vary greatly in degree of alienation and on four different types of alienation measures. As an example, workers who exhibit work alienation do not necessarily also feel powerless. Thus, Seeman feels that a one-dimensional view of an alienated urbanite is incorrect. He argues that of the various kinds of alienation, "powerlessness" has the most important consequences for individuals and society.

Community size and the powerlessness dimension of alienation were not associated in several different community studies. On the other hand, there was a small relationship between community size and alienation as measured by social isolation. Attendance at meetings was less important than knowing one's neighbors and having relatives living in the neighborhood in *not* having a feeling of social isolation (Fischer, 1973). This particular study, using several different samples, rejects the idea that urbanism is associated very strongly with alienation. In a study of white Appalachians living under a variety of conditions (urban and rural and migrant status), the level of anomia was relatively constant—between 32 and 35 percent. This same study, however, showed that other groups of rural southern migrants to Detroit and of native Detroiters had even lower proportions who were reported as being anomic (Nelsen and Whitt, 1972, pp. 382–383).

An analysis of three upstate New York communities varying along urban–rural dimensions also casts doubt on the assumption that anomia is more characteristic of urban than of rural life (Mizruchi, 1969), suggesting that differences between dwellers of large urban areas and those of less urbanized communities have often been exaggerated (Mizruchi, 1960, p. 653).

Finally, a study of a city and a small county seat in a southeastern state found that the relationship between urbanism and anomia is a tenuous one. According to this study, level of education accounts for apparent urban–rural differences in anomia among whites, while such differences do not exist at all for blacks (Killian and Grigg, 1962). Further specification of findings in this study show that "whites who place themselves in the upper or middle class are more likely to display high anomia if they live in the city rather than in the small town"

(p. 664). On the other hand, black white-collar workers are more likely than other blacks to display anomia if they live in rural areas. Thus, position in the social structure and urban–rural residence both may interact to influence anomia.

In summary, the simple proposition that mass society, or urbanism, is closely linked to alienation is not supported by currently available research evidence. There does appear to be some support for the idea that different socioeconomic circumstances and opportunity structures are linked to at least some types of alienation. Obviously, further theory and research are needed.

VARIATION IN ALIENATION WITHIN METROPOLITAN COMPLEXES

Given the extensive theoretical and speculative literature concerned with alienation, it is strange that so little information exists that examines alienation as it is differentially distributed within metropolitan complexes. That such differences may systematically exist was shown by one study reporting that 34 percent of residents in the city of St. Louis were anomic, while only 15 percent of suburban residents were anomic (James, 1969, p. 194). The greater degree of anomia in the city was accounted for by those in the lower social classes. However, gross differences between central city and suburb may be somewhat misleading, because there is great differentiation among neighborhoods in the central city and suburbs. On an individual level, persons with higher job, formal schooling, and household income levels were less likely to be anomic than their counterparts. This led James to conclude that "disorganization" in the larger community and lower socioeconomic status on the individual level are associated with anomia (p. 195).

Somewhat similar results between central city and suburb were reported for the larger Los Angeles metropolitan area, which showed that 45 percent of the residents were anomic, while in a suburb of the same metropolitan area, the proportion of anomics was 36 percent (Miller and Butler, 1966, p. 404). Another study of four different areas of the Los Angeles metropolitan complex (Greer and Kube, 1959, pp. 106–109), similar in socioeconomic status but varying along urbanism (proportion of multiple family housing units and females in the labor force) found that the more urbanized areas of Hollywood and Silver Lake had higher percentages of anomics (about 12 percent) than the more suburban areas of Eagle Rock and Temple City (about 9 percent), with additional variation in the percentage of "semi-anomics" and "non-anomics." The main determinant of anomia in this study appears to be socioeconomic status and educational level, with those deprived of income and education more likely than others to be anomic. Migrants to the Los Angeles metropolitan area generally were not any more likely to be alienated than were natives; however, lower-class migrants were more likely than natives to be alienated (Hunt and Butler, 1972).

In the Los Angeles metropolitan complex, when a sample of integrated middle-class blacks was compared with black ghetto residents, middle-class integrated blacks "had greater expectations for control of events that concerned them and less of a feeling of anomia." They also appeared to be oriented more toward the mainstream of society than toward segregated black institutions. "Alienation within the ghetto takes on a circular characteristic; not only is it a product of segregated living, it also acts to keep people locked in the traditional residential patterns" (Bullough, 1967, p. 477).

Finally, it appears that social class and education are closely linked to alienation. For example, in a San Francisco study, Bell (1957, p. 114) notes that "It seems clear from the results of this study that anomie is inversely related to economic status. This is true whether economic status is measured by individual or neighborhood variables." Similarly, anomia is related to social isolation. This relationship between neighborhood status and anomia indicates that the economic character of the neighborhood may play an important part in "sorting out persons having different degrees of anomie" (p. 115). Also, it appears that neighborhood influence on anomia persists even when individual variables such as social participation, rural–urban background, age, and individual economic status are controlled.

Despite pleas for a decent burial (Lee, 1972), it is likely that alienation as a concept will continue to be used in sociological and urban literature. Meanwhile, it would be wise for those who read this literature to understand what the particular author may mean when using the term in the context of a particular study or essay. For example, "work alienation and powerlessness, two of the varieties of alienation most discussed in the contemporary literature, function independently (and generally in opposite ways): *high* work alienation and low powerlessness" tend to produce different kinds of behavior (Seeman, 1972, p. 15).

The assumption that mass society has created an isolated, alienated population needs to be more adequately tested. However, it does appear that most people in the United States have meaningful social relationships with kin, friends, neighbors, and co-workers. Similarly, substantial proportions of the population participate in voluntary organizations. Nevertheless, it also would be inaccurate to portray everyone in this manner. Although estimates vary, evidently somewhere between 10 and 20 percent of the population can be considered as social isolates. An even greater percentage, probably about one-third at a minimum, are alienated from society or are self-alienated. In percentage terms, isolation and alienation may not appear to be major problems. However, if absolute population figures are considered, then if one-third of the population is alienated, somewhere around *seventy million* people in the United States are self-alienated or alienated from mass society, or both.

PROSPECTS
What does the future hold? It is difficult to imagine mass society changing drastically over the next several decades. Thus, it appears that the characteristics of mass society as we now know them probably will continue well into the future. There does not appear to be a future trend in the growth of stronger community ties, and all of the pressures weakening the traditional, monogamous family are expected to continue unabated. Available current information shows that divorce rates are increasing, and family patterns divergent from the traditional family are increasing in number (Butler, forthcoming). Similarly, the ties people have with organizations, churches, friends, neighbors, and co-workers, while not necessarily growing weaker, also are not growing stronger.

The most apparent trend is toward greater alienation from society, as indicated by an increasing proportion of the population withdrawing from participation in society. Withdrawal takes the form of an unwillingness to participate in voluntary organizations, to assist in charitable fund-raising drives, and being primarily concerned with one's self-interest rather than the general interest of the society at large.

My prognosis is that this trend of alienation from society will continue in the future, because there appears to be little effort to change the elements of mass society that help produce alienation—especially the feeling of powerlessness. Similarly, there is little recognition that alienation is a major urban problem. Although recognizing alienation as a major urban problem would not guarantee its solution, the first stage of awareness has not been accomplished. Thus, there has been little discussion of alternative solutions, and virtually no effort has been expended in solving this problem.

NOTES
1. Parts of this chapter were taken from Butler (1976).
2. A number of articles have dealt with the "meaning of alienation." See any of the following: Nettler (1957); Seeman (1959); Dean (1961); Browning, et al., (1961); McClosky and Schaar (1965); or Neal and Rettig (1967).
3. For a general theoretical treatment of the concept of *neighborhood*, see Keller (1968).
4. This definition of the neighborhood is similar to Hatt's (1946) conception of a *natural area*, which he defined as follows:
(1) A spatial unit limited by natural boundaries enclosing a homogenous population with a characteristic moral order, and (2) a spatial unit inhabited by a population united on the basis of interrelatedness among its residents.
5. *Anomia* is normlessness at the individual level; *anomie* is normlessness at the societal level. Not all authors make this distinction between the individual and societal level.

REFERENCES

Axelrod, Morris. "Urban Structure and Social Participation." *American Sociological Review* 21 (February 1956):13–18.

Babchuk, Nicholas, and Ralph V. Thompson. "The Voluntary Associations of Negroes." *American Sociological Review* 27 (October 1962):647–655.

Barber, Bernard. *Social Stratification.* New York: Harcourt Brace and Company, 1957.

Bell, Wendell, and Maryanne T. Force. "Urban Neighborhood Types and Participation in Formal Associations." *American Sociological Review* 21 (February 1956):25–34.

Bell, Wendell. "Anomie, Social Isolation, and the Class Structure." *Sociometry* 20 (June 1957):105–116.

Berado, Felix M. "Kinship Interaction and Migrant Adaptation in an Aerospace-Related Community." *Journal of Marriage and the Family* 28 (1966):296–304.

Blumberg, Leonard, and Robert R. Bell. "Urban Migration and Kinship Ties." *Social Problems* 6 (Spring 1959):328–333.

Bollens, John C., and Henry J. Schmandt. *The Metropolis: Its People, Politics, and Economic Life.* New York: Harper and Row, 1965.

Booth, Alan. "Sex and Social Participation." *American Sociological Review* 37 (April 1972):183–192.

Boskoff, Alvin. *The Sociology of Urban Regions.* New York: Appleton-Century-Crofts, 1970.

Browning, Charles J., Malcolm F. Farmer, H. David Kirk, and G. Duncan Mitchell. "On The Meaning of Alienation." *American Sociological Review* 26 (October 1961):780–781.

Bullough, Bonnie. "Alienation in the Ghetto." *American Journal of Sociology* 72 (March 1967):469–478.

Butler, Edgar W., Ronald J. McAllister, and Edward J. Kaiser. "The Effects of Voluntary and Involuntary Residential Mobility on Females and Males." *Journal of Marriage and the Family* (May 1973):219–227.

Butler, Edgar W. *Urban Sociology: A Systematic Approach.* New York: Harper and Row, 1976.

Butler, Edgar W. *Traditional Marriage and Emerging Alternatives.* New York: Harper and Row, forthcoming.

Chapin, F. Stuart, Jr., Edgar W. Butler, and Frederick C. Patten. *Blackways in the Inner City.* Urbana: University of Illinois Press, forthcoming.

Dackawich, S. John. "Voluntary Associations of Central Area Negroes." *Pacific Sociological Review* 9 (1966):74–78.

Dean, Dwight G. "Alienation: Its Meaning and Measurement." *American Sociological Review* (October 1961):753–758.

Dotson, Floyd. "Patterns of Voluntary Association Among Urban Working Class Families." *American Sociological Review* 16 (October 1951):687–693.

Durkheim, Emile. *Suicide.* Translated by John A. Spaulding and George Simpson. Glencoe: Free Press, 1951.

Faia, Michael A. "Alienation, Structural Strain, and Political Deviancy: A Test of Morton's Hypothesis." *Social Problems* 14 (Spring 1967):389–413.

Feagin, Joe R. "The Kinship Ties of Negro Urbanites." *Social Science Quarterly* 49 (December 1968):660–665.

_____ "A Note on the Friendship Ties of Negro Urbanities," *Social Forces* 49 (December 1970):303–308.

Fischer, Claude S. "On Urban Alienations and Anomie: Powerlessness and Social Isolation." *American Sociological Review* 38 (June 1973):311–326.

Freeman, Howard E., Edwin Novak, and Leo G. Reeder. "Correlates of Membership in Voluntary Associations." *American Sociological Review* 22 (October 1957):528–533.

Gans, Herbert J. *The Urban Villagers.* New York: Free Press, 1962.

Greer, Scott, and Ella Kube. "Urbanism and Social Structure: A Los Angeles Study." In *Community Structure and Analysis,* edited by Marvin B. Sussman. New York: Thomas Y. Crowell, 1959, pp. 93–112.

Gusfield, Joseph R. "Mass Society and Extremist Politics." *American Sociological Review* 27 (February 1962):19–30.

Hannerz, Ulf. *Soulside: Inquiries Into Ghetto Culture and Community.* New York: Columbia University Press, 1969.

Hatt, Paul. "The Concept of Natural Area." *American Sociological Review* 11 (August 1946):423–427.

Hausknecht, Murray. *The Joiners.* New York: Bedminster Press, 1962.

Hawley, Amos H. *Human Ecology.* New York: Ronald Press, 1950.

Hillery, George A. "Definitions of Community: Areas of Agreement." *Rural Sociology* 20 (June 1955):111–123.

Hunt, Gerard, and Edgar W. Butler. "Migration, Participation, and Alienation." *Sociology and Social Research* 56 (July 1972):440–452.

James, Gilbert. "Community Structure and Anomia." In *The New Urbanization,* edited by Scott Greer, Dennis McElrath, David W. Minar, and Peter Orleans. New York: St. Martin's Press, 1969, pp. 189–197.

Josephson, Eric and Josephson, Mary, eds. *Man Alone: Alienation in Modern Society.* New York: Dell, 1962.

Keller, Suzanne. *The Urban Neighborhood.* New York: Random House, 1968.

Killiam, Lewis H., and Charles H. Grigg. "Urbanism, Race and Anomia." *American Journal of Sociology* 67 (May 1962):661–665.

Komarovsky, Mirra. "The Voluntary Associations of Urban Dwellers." *American Sociological Review* 11 (December 1946):686–698.

Lee, Alfred McClung. "An Obituary for 'Alienation.'" *Social Problems* 20 (Summer 1972):121–127.

Liebow, Elliot. *Tally's Corner.* Boston: Little, Brown, 1967.

Litwak, Eugene. "Reference Group Theory, Bureaucratic Career, and Neighborhood Primary Group Cohesion." *Sociometry* 23 (March 1960):72–84.

Litwak, Eugene, and I. Szelenyi. "Primary Group Structures and Their Functions: Kin, Neighbors, and Friends." *American Sociological Review* 54 (August 1969):465–481.

McClosky, Herbert, and John H. Schaar. "Psychological Dimensions of Anomy." *American Sociological Review* 30 (February 1965):14–40.

Meadow, Kathryn P. "Relationship of Neighborhood Friendship Formation to Other Types of Social Contact." *Journal of Intergroup Relations* 4 (Summer 1965):171–184.

Miller, Curtis R., and Edgar W. Butler. "Anomia and Eunomia: A Methodological Evaluation of Srole's Anomia Scale." *American Sociological Review* 31 (June 1966):400–406.

Mizruchi, Ephraim H. "Social Structure and Anomia in a Small City." *American Sociological Review* 25 (October 1960):645–654.

_____ "Romanticism, Urbanism, and Small Town in Mass Society: An Exploratory Analysis." In *Urbanism, Urbanization, and Change: Comparative Perspectives,* edited by Paul Meadows and Ephraim H. Mizruchi. Reading, Mass.: Addison-Wesley, 1969, pp. 243–251.

Mydral, Gunnar. *An American Dilemma: The Negro Problem and Modern Democracy.* New York: Harper and Row, 1944.

Neal, Arthur G., and Solomon Rettig. "On the Multidimensionality of Alienation." *American Sociological Review* 32 (February 1967):54–64.

Nelsen, Hart M., and Hugh P. Whitt. "Religion and the Migrant to the City: A Test of Holt's Cultural Shock Thesis." *Social Forces* 50 (March 1972): 379–384.

Nelson, Joel I. "Anomie: Comparisons Between the Old and New Middle Class." *American Journal of Sociology* 74 (September 1968):184–192.

Nettler, Gwenn. "A Measure of Alienation." *American Sociological Review* 22 (December 1957):670–677.

Nisbet, Robert A. *The Quest for Community.* New York: Oxford University Press, 1953.

Nohara, Shigeo. "Social Context and Neighborliness: The Negro in St. Louis." In *The New Urbanization,* edited by Scott Greer, Dennis L. McElrath, David W. Minar, and Peter Orleans. New York: St. Martin's Press, 1968, pp. 179–188.

Palisi, Bartolomeo J. "Ethnic Patterns of Friendship." *Phylon* 27 (Fall 1966):217–225.

Reissman, Leonard. "Class, Leisure, and Social Participation." *American Sociological Review* 19 (February 1954):76–84.

Riemer, Svend. "Urban Personality—Reconsidered." In *Community Structure and Analysis,* edited by Marvin B. Sussman. New York: Thomas Y. Crowell, 1959, pp. 433–444.

Rose, Arnold. *Theory and Method in the Social Sciences.* Minneapolis: University of Minnesota Press, 1953.

Rose, Arnold M. *The Power Structure.* New York: Oxford University Press, 1967.

Scanzoni, John N. *The Black Family in Modern Society.* Boston: Allyn and Bacon, 1971.

Seeman, Melvin. "On the Meaning of Alienation." *American Sociological Review* 24 (December 1959):783–791.

———. "The Urban Alienations: Some Dubious Theses from Marx to Marcuse." *Journal of Personality and Social Psychology* 19 (August 1971):135–143.

———. "Alienation and Knowledge-Seeking: A Note on Attitude and Action." *Social Problems* 20 (Summer 1972):3–17.

Shils, Edward A. "Mass Society and Its Culture." *Daedalus* 89 (Spring 1960): 288–314.

Srole, Leo. "Social Integration and Certain Corollaries: An Exploratory Study." *American Sociological Review* 21 (December 1956):709–716.

Sussman, Marvin B. "The Help Pattern in the Middle Class Family." *American Sociological Review* 18 (February 1953):22–28.

Suttles, Gerald D. *The Social Order of the Slum.* Chicago: University of Chicago Press, 1968.

Taviss, Irene. "Changes in the Form of Alienation: The 1900s vs. the 1950s." *American Sociological Review* 34 (February 1969):46–57.

Thomlinson, Ralph. *Urban Structure.* New York: Random House, 1969.

Warner, W. Lloyd, and Paul S. Lunt. *The Social Life of a Modern Community.* New Haven: Yale University Press, 1941.

Wilensky, Harold L. "Mass Society and Mass Culture: Interdependence or Independence?" *American Sociological Review* 29 (April 1964):173–197.

Wright, Charles R., and Herbert H. Hyman. "Voluntary Association Memberships of American Adults: Evidence from National Sample Surveys." *American Sociological Review* 23 (June 1958):284–294.

Young, Michael and Peter Willmott. *Family and Kinship in London.* Baltimore: Penguin, 1957.

PART II
POPULATION AND
URBAN PROBLEMS

3
URBANIZATION
AND POPULATION
GROWTH

INTRODUCTION

The very earliest cities had conditions that make many current urban problems appear insignificant.[1] For example, the problems of waste disposal and of furnishing an adequate water supply were difficult to surmount until the twentieth century. Thus, it is no surprise that large-scale illnesses, the Black Death, and high mortality rates occurred periodically in early cities. Beginning in the 1340s, the Black Death was carried into Europe by Italian traders (East, 1966, p. 317), and periodically, for the next several hundred years, epidemics decimated populations of entire cities. After the Black Death era, the population expanded from about 100 million in 1650 to 187 million in 1800 (East, 1966, p. 392).

Feudal and medieval cities, like their modern counterparts, required agricultural hinterlands that produced surpluses, transportation networks to facilitate the movement of goods, and increasing division of labor to manufacture goods for trading. Changes in agricultural production and transportation modes occurred slowly. But as technology became more sophisticated, the division of labor increased. In England during the eighteenth and nineteenth centuries, these changes came together to produce the first industrial revolution.

During the Middle Ages, requirements of defense and communications limited the area of cities. As in earlier Rome, high, closely packed tenements were the standard dwellings for most of the population of medieval Paris, the cities of Renaissance Italy, and most other cities in Europe. The working-class quarters of the newly developing industrial cities of Edinburgh and Birmingham, England, may have consisted of the "most depressing and unsanitary environments man has ever invented" (Passoneau, 1963, p. 13; Rowntree, 1922).

Much of the growth of urban places was made possible by more efficient transportation modes and industrialization, and industrialized cities have been compared with preindustrial cities primarily along these dimensions (Sjoberg, 1955). Comparatively few cities in the United States were settled before the nineteenth century, and few that had could be considered industrialized. At the beginning of the nineteenth century only 4 percent of the population in the United States lived in cities of eight thousand or more. One reason cities did not grow as rapidly before the nineteenth century as thereafter was the excessively high death rate. Poor sanitation and accompanying periodic plagues resulted in high death rates that counteracted migration to cities. Migration from the countryside "did little more than fill the vacant places caused by death" (Weber, 1899, p. 233). However, migrants from rural areas continued to replenish urban populations no matter what percentage of the urban population died as a result of epidemics and plagues.

A reduction in the urban death rate resulted in higher rates of natural increase (more births than deaths created a population increase). There was a large influx of migrants from rural areas in the United States to cities, and immigrants from other lands populated both urban and rural areas. Death rates in early large cities of the United States were substantially higher than in smaller cities; and all cities, large and small, had higher death rates than did the rural areas. (For data on New England in 1892, see Weber, 1899, pp. 344–346.) In addition, these death rate differentials appeared to hold for all ages. However, Weber, (1899, p. 348) concluded that "excessive urban mortality is due to lack of pure air, water and sunlight, together with uncleanly habits of life induced thereby. Part cause, part effect, poverty often accompanies uncleanliness: poverty, overcrowding, high rate of mortality, are usually found together in city tenements." Nevertheless, he also concluded that there is "no inherent eternal reason why men should die faster in large communities than in small hamlets, provided they are not too ignorant, too stupid, or too selfishly individualistic to cooperate in the security of common benefits. . . . The real checks upon the growth of population in previous centuries were war, famine, pestilence, and unsanitary cities involving particularly high infantile mortality" (Weber, 1899, p. 155). Thus, medical and sanitary progress reduced several of these checks. Pestilence and unsanitary conditions no longer result in higher (infant) mortality and limitations on population growth in the United States.

Until the early 1800s, cities in the United States had a relative lack of congested areas, dark alleys, slums, and for the most part, crime. However, slums began to be reported in New York City, and Boston had areas inhabited only by the poor. As cities grew larger, so did their problems. Few streets were paved and mud was a prominent feature during the wet season. A number of personal journals by writers who visited or lived in cities of the middle 1800s report that animals roamed the city streets. And at least one observed that, without these animals who served as garbage disposals, streets would be choked with filth. Cities of this era were virtually without sewage facilities. New York City, which created its department of sewers in 1849, was one of the first in the United States to do so. It is not too surprising, then, that epidemics occurred frequently. Diseases that could be carried by the water system or by ditches and streets with garbage in them were especially prominent. Among diseases that reached epidemic proportions were dysentery, typhoid, and typhus. Cholera becomes epidemic primarily through water contamination, and large scale epidemics occurred in 1832, 1849, and 1866. Yellow fever, which propagates in fetid pools of water and is transmitted by mosquitoes, claimed many lives after the turn of the century, and it persisted in northern cities until around 1825. Yellow fever epidemics claimed thousands of lives. Four thousand died in Philadelphia in 1793, in New Orleans, two thousand people died in 1847, and over eight thousand died during the summer of 1852. These large-scale epidemics led many people to suspect that increasing population density was responsible. Others believed that "In the early years of the century, poverty, like disease, was ordinarily considered the result of an individual's moral failure" (Glaab and Brown, 1967, pp. 90–91).

Early cities were characterized by inadequate traffic and transportation facilities. As cities grew and became more crowded, more complicated and sophisticated administrative systems were needed to handle complex problems that the changes were creating in the social institutions of society. City government in the early United States was alternatively viewed as being very good or virtually beyond redemption. The large increase in urban population created tremendous problems and made it mandatory that new forms of social organization be created to take care of problems that larger populations generated. Similarly, changing technology intensified urban problems and created new forms of social organization. Governmental costs increased faster than the population because the demand for municipal services in cities made capital investment a necessity. Many functions not performed previously or performed formerly by private organizations came under the city government. These required expanded facilities and more resources.

As poverty and slums grew in cities, there also was an increase in crime rates. Previously cities used a combination of day policemen and part-time, hired night watchmen, both of whom had little training and typically did not wear uniforms. But in 1844 many cities followed the lead of New York City in abolishing this informal system and forming a single body of policemen. This change in social organization was further modified when a Board of Police Commissioners was established and, for the first time, over bitter opposition, policemen were required to wear uniforms. Crime increased in cities, and violence on a large scale also occurred in some places. Many violent episodes were between workers, their organizers, and employers.

Other public services, such as fire protection, water, and sewage, gradually came under the jurisdiction of municipal governments. In addition, bridges, streets, street lights, sewage facilities, and educational facilites all required large capital outlays that had to be paid for by city residents. Demands for these new and expanded services and a lack of institutionalized means in dealing with them led to large-scale graft, and only gradually did "reform" governments come into being which attempted to deal with these problems. Cities absorbed large population increases, and the technological changes accompanying this demographic phenomenon required changes in the human institutions of the family, religion, education, and government, and in how people viewed the world. Demographic changes were a result of two migrations—migration into cities from the rural areas of the United States and migration from abroad, primarily Europe (Davis, 1966). The United States census reported that between 1900 and 1910 there were almost twelve million new city residents. Of these, 41 percent were migrants from other nations, about 30 percent were migrants from rural areas of the United States, and slightly less than 22 percent were from natural increase—excess of births over deaths in cities. The remainder of the increase (7 percent) was a result of incorporation of what had been fringe areas into the city proper. It should be noted that the rural population in the United States increased in absolute numbers, even though the percentage decrease in rural population was substantial.

The impact of the immigration to the United States is shown by the following:

> In 1890, New York (including the still legally separate municipality of Brooklyn) contained more foreign-born residents than any city in the world. The city had half as many Italians as Naples, as many Germans as Hamburg, twice as many Irish as Dublin, and two and a half times the number of Jews in Warsaw. In 1893, Chicago contained the third largest Bohemian community in the world; by the time of the First World War, Chicago ranked only behind Warsaw and Lodz as a city of Poles. Notable also was the fact that four out of five people living in greater New York in 1890 had either been born abroad or were of foreign parentage (Glaab and Brown, 1967, p. 139).

These immigrant populations did not live all over the cities but formed immigrant neighborhoods and ethnic ghettos. The impact of immigration was greater on eastern seaboard cities than it was on western and southern cities.

Several technological innovations occurred around 1850 that made it possible for cities to grow upward as much as horse-drawn buses, and later railroads, made it possible for them to expand horizontally. Horizontal expansion was greatly aided by railway electrification. Cast iron columns made it possible to build higher buildings, the first skyscrapers. And the invention of an efficient elevator helped move people up and down faster in these higher buildings. Earlier cities were rather compact, and expanded populations lived near their sites of work. With the advent of the electric railway around the turn of the century, the city began its outward expansion in earnest. That expansion led to the first large-scale suburban developments. Early suburbanites were primarily from the middle and upper stratums of society. As cities grew and expanded upward and outward, areas of formerly high population concentrations lost population. This probably happened because the central parts of the cities were taken over by commercial facilities and office buildings, rather than because of any particular dissatisfaction with city life by its inhabitants. In other words, population loss in what had been densely populated areas was a consequence of intensified land use and the fact that central district land became too valuable for residential use.

TWENTIETH CENTURY URBAN AND METROPOLITAN GROWTH

In the United States in 1800, only about 6 percent of the population lived in urban places. On the eve of the Civil War, only one city contained more than a million residents—New York City. Philadelphia had half a million, and Baltimore had two hundred fifty thousand. By 1920, over half of the people in the United States were living in urban places. A sharp rise in birth rates and declining death rates gave an added push to the suburbanization process in the 1920s. In the 1930s, suburban development dominated the economic, social, and political life of the United States (Wade, 1963, p. 75). The automobile was important in this suburban expansion. Previously, the shape of urban growth was primarily determined by the capacity of public conveyances to transport the population. Thus, early suburban expansion occurred along railroad lines that radiated out from the core. The automobile made possible a different kind of expansion, one not bounded by railroad lines, and urban sprawl began in earnest. Along with urban sprawl, the appearance of a shrinking revenue base for cities came into focus for the first, but not last time.

As westward expansion took place, there was a continued increase in the proportion of population classified as urban, except for the decade between 1930 and 1940. During those years the percentage of urban remained virtually unchanged. However, increasing urbanization of the population began anew during the 1940s, probably as a result of World War II. By 1970, well over 70 percent of the population lived in urban areas.

Larger cities, and areas around them, continued to grow. By 1970 there were over twenty-five urban complexes with more than one million inhabitants, over fifty with more than half a million population, and several hundred had a population of one hundred thousand or more. Actually, there are many more cities of one hundred thousand or more; many cities of this size are classified as suburbs when they are near larger central cities, such as Los Angeles. As the United States population increased, a larger and larger proportion of the total population lived in urban areas. Table 3–1 illustrates the increasing total population of the United States and the increase in the number of urban territorial units, defined as places with 2,500 or more inhabitants. On a regional basis, the northeastern part of the country was the first to urbanize, and it maintained its urbanization lead over the rest of the country. However, during the 1950–1960 decade, five million urban residents were added to the California population, and this population growth continued between 1960 and 1970. Similarly, other urban areas in the South (especially Florida) and West grew rapidly.

Table 3–1 United States Population Growth: 1790–1970

Year	Total Population	Urban Territory[a]	Immigrants
1790	3,929,000	24	
1800	5,297,000	33	
1820	9,618,000	61	8,385
1840	17,120,000	131	84,066
1860	31,513,000	392	153,640
1880	50,262,000	949	457,257
1900	76,094,000	1,737	448,572
1920	106,466,000	2,722	430,001
1940	131,954,000	3,464	70,756
1950	151,326,000	4,741	326,867
1960	179,323,000	6,041	265,000
1970	203,212,000	7,062	373,000

Sources: *Historical Statistics of the United States: Colonial Times to 1957*, U.S. Department of Commerce, Bureau of the Census, Washington, D.C., 1960; and U.S. Bureau of the Census, *Statistical Abstract of the United States: 1973* (94th edition), Washington, D.C., 1973.

[a]2,500 or more

The increasing urbanization of population and the coalescence of some population concentrations into contiguous urban areas has led to the notions of conurbation and metropolitanism. The term conurbation has been used to describe areas that previously had been distinct political and geographic units but whose population grew and joined together to form dense population masses. Although typically political jurisdictions remained the same, geographic separation no longer existed (Mumford, 1955, p. 391). The metropolitan concept includes a large central city and a much larger surrounding geographic area with a population whose social and economic activities form a more or less integrated system centered around the central city.

Metropolitan areas have grown at a fast pace, although in some instances the central city has actually lost population. In other cities, specific areas within the central city have lost population while the central city, as a whole, has gained population. Some have suggested that the central city is declining, but it is more appropriate to examine land use changes taking place in the entire city and metropolitan complex. It then becomes apparent that the central city is not declining but that its function and form are changing. Within those central cities not losing population, there are some areas that are losing residential population. However, the land is not remaining vacant. The function of such land is changing as it is being used more intensely for such purposes as offices, shopping centers, and convention centers. One very obvious pattern that has been established over the past three or four decades is the increasing proportion and segregation of the population living in central cities that is black, and in some other cities, especially in the Southwest and West, chicano (see Grebler, et al., 1970, p. 115).

The twentieth-century metropolitan city is the product of the extensive application of science to industry, the diffusion of electric power, and the advent of the automobile. The metropolitan city, as compared with earlier forms, is a product of the accelerating technological revolution that permeates virtually all phases of life. The combination of electric power, the automobile, and modern communication technology set centrifugal forces in motion that simultaneously diffused population and industry widely over the landscape and permitted larger agglomerations of both (Hauser, 1965, p. 4).

URBAN GROWTH AND SOCIAL ORGANIZATION

As the population became increasingly urbanized, specialization in social organization became more prominent. Originally the family took care of virtually all of its own needs, including producing most of its own food. However, in some early cities the increasing specialization that accompanied urbanization resulted in the breaking down of functions originally performed by the family unit. Subsequently, changing technology made it difficult for household enterprises to compete with larger-scale manufacturers. The loss of the productive function by the family was accompanied by radical changes. Most family members were no longer part of the labor force and "children were converted from a valuable resource to a charge against a wage or salary income" (Hawley, 1971, p. 121). No longer did the family unit process food or make clothes, nor was it any longer the focus of recreational activities.

Along with the family, other institutions became more specialized. These changes took place over a period of several centuries, and even today some families have resisted this aspect of urbanization and industrialization. However, most families and their members had to develop an increasingly wider social space. Population movement and circulation was increasingly required if the family was to survive. Thus, family members were exposed to a wider world beyond the immediate family and neighborhood. In addition, a substantial part of urban growth was made up of rural migrants. Similarly, there was a great deal of residential movement within cities from one area to another. Spatial movement, both migration to the city and movement within the city, resulted in the breakdown, in many instances, of kinship networks, mutual aid by neighbors, and primary group social controls on behavior.

The emergence of mass society, with increasing specialization and differentiation, ultimately resulted in a variety of relatively homogenous areas within the metropolitan complex with differing degrees of neighboring and a whole variety of life styles unlike those known previously. Social participation patterns changed markedly and voluntary organizations, for many, became the focus of social interaction, with a decline in extended family participation. Participation in and adherence to the traditional religious order declined and for many became nonexistent. For others, religious participation became devoid of religious content, and religious affiliation was used as another voluntary organization.

As urbanization of the United States took place, government and services became more specialized and increasingly took more of the earned dollar. Governmental complexity, overlap, and inefficiency became a way of life. Environmental hazards, slums, poverty, deteriorated housing and neighborhoods, and crime and violence all became important urban problems in the United States during the nineteenth and twentieth centuries. Planning became a byword, and in spite of planning that did take place in many metropolitan areas, urban problems continued to proliferate.

PROSPECTS

Two facets of the future population in the United States need to be explored. First, the question how many people there will be in the future is an important one, because it has implications for virtually all other urban problems discussed in this book. Associated with the question of how many is what age distribution or age structure the population will have. Second, the concern with what proportion of these people will be living under urban conditions is important.

How many people will there be in the United States in the future? Currently in the United States, birth rates are down and age at first marriage is up, yet even now the population is increasing each year. Zero population growth has not yet occurred in the United States.[2] Also, it should be noted that by 1980 the number of women in the heaviest childbearing ages of twenty to twenty-nine will be twice as great as in 1960 (Hartley, 1973). Thus, if a two-child family soon became the average family norm, the United States would have 250 million residents by the year 2000 and 350 million by the year 2050 (Frejka, 1973, p. 165). If this norm is not reached rather quickly, U.S. population growth will be greater than these figures! To actually achieve zero population growth requires a one-child family at least for the next several decades. Population growth in the United States has continued at about 1 percent per year—which is twice the rate of most other technologically advanced countries. This growth is especially important because the U.S. population represents about 6 percent of the world's population but uses from about one-third to one-half of the world's resources (Hartley, 1973).

In the United States in the future there will have to be a trade-off between population growth and quality of life, unless the United States is able to command an even greater proportion of the world's resources. However, there are at least two conditions militating against this possibility. First, population growth throughout the rest of the world, especially in countries not yet technologically advanced, also requires resources. Second, populations of other countries are beginning to demand a larger share of resources. Thus, there are several converging conditions that make it highly unlikely that the United States in the future will be able to increase its proportion of the world's resources. In fact, the proportion probably will be reduced. Thus, any population increase in the United States will result in a lowered quality of life for some, because fewer resources will be available. Also, it should be noted that while a reduction in the population growth rate would not necessarily solve some of the other urban problems discussed in this book, any population increase probably will create more problems and make the solutions of other problems more difficult if not impossible (Hartley, 1973).

Perhaps the best solution to population growth would be to have a rational population policy adhered to by the population. However, given our society, this probably will not happen. A balanced population structure would be one in which the productive population—that is, those who are able to and do work, generally between the ages of twenty-one to sixty-five—is in balance with the non-producing population, or at least with the very young and the aged. A population out of balance in regard to production also poses other kinds of problems, whether the population is increasing, remaining stable, or decreasing. Problems associated with a stable or declining population are not likely to be part of the foreseeable future of the United States.

While the U.S. population may be expanding, the distribution of that population also is related to urban problems. Almost since the very beginning of this country's history, an increasing proportion of the population has lived under urban conditions. This trend carried through the 1930s, when about half the population lived in urban areas, and continued up until the 1970s. By 1980 it is expected that well over three-fourths of the population will be living in urban areas. Despite the publicity surrounding some families that have moved back to the farm, the overall net urban increase has continued unabated. Especially remarkable over the past several decades has been the growth of larger metropolitan complexes, especially in their rings or suburbs. This urban sprawl appears likely to continue in the future—especially along the warmer coastal zones of the Pacific Coast and the Gulf of Mexico as well as along the Atlantic Coast and Great Lakes. This increasing urban and metropolitan population concentration has helped to multiply the number of local governments that are necessary to deal with this population and its needs, and has added to traffic congestion, increased pollution, and other problems. (National Academy of Sciences, 1965, pp. 7–8).

It appears that the U.S. population is going to grow in the future. Although this growth may not be as rapid as in the past, resources needed to maintain the quality of life expected by this population will be extremely difficult to come by. The vast majority of the population will continue to live under distinctly urban conditions. Many will continue to drift to the seacoasts and Great Lakes, creating increasingly greater metropolitan concentrations that will be accompanied by a growth in governments and of conditions that are considered as problems.

NOTES

1. For a more extensive historical description of earlier cities, see Chapter 3 of Butler (1976).

2. Some demographers believe that zero population growth has already been achieved. I believe that the 1980 U.S. Census will show that they are incorrect and that the population will have increased at about 1 percent per year during the period from 1970 to 1980—or more than twenty million people. For a reasoned analysis of U.S. population growth alternatives, see Frejka (1973).

REFERENCES

Butler, Edgar W. Urban Sociology. New York: Harper and Row, 1976.

Davis, Kingsley. "The Urbanization of the Human Population." In Cities, A Scientific American Book. New York: Alfred A. Knopf, 1966, pp. 3–24.

East, Gordon. An Historical Geography of Europe. 5th ed. London: Methuen, 1966.

Frejka, Tomas. The Future of Population Growth. New York: Wiley, 1973.

Glaab, Charles N., and A. Theodore Brown. A History of Urban America. New York: Macmillan, 1967.

Grebler, Leo, Joan W. Moore, and Ralph C. Guzman. *The Mexican-American People.* New York: Free Press, 1970.

Hartley, Shirley F. "Our Growing Problem: Population." *Social Problems* 21 (Fall 1973):190–206.

Hauser, Phillip M. "Urbanization: An Overview." In *The Study of Urbanization,* edited by Phillip M. Hauser and Leo F. Schnore. New York: Wiley, 1965, p. 1–47.

Hawley, Amos H. *Urban Society: An Ecological Approach.* New York: Ronald Press, 1971.

Mumford, Lewis. "The Natural History of Urbanization." In *Man's Role in Changing the Face of the Earth,* edited by W. O. Thomas, Jr. Chicago: University of Chicago Press, 1955, pp. 382–398.

National Academy of Sciences. *The Growth of U.S. Population.* Washington, D.C.: National Academy of Sciences-National Research Council, 1965, Publication 1279.

Passonneau, Joseph R. "Emergence of City Form." In *Urban Life and Form,* edited by Werner Z. Hirsch. New York: Holt, Rinehart and Winston, 1963, pp. 9–27.

Rowntree, B. Seebohm. *Poverty: A Study of Town Life.* London: Longmans, Green, 1922.

Sjoberg, Gideon. "The Preindustrial City." *American Journal of Sociology* 60 (March 1955):438–445.

Wade, Richard C. "The City in History—Some American Perspectives." In *Urban Life and Form,* edited by Werner Z. Hirsch. New York: Holt, Rinehart and Winston, 1963, pp. 59–79.

Weber, Adna F. *The Growth of Cities in the Nineteenth Century.* Ithaca, N.Y.: Cornell University Press, 1963 (original publication date, 1899).

4
POPULATION SEGREGATION AS AN URBAN PROBLEM

INTRODUCTION

One of the basic assumptions of much sociological and ecological literature is that social, economic, and ecological characteristics of areas within urban and metropolitan regions are systematically interrelated to social behavior, to demographic factors such as fertility, infant mortality, age structures, and to ethnic and racial residential segregation. Several frames of reference have been developed to account for the variety and types of segregated areas found within the metropolitan complex. Early traditional frames of reference—such as the Burgess (1925) concentric zone theory, Hoyt's (1939) sector theory, and the multiple nuclei theory (Harris and Ullman, 1945)—postulated homogeneous areas within the urban complex. Quinn (1950, pp. 116–137) showed that a variety of homogeneous areas within the urban complex would require the presence of widely varying populations such as the minorities, foreign born, and aged living in segregated areas.

Other recent orientations used in the study of areas within metropolitan and urban complexes showed that even though a city may become more heterogeneous across time, subdivisions within become more homogeneous (Shevky and Williams, 1949; Shevky and Bell, 1955). From this social area frame of reference the city becomes more homogeneous over time in (1) social rank, (2) urbanization/familism, and (3) segregation.

Social Rank. A socioeconomic factor accounts for the largest proportion of variation. That is, it explains more of the differences that occur among city areas than any other dimension.

Familism/Urbanization. A second factor that is postulated and inevitably emerges describes family size, age composition, and "residential environments for different kinds of families at different stages of their life cycles" (Abu-Lughod, 1969, p. 202). In a few cities, this factor appears to be mixed with social rank.

Segregation. Most often measured by ethnicity, this factor is the least independent of the three dimensions and has been reported very rarely outside the United States. This may be a function of the cities selected for study both in and outside the United States; it may be a result of the selection of variables; or it may be representative of the real world in the United States and elsewhere.

The city from this perspective is seen as a product of the complex whole of society. Changes taking place in that society, such as (1) in the distribution of skills, (2) in the organization of productive activity, and (3) in population composition. Social segregation becomes more marked over time. Each trend contributes to the process of social differentiation—segregation.

A changing distribution of skills leads to a more definitive ordering of people in society according to the socioeconomic status of their occupations. Changes in the organization of productive activities are associated with changes in styles of living, and these are characterized by a decline in family life. Changes in population lead to residential concentration or segregation of like types of people (for example by ethnicity and age). As the city becomes more heterogeneous, *subdivisions within it become more homogeneous,* that is, the subdivisions become segregated.

Although the theoretical relevance of social area analysis has been questioned, it does appear appropriate to accept the constructs of social rank, urbanization/familism, and segregation as useful dimensions for describing areas within most cities in the United States (Goldsmith and Unger, 1970, p. 5).

Another model of urban area differentiation was advanced by Hoover and Vernon (1962). Using observations covering thirty-five years and twenty-two counties that constitute the New York metropolitan region, they showed that variation among urban areas and the development of homogeneous neighborhoods can be accounted for by job type, income, and age structure of households. Since the Hoover-Vernon model is longitudinal, it is necessary to use an index of date of settlement. Beverly Duncan and her colleagues (1962) used the date an area first had two dwelling units per acre. Several recent studies based on the entire Los Angeles County metropolitan area suggests that the Hoover-Vernon model—based on New York—has substantial applicability to Los Angeles. Data for Los Angeles show that the earliest settled areas contain the highest proportion of older population and females in the labor force, lower proportion of owner occupied single family housing units, and low fertility rates (Duncan, et al., 1962; Butler and Barclay, 1967). Furthermore, earliest settled areas were characterized by lower social levels as measured by occupational and educational status and by housing value and median rent paid for housing, as well as by higher spatial mobility rates and proportion minorities—for example, blacks and chicanos.

While these and virtually all other frames of reference focus on the homogeneity of urban areas, the emphasis should be placed on the *relative* degree of homogeneity and segregation, which changes over time (Duncan and Duncan, 1957). For example, most first settled areas, therefore old areas, are characterized by fewer young children, more older people, more minorities, and fewer single family housing units. They also are characterized by persons in lower level occupations, lower housing value as reflected in rents, and a lower percentage of owner occupied housing units. Yet, these first settled areas have reached their current state by going through transitional stages without ever being completely homogeneous. At the initial stages, the black population and aged population decrease and then a steady increase begins across time as housing becomes older and starts to deteriorate. Similarly, at the initial building-up stage, areas typically increase in proportion of white-collar workers but gradually decrease thereafter. In addition, housing characteristics and tenure change across time. In early stages the proportion of owner-occupants increases and then decreases as areas go through various transitional stages. It appears that populations and housing are always in a state of relative homogeneity, so all of our discussion concerning segregated areas is concerned with relative degrees of segregation.

There are different types of segregation patterns in the United States. Most of these patterns reflect differences that are meaningful to people in defining other people. Thus, race and ethnic status, social class, and age residential segregation patterns are apparent in most U.S. cities. These residential segregation patterns represent social categories that are systematically made in our society in everyday interaction with other people.

Explanations of residential segregation generally revolve around three causes. First, there is the notion of *voluntary* concentration of people who want to live with similar individuals. Second, there is *involuntary* segregation patterns in which various kinds of populations—Norwegians, Jews, blacks, chicanos, or the aged—are forced to live in particular areas of the city. Third, there is an *economic* determinism point of view stressing the disadvantaged economic position of a population and the consequence of that population living in areas with deteriorated housing and neighborhoods.

ETHNIC/RACIAL SEGREGATION

Closely allied with the growth and internal differentiation of cities and urban complexes in the United States is ethnic/racial segregation. Although racial segregation does not take the form of a reservation (except for Native Americans), it can be described as "a form of partial ostracism" (Johnson, 1943). For most racial minorities in the United States, segregation has to be considered as external—imposed and involuntary. While some earlier immigrant populations to some degree voluntarily lived in segregated enclaves, some of these enclaves disappeared as immigrants became Americanized. On the other hand, segregation of blacks and chicanos in particular has been enduring and can, for the most part, be considered as involuntary. The most obvious segregation patterns and those most easily measured are physical or spatial separation. However, segregation refers to "all conventions and social ritual designed to enforce social isolation and social distance, and for this reason embedded in racial traditions" (Johnson, 1943). In the discussion that follows, the focus is on *residential segregation*, but it should not be forgotten that many other kinds of social segregation are related to residential segregation. School integration and school busing problems, occupational discrimination, and social relationships are all influenced by segregated residential patterns. Thus, "racial segregation in residential areas provides the basic structure for other forms of institutional segregation" (Johnson, 1943). Some of the various forms that residential patterns of segregation may take were enumerated a number of years ago by Johnson (1943). They included the following:

1. In the *rural south* small dwellings are scattered over the open country. These dwellings are generally owned by a white landowner who allows a black family to become a tenant farmer on his land.

2. A *small town* pattern which shows a more definitive clustering of the black population. These clusters may be scattered throughout the town but they are quite definitive areas of black population. Most of these clusters are located on the *edge of town* and many have intervening white neighborhoods which have paved streets, street lights, water, and sewerage connections which for some reason seldom reach black residential neighborhood clusters. In contrast to larger cities, these areas of residence were built and developed for black residents rather than being passed down to blacks by white residents who have moved on to better areas.

3. The *back-yard residence pattern* also existed at least in some southern cities. This pattern found in Charleston, South Carolina, for example, had black residences located among white residences and thus blacks were scattered relatively uniformly throughout the city. Generally homes of blacks were located in the back yards of white families for whom they worked as servants.

4. In some cities there is a *concentration* of blacks to such a degree

that it approaches complete segregation. At least a number of years ago Tulsa, Oklahoma and Durham, North Carolina (Johnson, 1943) were such cities; today many large cities have such concentrations.

5. Most urban complexes, however, have one large black *concentration with smaller clusters* scattered about throughout the city and its suburbs.

Again, it should be noted that many other segregated patterns are substantially related to segregated residential patterns. If, in the future, segregated residential patterns begin to disappear, it will, of course, be of further interest to note that whether other areas of institutional racism, such as in the schools, work, and welfare, also break down.[1]

Black Segregation

One of the earliest longitudinal studies of residential racial segregation was conducted in Chicago (Duncan and Duncan, 1957). In Chicago, as the black population increased in numbers, it expanded into what had been all anglo neighborhoods. At the same time, blacks tended to gather in areas and neighborhoods already heavily populated by blacks, thus substantially increasing the density of already over-populated areas. In Chicago, black population movement generally occurred radially outward from areas already heavily populated by blacks. The black movement into nearby neighborhoods did not alter the socioeconomic character of the areas. Similarly, the outmovement of anglos and the inmovement of blacks did not alter problems in the area or increase them. These problems remained relatively constant regardless of population's racial composition.

Blacks who first entered former anglo areas tended to be natives of the city and generally better off economically than those who remained behind in predominantly black residential areas. Migrants from the South and rural areas typically moved into already well-established black neighborhoods. The differential distribution of black natives and migrants in Chicago suggest that there are substantial differences in residential patterns within the black community. A study of Milwaukee (Edwards, 1970) showed that the residential distribution of black families varied by income and by stage of the family cycle. Black residential patterns resembled those of the larger anglo population. The greatest variation was found with families having higher incomes and couples with children. These families were living in areas, contiguous to the black core, that were serving as suburbs for wealthier black families with children.

Recently, Van Arsdol and Schuerman (1971) showed that in Los Angeles County, the segregation of Mexican-born and nonwhites other than blacks decreased slightly over the past several decades. However, as anglos moved to newly developed suburban areas and neighborhoods in the urban complex, blacks tended to move into vacated areas, and they became more concentrated and segregated as these areas developed ghetto characteristics. As a result of their study, Van Arsdol and Schuerman (1971, p. 477) conclude that "increased de facto segregation can be expected in neighborhoods where there is a conversion, downgrading, or a thinning out of housing units." In more recently developed areas, segregation is greater for blacks than for the Mexican-born or nonwhites other than blacks. Blacks show the greatest proportional increase in neighborhoods where they already were highly concentrated, a pattern not applicable to other minority populations.

As shown in Figure 4–1, the earliest settled areas in Los Angeles County (DS-1) have almost twice the proportion of black population as areas settled more recently (DS-2, 3, and 4). These data show that the black population inherits older housing—and that this pattern exists throughout the County, not just in the central city of Los Angeles. Figures 4–2, 4–3, and 4–4 show how the black population expanded in Los Angeles County between 1940 and 1960. Particularly noticeable is the joining together of several larger areas of black population concentration and many peripheral areas of black population

Figure 4–1 Date of Settlement in Los Angeles County
and Percentage Black Population

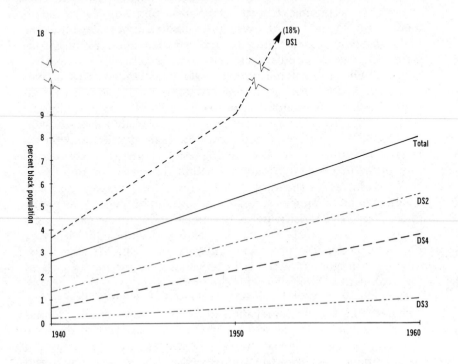

Figure 4–2 Distribution of Negroes: Comparability Grid for Los Angeles County, 1940 (N=474)

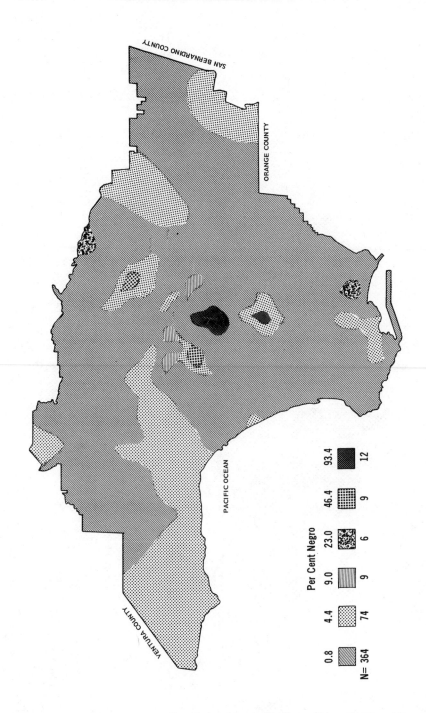

Figure 4–3 Distribution of Negroes: Comparability Grid for Los Angeles County, 1950 (N=474)

Figure 4–4 Distribution of Negroes: Comparability Grid
for Los Angeles County, 1960 (N=474)

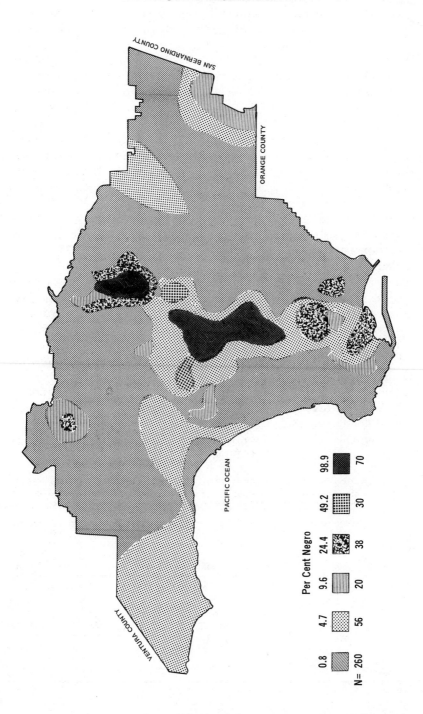

concentration which are (as might be expected from Figure 4–1) suburbs with older housing.

Obviously, increasing segregation and such large-scale concentrations of blacks have a negative aspect on the assimilation of blacks into the larger society. The 1970 United States census showed that blacks were becoming increasingly suburbanized. However, this suburbanization is misleading. Blacks who are suburbanizing are moving into older suburban areas with declining neighborhoods and deteriorating housing, much like that available to them in central cities. Thus, some blacks are merely trading these kinds of conditions in the central city for similar ones in the outer city or suburbs. Van Arsdol and Schuerman (1971, p. 478) argue that their Los Angeles County data support a contention that "ethnic residential segregation is not confined to the central city but pervades the entire metropolis" (see also Aldrich, 1975).

A recent study examined residential segregation of nonwhite households for 109 cities from 1940 through 1970 (Winsborough, et al., 1975). As shown in Table 4–1, residential segregation in these cities remained relatively similar in 1940, and 1950, and 1960 with only a slight increase or decrease noted. However, between 1960 and 1970, there was a decrease in segregation. Thus, segregation in 1970 appears to be lower than at any previous period for which comparable data are available. Since the index used to measure segregation in this study was the *index of dissimilarity*, [2] complete desegregation in 1970 would require that 80 percent of the nonwhite population be redistributed into white neighborhoods. Regional differences in residential segregation remained virtually unchanged between 1960 and 1970; segregation in the South remained the highest, and segregation in the West continued to be the lowest.

Generally, this study confirms earlier reports that the basic description of segregation of nonwhites in cities in the United States is of

Table 4–1 Means of the Index of Residential Segregation Between White and Nonwhite Household Heads for 109 Selected Cities and for Census Regions, 1940 to 1970*

		Means				
			Regions			
Date	All Cities	NE	NC	W	S	Non South
1970	81.55	74.30	2.58	67.89	87.96	77.05
1960	86.12	78.86	88.40	76.41	90.84	82.80
1950	87.26	83.60	89.91	82.95	88.54	86.36
1940	85.23	83.18	88.43	82.70	84.86	85.48
Number of Cities	109	25	29	10	45	64

*From Winsborough, et al.

56 The Urban Crisis: Problems and Prospects in America

nearly complete segregation and that departures from this pattern are a result of nonwhites expanding outside neighborhoods of previous concentration. Thus, as the nonwhite population expands, it moves into former all white neighborhoods that are briefly desegregated.

Generally, the extent and composition, white or nonwhite, of urban population growth has a lot to do with whether or not a particular city reports greater or lesser segregation. The population dynamics of the time period under consideration influence the direction and pattern of segregation. For example, in the South, generally first settled or older southern cities are less segregated than are newer cities (Schnore and Evenson, 1966). In addition, during the 1940s and 1950s, non-white growth rates in most cities were quite high as were white growth rates which put great pressure on the existing housing market with intense competition for existing housing, resulting in increased seg-regation. However, during the 1960s, nonwhite population growth declined some and white populations declined more, especially in central cities, as whites moved to the suburbs in increasing numbers. Thus, there was more housing available for nonwhites in the central city. Similarly, during this decade some anti-discrimination and equal housing opportunity laws had some effect. If the decrease in segrega-tion patterns between 1960 and 1970 is extrapolated to the 1980s, an index of 75 is expected by that time.

Several studies suggest that within black neighborhoods, substan-tial income segregation exists (Marston, 1969). In Milwaukee, residen-tial segregation of black families by income (Cottingham, 1975) and by stage in the family life cycle resembles patterns found in white neigh-borhoods (Edwards, 1970). Segregation was greatest between those families that had the greatest disparity in income, with stage in the family life cycle being a secondary but important factor. Also, it ap-pears that changing areas—those areas in which the black population is expanding outward—serve the black population much as suburban areas serve the white population. That is, these areas that are changing from white to black population serve as suburbs for blacks in higher income categories and families with children—much as white suburbs appeal to whites with higher incomes and families with children.

Most black migration to metropolitan complexes has been to the central city. Thus, in 1950 blacks made up only 4.5 percent of the sub-urban population; during the twenty year period between 1950 and 1970 this figure had increased to 4.9 percent. Nevertheless, there are suburban neighborhoods in many larger urban complexes with a black population; these suburbs are occupied primarily by blacks and are segregated from the white population. In examining the historical trends of black suburbanization, Farley (1970) shows that, although virtually all economic levels of blacks have moved to the suburbs, they, like their white counterparts, tend to have higher socioeconomic status.

Three major types of suburban areas have increased in black population: (1) Particularly in the North, older, densely settled suburbs have increased in black population while typically the white population in the same suburbs has decreased. Although the housing in these older suburbs is older, generally it is better than housing that could have been purchased in the central city. (2) Some new suburban developments are being built exclusively for black residents and, of course, some blacks moved into previously all white residential neighborhoods. (3) A growing black population is moving into areas on the periphery of the city and metropolitan complex that can be characterized as lacking adequate sewer and water facilities, containing dilapidated homes of low value, and having a population almost exclusively black. It should be noted that two of these three types of movement are into older, dilapidated housing that whites and others have abandoned to the black population. Generally, the exchange of central city for suburban residence has not substantially altered the quality of housing occupied by most blacks.

A study of suburban communities that more than doubled their number of black inhabitants and reached a population of 10 percent blacks between 1960 and 1970 shows that generally such places were located in the suburban areas of Chicago, Los Angeles, New York, Cleveland, Newark, and Washington, D.C. (Connolly, 1973). This expansion into suburban neighborhoods was principally into areas contiguous to a city that already had a substantial black population. Thus, this suburban expansion was primarily a physical expansion of central city black neighborhoods into nearby areas that happened to be outside the central city. City boundaries were relatively meaningless in this expansion. A similar growth was experienced in several larger suburbs with already existing black populations. Some suburban black populations expanded during the 1960s into more visible black suburbs. In both of these instances, black population concentration in suburbs can be attributed to expansion of a contiguous concentration of blacks.

Generally, it must be concluded that the suburbanization of the black population to date does *not* signify a change in segregation patterns within metropolitan complexes. Rather it appears that most blacks who move into a suburban location are moving from a segregated central city neighborhood to a segregated suburban neighborhood, and generally to a neighborhood that is contiguous to an already existing concentration of black population. In some instances, housing is upgraded, but in general the move also is from one lower quality housing area to another one located nearby in the suburbs.

Farley (1970, pp. 525–526) argues that future expansion of the black suburban population will depend on the rate at which the economic status of blacks improves, the rate at which new housing is constructed, the federal government's housing policies, and the rapidity with which suburban housing becomes available to blacks.

Mexican Americans[3]

Mexican-Americans live throughout the United States, but the largest proportion of them live in the southwestern part of the country. In addition, this region of the United States has a large black population. The concentrations of Mexican-Americans in southwestern cities is highly varied and complex. Some concentrations follow the traditional patterns of other minorities in moving into older areas of deteriorating housing. However, many other areas of Mexican-American concentration have different patterns (Grebler, et al., 1970). Some cities in the Southwest first settled by Mexicans were organized around a *plaza*. These plazas subsequently gave way in many instances to other central business districts but remained the focal point of the Mexican-American population. While some early established *barrios* were absorbed by expanding urbanization, others continue as Mexican-American enclaves in what are now larger urban places. Pacoima, among the vast San Fernando Valley housing tracts of Southern California, is one such example. Others are such places as El Monte, California, and pockets of Mexican-Americans in various other cities. In addition, there are a few cities in which Mexican-Americans dominate both numerically and socially—for example, Rio Grande City and Presidio, Texas, and perhaps Laredo, Texas.

In all cities of the Southwest, Mexican-Americans are *less* segregated from anglos than are blacks. However, there is substantial variation in the extent of segregation as measured by the index of dissimilarity. For example, almost two-thirds of Mexican-Americans in the more segregated cities of Riverside, San Bernardino, Corpus Christi, Dallas, Houston, Lubbock, Odessa, San Angelo, and Wichita Falls would have to be relocated before integration would have taken place. The distribution of the Mexican-American population in Riverside is shown in Figure 4–5. Cities in the Southwest with *relatively* little segregation (that is, with only about one out of three to one out of two Mexican-Americans to be relocated before complete integration) are Oakland, Sacramento, San Diego, San Francisco, Pueblo, Galveston, and Laredo. Other cities, of course, fall in between these lower values and those of the more segregated cities.

Segregation of Mexican-Americans from anglos is closely associated with segregation patterns of blacks. That is, "where one minority is highly segregated, the other is also likely to be highly segregated" (Grebler, et al., 1970, p. 277). However, this does not mean that Mexican-Americans and blacks necessarily are living in the same residential areas. There is inconsistency in this regard. Generally cities in which Mexican-Americans and blacks are living in the same residential areas are middle-sized or smaller cities such as Abilene,

Figure 4–5 Percent of Mexican-American Population
in the City of Riverside, By Census Tract (1962 Survey Data
Based on Ten Percent Sample)

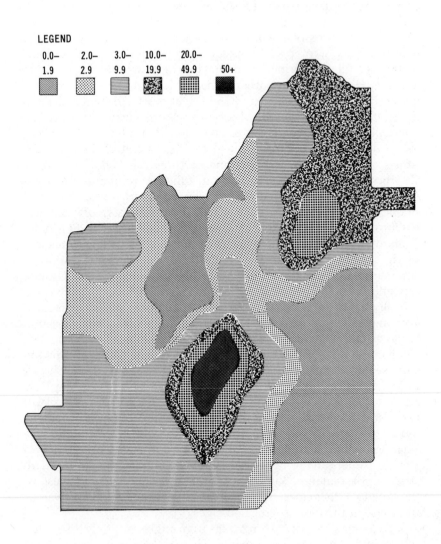

Corpus Christi, Odessa, Riverside, San Bernardino, and Wichita Falls. The most segregated cities—that is, anglos from Mexican-Americans and Mexican-Americans from blacks—are typically larger cities such as Dallas, Fort Worth, Denver, Houston, Los Angeles, Lubbock, Phoenix, San Antonio, and Tucson. Cities in which relatively little segregation occurs are of mixed sizes.

Mexican-American families that move into anglo neighborhoods appear to be those who have begun to utilize birth control, to have small families, to cut extended-family household arrangements, and to accept anglo cultural patterns. Nevertheless, the larger the city, the less likely that residential integration has taken place. In addition, when there are relatively few Mexican-Americans in relation to the black population, segregation from anglos is accentuated, and Mexican-Americans are treated like blacks. On the other hand, where there are relatively few blacks compared to Mexican-Americans, there is a lower level of segregation and blacks are treated substantially the same as the Mexican-American population (Grebler, et al., 1970, p. 285).

Other Ethnic Segregation Patterns

A study of segregation patterns of ethnic populations in ten northeastern and midwestern central cities reported substantial evidence that segregation of immigrant ethnic populations decreased as their relative income and socioeconomic status increased (Lieberson, 1963).[4] Generally, in the time span covering the period of 1910 through 1950, residential segregation decreased slightly. Because these decreases in residential segregation patterns for such populations as the Irish, Italians, and Russians were rather small, these ethnic enclaves remain as important ethnic oriented neighborhoods. (For similar results in Chicago, see Taeuber and Taeuber, 1954.) An analysis of New York as of 1960 (Kantrowitz, 1969) produced consistent results with the earlier study of ten other cities. In New York, the two most highly segregated ethnicities (other than blacks) were Italians and Scandinavians. Norwegians were highly segregated from other ethnic populations.[5] Their lowest segregation was from Swedes and their segregation, from Slavic Jews from the USSR, almost approached their segregation from blacks. As a result of the New York metropolis study, Kantrowitz (1969, p. 695) argues that it is "a fair speculation that Norwegian segregation from Negroes differs in degree, but not in kind, from their separatism from Slavic Jews." He further argues that strong prejudice against blacks on the part of whites compounds an already strong separatism that exists with some white populations. That is, if Norwegians don't particularly want to integrate with Protestant Swedes and Catholic Italians, they certainly are even less likely to accept black neighbors.

Segregation of the Aged

Segregation of different age categories in urban and metropolitan complexes has been a relatively neglected area of study. But, at least one report has shown that the story about the little old lady from Pasadena was based on fact (Smith, 1960, p. 241). Other cities such as St. Petersburg, Florida, also have more than their share of older people. Within metropolitan regions there also is substantial variation in where older people live. Generally, concentrations of older people are a result of both a residual population remaining in the area and older persons moving in. In Los Angeles County, as shown in Figure 4–6, there are areas with substantial concentrations of the older population. In 1960, 9.2 percent of the population was sixty-five years of age and over, and many areas had substantially greater percentages. Generally, the aged population formed a belt across the central part of the county from Santa Monica on the ocean through the central part of the city of Los Angeles, continuing northward to Pasadena. Similarly, there was a concentration in Long Beach (at the bottom of the map). In addition, there were smaller clusters of older people scattered throughout the county. Most of these clusters were areas of older, first settled housing. Figure 4–7 shows that DS-1 (the first settled areas of Los Angeles County) were the only areas to have above average population concentrations of older people.

Statistical analyses show that the percentage of aged population in Los Angeles County is associated with older housing, apartments, and negatively associated with younger children. Interestingly, the older population lives in areas heavily populated by people who are in the age category of fifty-four to sixty-five and thus approaching old age. A 1970 study of Terre Haute, Indiana reports virtually the same results as did these earlier analyses of Los Angeles County (Cox and Bhak, 1975).

It appears from the limited evidence available that the aged, and those approaching aged status, are highly segregated in many metropolitan complexes.

PROSPECTS

In the past, minorities were segregated and excluded from full social participation in the United States. Yet, clearly discriminatory behavior is contrary to professed ideals and objectives of our society. The most clear differentiation between the ideals of the society and actual behavior of the dominant white majority is in relationship to Native Americans. For the most part they remain on reservations that keep them clearly outside the mainstream of society. Blacks are not segregated to this great a degree, but black neighborhoods of many larger cities in the United States are becoming near-reservations.

Although there is no question that blacks continue to be segregated from other populations in most urban complexes, it is less certain that

Figure 4–6 Distribution of the Aged in
Los Angeles County, April 1, 1960

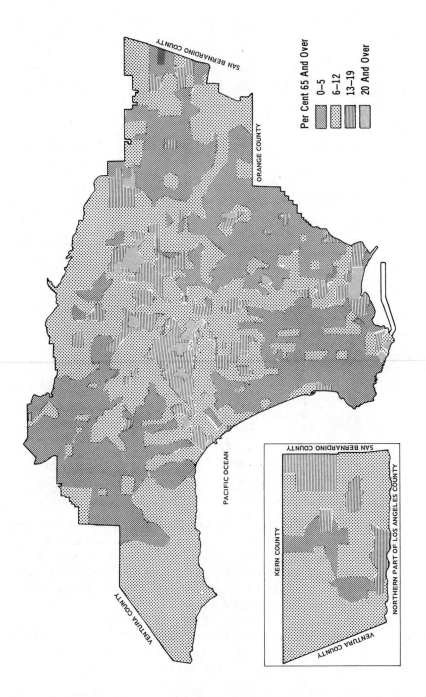

Base map by the Research Department of the Los Angeles Chamber of Commerce. Aged overlay by Edgar W. Butler.

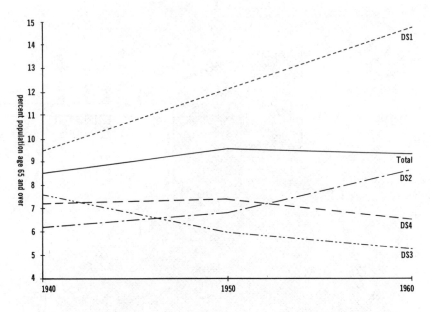

Figure 4–7 Date of Settlement in Los Angeles County and Percent Population Age Sixty-Five and Over

other ethnic minorities are remaining segregated. There appears to be a variable segregation pattern in regard to Mexican-Americans. Where they are relatively few in number, discrimination and residential segregation patterns are nearly absent. However, where there is a larger population of Mexican-Americans, discrimination and segregation patterns experienced by blacks also appear to apply to Mexican-Americans. On the other hand, it should not go unnoticed that in many cities, the aged may be more segregated than blacks and qualify for the most segregated population category. Currently it appears that in most cities and urban regions in the United States, the segregation patterns of the black and aged populations are changing very slowly.

For many years the legal codes, procedures, and processes helped maintain segregation patterns, but virtually all of these laws have been eroded over the past several decades. Some laws have been passed that make segregation and discriminatory practices illegal—for example, affirmative action and voting rights laws. However, it should be noted that the passage of laws does not automatically end such practices. Many of these laws have been neglected by those who are supposed to enforce the law, and others have not been uniformly applied throughout all regions of the country. (For the documents relating to actual United States Supreme Court decisions, see Berger, 1970.)

Part of the problem, of course, is that there has continued to be a value conflict over racial segregation and integration of housing (Bressler, 1960; Rose, et al., 1953). Recent conflicts, sometimes reaching violence, over busing of students, integration of schools, admission of minorities to union membership, and housing integration all illustrate the value conflict that remains in the United States over segregation. Segregation patterns in the United States probably will continue to exist in spite of the ideals that many profess to hold in regard to democracy, equal opportunity, and humanitarian doctrines. These ideals are pitted against contrasting values and behavior that have evolved over several centuries and established a firm grip on the emotions and attitudes of many people. Emotions and attitudes are generally not open to persuasion or reason, and thus it is doubtful that they will be changed over the next several decades.

The major forces moving toward change are increasing urbanization and industrialization, which tend to break down prevailing values and behavior patterns. Segregation patterns and discrimination, however, have been very resistant to these forces. Segregation and discriminatory behavior probably will be most likely to change if and when minorities achieve *economic* parity with the white population. One mechanism whereby minorities may achieve parity is by increasing educational levels. However, without parallel occupational opportunities, education becomes only one more reason for increased dissatisfaction with society. In other words, occupational and economic opportunity must also be available, or education is worthless and can only increase dissatisfaction and alienation from society.

One alternative is for blacks to form a separate, autonomous state in which the ideal of mutual segregation without discrimination might exist. Another possibility, of course, is for the ideals of equal opportunity, humanitarianism, and democracy to be put into actual practice, so that the segregation discussed in this chapter would no longer exist. However, what is most likely to happen is that current practices will be continued, accompanied by a slow evolution toward the ideals of democracy and equal opportunity. This will be a slow, arduous route. Thus, we can expect that well into the future controversy will rage over the forms that segregation and discrimination will take, because many people judge these right and proper while others do not. And there will continue to be conflict over the best solutions to the problems of prejudice, residential segregation, and discrimination.

NOTES

1. Carmichael and Hamilton (1967) define *institutional racism* as discrimination rooted in the social structure and social processes, whereas *individual racism* is discrimination as practiced by individuals. Thus, a person may not practice individual racism but may be involved in a social structure or social process that is discriminatory.

2. The index of dissimilarity is calculated by taking differences between two contributions, category by category, and summing either the positive or the negative differences. For example, an index of 20.0 would mean for a particular area within a city to have essentially the same distribution as the entire city (for example), it would be necessary to shift one-fifth of the population category under consideration to equalize the spatial distribution of the population. Therefore, this means that the *lower* the index, the more alike the categorical distributions are.

3. Most of the material in this section was derived from chapter twelve, "Residential Segregation," of Grebler, et al., (1970). For a more detailed analysis than was possible to present here, see that excellent discussion.

4. Cities included in this study were Boston, Buffalo, Chicago, Cincinnati, Cleveland, Columbus, Philadelphia, Pittsburgh, St. Louis, and Syracuse.

5. Jonassen (1949) shows how this New York Norwegian community maintained itself over time by moving from Manhattan across Upper New York Bay and the East River to Brooklyn.

REFERENCES

Abu-Lughod, Janet L. "Testing the Theory of Social Area Analysis: The Ecology of Cairo, Egypt." *American Sociological Review* 34 (April 1969):198–212.

Aldrich, Howard. "Ecological Succession in Racially Changing Neighborhoods: A Review of the Literature." *Urban Affairs Quarterly* 10 (March 1975): 327–348.

Berger, Stephen D. *The Social Consequences of Residential Segregation of the Urban American Negro.* New York: Metropolitan Applied Research Center, 1970.

Bressler, Marvin. "The Myers' Case: An Instance of Successful Racial Invasion." *Social Problems* 8 (Fall 1960):126–142.

Burgess, Ernest W. "The Growth of the City: An Introduction to a Research Project." In *The City,* edited by Robert E. Park, Ernest W. Burgess, and Roderick D. McKenzie. Chicago: University of Chicago Press, 1925, pp. 47–62.

Butler, Edgar W. and William J. Barclay. "A Longitudinal Examination of Two Models of Urban Spatial Differentiation: A Case Study of Los Angeles." *Research Previews* 14 (March 1967):2–25.

Carmichael, Stokley and Charles V. Hamilton. *Black Power: The Politics of Liberation in America.* New York: Vintage Press, 1967.

Connolly, Harold X. "Black Movement into the Suburbs." *Urban Affairs Quarterly* 9 (September 1973):91–111.

Cottingham, Phoebe H. "Black Income and Metropolitan Residential Dispersion." *Urban Affairs Quarterly* 10 (March 1975):273–296.

Cox, Harold and Albert Bhak. "Determinants of Age Based Residential Segregation." Department of Sociology, Indiana State University, 1975.

Duncan, Otis Dudley, and Beverly Duncan. *The Negro Population of Chicago, A Study of Residential Succession.* Chicago: University of Chicago Press, 1957.

Duncan, Beverly, Georges Sabagh, and Maurice D. Van Arsdol, Jr. "Patterns of City Growth." *American Journal of Sociology* 67 (January 1962):418–429.

Edwards, Ozzie L. "Patterns of Residential Segregation Within a Metropolitan Ghetto." *Demography* 7 (May 1970):185–193.

Farley, Reynolds. "The Changing Distribution of Negroes Within Metropolitan Areas: The Emergence of Black Suburbs." *American Journal of Sociology* 75 (January 1970): 512–529.

Goldsmith, Harold F., and Elizabeth L. Unger. "Differentiation of Urban Subareas: A Reexamination of Social Area Dimensions." Mental Health Study Center, National Institute of Mental Health, November, 1970.

Grebler, Leo, Joan W. Moore, and Ralph C. Guzman. *The Mexican-American People.* New York: Free Press, 1970.

Harris, Chauncy D., and Edward L. Ullman, "The Nature of Cities." *The Annals* 242 (November 1945):7–17.

Hoover, Edgar M., and Raymond Vernon. *Anatomy of a Metropolis.* New York: Anchor Books, 1962.

Hoyt, Homer. *The Structure and Growth of Residential Neighborhoods in American Cities.* Washington, D.C.: Federal Housing Administration, 1939.

Johnson, Charles S. *Backgrounds To Patterns of Negro Segregation.* New York: Harper and Row, 1943.

Jonassen, Christen T. "Cultural Variables in the Ecology of an Ethnic Group." *American Sociological Review* 14 (February 1949):32–41.

Kantrowitz, Nathan. "Ethnic and Racial Segregation in the New York Metropolis, 1960." *American Journal of Sociology* 74 (May 1969):685–695.

Lieberson, Stanley. *Ethnic Patterns in American Cities.* New York: Free Press, 1963.

Marston, Wilfred G. "Socioeconomic Differentials Within Negro Areas of American Cities." *Social Forces* 48 (December 1969):665–676.

Quinn, James A. *Human Ecology.* Englewood Cliffs, N.J.: Prentice-Hall, 1950.

Rose, Arnold M., Frank J. Atelsek, and Lawrence R. McDonald. "Neighborhood Reactions to Isolated Negro Residents: An Alternative to Invasion and Succession." *American Sociological Review* 18 (August 1953):497–507.

Schnore, Leo F., and Philip C. Evenson. "Segregation in Southern Cities." *American Journal of Sociology* 72 (July 1966):58–67.

Shevky, Eshref, and Marilyn Williams. *The Social Areas of Los Angeles.* Berkeley and Los Angeles: University of California Press, 1949.

Shevky, Eshref, and Wendell Bell. *Social Area Analysis.* Berkeley and Los Angeles: University of California Press, 1955.

Smith, T. Lynn. "A Comparative Study of the Age Distributions of the Populations of Major Cities in the United States." *Social Forces* 38 (March 1960):240–245.

Taeuber, Karl E., and Alma F. Taeuber. "The Negro as an Immigrant Group: Recent Trends in Racial and Ethnic Segregation in Chicago." *American Journal of Sociology* 69 (January 1964):374–382.

Van Arsdol, Jr., Maurice D., and Leo A. Schuerman. "Redistribution and Assimilation of Ethnic Populations: The Los Angeles Case." *Demography* 8 (November 1971): 459–480.

Winsborough, Halliman H., Karl E. Taeuber, and Annamette Sorensen. "Models of Change in Residential Segregation, 1940–1970." Madison: Center for Demography and Ecology, University of Wisconsin, August 1975, Paper 75-27.

5
POPULATION DENSITY AS AN URBAN PROBLEM

INTRODUCTION

Another element of the relationship of population to urban places is its *density*. There is general agreement among demographers and social scientists that high population concentration in specific areas has a profound effect on individuals. Thus, many believe that increased violence and social disintegration take place under highly dense conditions as a result of population pressure. In this chapter we will examine some of the specific consequences that density and overcrowding have on behavior, mental well-being, mental disorders, crime, and other social pathologies.

Some researchers have written about the effect crowding has on human behavior, but there is a paucity of good research. Schorr (1963) carried out a careful review of existing literature on the effect poor housing has on social pathology and reported:

> *A perception of one's self leads to pessimism and passivity, stress to which the individual cannot adapt, poor health, and a state of dissatisfaction; pleasure in company but not in solitude, cynicism about people and organizations, a high degree of sexual stimulation without legitimate outlet, and difficulty in household management and child-rearing . . . (Schorr, 1963, pp. 31–32).*

This summarizes the prevailing view up until that time. Thus, high density has been thought of as an important environmental factor related to various kinds of social and mental breakdowns and ill-nesses. This relationship has existed for a long time and was even greater when sanitary conditions were not under control and life in densely settled areas of cities was extremely hazardous. At that time, epidemics took a severe toll of the population. Even today, a sub-stantial number of studies report that people with mental and phys-ical ailments are concentrated in areas of high density. A question that needs to be answered is whether this relationship is caused by high density or if it is only an association between high density and the kinds of people who move, drift, or are left to live in such highly dense areas—minorities, the aged, and lower classes.

URBAN GROWTH AND CHANGING POPULATION DENSITY

There are several points of view regarding how population density came into being in U.S. cities. One perspective examines the process whereby the land in short supply in central cities becomes the focus of an intense economic struggle. Thus, land at the edge of the city is not nearly as valuable, yet the general pattern of population is one of density decreasing as the distance from the central business district increases. Another orientation stresses that as the overall density increases in metropolitan areas, a general shortage of land occurs and the increasing population is spatially limited because they want to live near the central business district and accessible transporta-tion. This point of view generally stresses that population growth eventually must lead to some population deconcentration, because increasing competition for central business district land for business and industrial uses forces the population out to peripheral districts where land is less expensive.

Another somewhat revised view suggests that more recent metro-politan population growth is not influenced greatly by competition for the central business district land. This perspective suggests that since the advent of modern transportation, most urban activities can locate almost anywhere in the metropolitan region and people can live just about anywhere in that metropolitan region and still be close to work, various amenities, or transportation points.

A historical factor in increasing the density of cities was the massive movement of people from other countries to the United States. His-torically, the United States is a nation populated by immigrants and descendants of immigrants—Puritans, Dutch colonists, prisoners, ne'er-do-wells, enslaved Africans, and so on. Beginning in the early 1800s, European immigrants arrived in great numbers. This immigra-tion overshadowed any movement that preceded it or has occurred since. Some early immigrants to the United States moved to rural areas. But the great immigration of the 1800s consisted primarily of immigrants from Europe who settled in large eastern U.S. cities. These immigrants numbered well over forty-two million (through 1964), although some of them eventually returned to their countries of origin (Taeuber and Taeuber, 1958, pp. 48–70).

Immigrants to the United States in the early nineteenth century lived a hard life. If they survived the diseases of the voyage across the ocean, they faced exploitation when they arrived. A high proportion of immigrants during this period entered the United States through New York, and many of them sought employment and remained in that city. Overcrowding became prevalent, and "the density of the seven lower wards of Manhattan increased from 94.5 to 163.5 persons per acre in the period from 1820 to 1850" (Glaab and Brown, 1967, pp. 93–95). Substantial numbers of people were living underground in cellars. Slums developed and began to change the character of the city. Other immigrants, especially the Irish who fled from the potato famine of the 1840s, arrived in Boston, where they faced similar dismal living and working conditions.

By 1890, New York contained more foreign born residents than any city in the world. It had as many Italians as Naples, as many Germans as Hamburg, twice as many Irish as Dublin, and two and a half times as many Jews as Warsaw (Glaab and Brown, 1967, p. 139). The structure of many U.S. cities changed markedly as a result of this large influx of immigrants. Residential segregation of immigrants created ethnic ghettos. The inhabitants of many residential areas moved out under the onslaught of thousands and thousands of immigrants seeking housing.

There were a number of consequences of the large-scale immigration to U.S. cities. In 1852, more than half of those requiring public assistance in eastern cities were Irish and German, and by 1860, 86 percent of "paupers" were of foreign birth (Glaab and Brown, 1967, p. 95). Closely associated with the growth of the immigrant population and slums in eastern cities was an increase in crime. In 1828 John Pintard wrote to his daughter that "as long as we are overwhelmed with Irish emigrants, so long will the evil abound" (Glaab and Brown, 1967, p. 95).

Political and municipal change abounded during the great immigration period. It is difficult to establish a cause and effect relationship, but many institutional changes in U.S. cities occurred at the same time the large influx of immigrants was taking place. About the time of the great immigrations to the United States, the development of slums, poverty, and crime led to formalized police systems. In addition, it was about this time that increased public assistance and increased public and municipal services such as water, fire protection, and maintenance of streets and roadways became the standard rather than the unusual. Another aspect of the great immigration was the increasing diversity found in cities in the United States. With immigrants arriving from many different countries with a variety of languages and social customs, the cities became a virtual mosaic of all Europe. Most European immigrants were peasants and thus rural oriented. Nevertheless, one aspect of their homeland that they transplanted was reflected in native organizations, banks, and mutual aid societies organized along ethnic and national origin.

The great increases in population of U.S. cities prior to the 1900s were substantially a result of migration into cities by immigrants, primarily from Europe. At the same time there was a strong migration stream within the United States from the countryside to cities. Further, immigrants from foreign lands and rural to urban migrants reproduced at a greater rate than the native urban population, further helping populate cities. "Of 11,826,000 *new* city dwellers in 1910, some 41 percent were immigrants from abroad, 29.8 percent were native rural-to-urban migrants, 21.6 percent represented natural increase, and the remaining 7.6 percent were the result of incorporation of new territories into existing cities. Virtually all demographic evidence indicates that the growth of cities in the period 1860 to 1910 was sustained by high birth rates on the farm, including the rural areas of Europe, and among people newly arrived in the city" (Glaab and Brown, 1967, p. 135).

Several of the great rural to urban streams were made up of southern blacks. The first substantial black movement occurred in the late 1700s, as slaves moved north to escape their southern masters. In the 1890s another black urban migration spurt took place (Hamilton, 1964). In the early 1900s, New York City, Philadelphia, Chicago, Cleveland, Baltimore, Washington, D.C., and St. Louis had a large influx of black population. Also, to some degree, southern cities, especially Birmingham and Norfolk, had substantial in-migration of rural blacks. This stream was brought about primarily by the cotton crop failure just prior to World War I, which was accompanied by an increased industrial labor demand in cities of the Northeast as a result of World War I (Groh, 1972, pp. 50–51).

This northward and urban migration by rural, southern blacks continued during the 1920s and 1930s. It was intensified in the 1940s by the increased demand for industrial labor in northeastern and midwestern cities brought about by World War II. Like immigrants to the United States from foreign countries, southern migrant blacks formed ethnic ghettos in receiving cities. From the very beginning these black ghettos were more dense, homogeneous, and permanent ghettos than were the immigrant enclaves. In contrast to European immigrant colonies, black ghettos did not break up over time but remained predominantly black in character and began to increase in density as well as spread outward.

One factor leading to lower density in the city was the movement of families to the suburbs. During the post World War II era, mass-produced suburbs were populated by large numbers of married couples with children. At this stage, births helped account for a greater proportion than previously of the increasing suburban population.

Demographically the suburban population is somewhat different from the city population. Even though suburban movement includes people with a wide range of social and economic characteristics, there does appear to be concentration of persons in certain categories, and more and more of the suburban population has had previous suburban living experience. So, while there are differences in suburbs, there apparently is a selectivity of population taking place as the urban center expands. Currently, families moving to the suburbs are likely to be composed of anglo adults who are in the early stages of the life and family cycles, who either bring large numbers of children with them or are having them once they have arrived in the suburbs.

Reasons given for moving to the suburb invariably include primary reference to evaluations of suburbs as more desirable places than cities to raise children because there is less congestion and there are places for children to play. Occasionally a statement is made that few desirable houses or neighborhoods are available in the city. Others report that it is cheaper to live in the suburbs because land and taxes cost less. However, this may be a misperception, inasmuch as it may actually cost more to live in suburbia than in the city.

These all are social psychological reasons advanced by respondents. Another point of view is that the main reason the suburbs and fringe areas have grown is that that is where contractors have built new houses. After available space in the city is used up and density has increased to intolerable limits, expansion has to occur at the periphery. The only other alternative is to increase urban density by increasing crowding of the existing housing supply and by building vertically. Vertical expansion, of course, is limited by the technology available at a particular point in time.

Interrelated with the mass immigrations, the southern black migration to cities, the rural-urban migrations, and suburban expansion are three important transportation eras in U.S. history that affected the density of cities: (1) the pre-1880 era—the years before electric streetcar systems came into prominence in most metropolitan areas; (2) the period between 1880 and 1920, when the streetcar was widely used in most metropolitan areas and before the automobile made its first appearance, and (3) the years since 1920, when the automobile has come to have mass acceptance (Guest, 1973, p. 57).

From this point of view, population density in cities corresponds to when they first grew to a large size and this is related to the transportation era to which they belonged. Older places—those first settled— have higher overall densities than newer places that relied on streetcars. Emerging contemporary cities have been most influenced by the automobile and have even lower densities.

In an examination of the Cleveland metropolitan area, Guest found that the three basic transportation eras were related quite systematically with the housing patterns of that metropolitan complex. His analyses of Cleveland and thirty-seven other metropolitan regions showed that population growth before streetcars led to a relatively steep density gradient; the central business district was highly dense and there was a rapidly decreasing density toward peripheral districts. However, during both the streetcar and automobile eras there was a deconcentration, or a spreading out of the population, which then resulted in a lower density in the central areas and decreasing density as one moved toward the periphery. Thus, population growth before 1880 led to a relatively congested and highly concentrated population. Population in newer cities and growth since 1880 has little effect on congestion or density and has led to a pattern of deconcentration, or the "spread city."

This research shows that urban density patterns, both in the Cleveland metropolitan area and the thirty-seven other metropolitan areas, can only be understood within the context of changing transportation trends (Guest, 1973). This is because population density patterns across metropolitan regions generally appear to have adapted to population growth differently depending on the transportation era in which they grew up. Currently, it appears that density of metropolitan regions is on a continual and gradual decrease. There is little evidence to suggest that there will be any immediate change in this pattern in the future.

DENSITY AND SOCIAL PATHOLOGIES

Schmitt (1966) studied Honolulu using an *overcrowding* measure (number of persons per room) and a *density* measure (number of persons per acre). He found that these measures corollated with the following rates: (1) deaths from all causes, (2) infant deaths, (3) suicide, (4) tuberculosis, (5) venereal disease, (6) mental hospitalization, (7) illegitimate births, (8) juvenile delinquency, and (9) imprisonment. While both overcrowding and density varied systematically with these rates, high density was more important in Honolulu. He found that the closest association with the health and disorganization rates he used was that shown by population per net residential area or high density. The relationships were particularly great with venereal disease and mental hospitalization, and low only for suicide and infant mortality. As a result of this study, Schmitt concludes that in Honolulu the population per net residential area, or density, is closely associated with morbidity, mortality, and social breakdown even when overcrowding is held constant. On the other hand, the reverse was not true. Thus, density is obviously a more important dimension than overcrowding. He reported somewhat similar results for delinquency and crime in Honolulu (Schmitt, 1957). Nevertheless, in Hong Kong, Schmitt (1963) found that density of persons per acre was not always associated with pathologies. The density of some residential areas of Hong Kong was four times that of the most densely populated areas in U.S. cities. Yet death and disease rates in the highly dense districts of Hong Kong were relatively low, and the rate for serious crime was half that of the United States.

In the study of a community within Manila, Philippines, Marsella, et al., (1970) report several factors associated with the density of people residing in a dwelling. The first factor associated with density was number of symptoms (complaints) revolving around psychosomatic illness, alienation, and anxiety. A second factor associated with density concerned physical and psychological arousal—for example, breaking things in anger, having a lack of energy, withdrawal, and so forth. It means the person bites his fingernails, has pains in his stomach, and overindulges in alcoholic beverages. A third factor, and the one most clearly associated with density, revolved around the theme of anxiety and disruptive violence. These two factors, in addition, were associated with low social class. A cautious conclusion is that "although the number of people in the dwelling is undoubtedly associated with the development of certain patterns of mental disorder, it operates as only one of a wide number of variables" (p. 292). Another important factor was social class. Lower class, as well as density, was associated with mental disorders in Manila. Part of the reason, of course, is that lower-class people face many stresses related to poor housing, financial deprivation, and status difficulty. These stresses also may contribute to mental disorders. On the other hand, anxiety and erupting violence were only associated with housing density and not social class.

There are two possible reasons for the effects of overcrowding on development of mental disorder symptoms. The number of people residing in the dwelling is likely to have implications for the patterns, styles, and motives of interpersonal relations within the household. All of these, in turn, may be related to the quantity of stress expressed by individuals in the household. Thus, the greater the number of people in the household the greater are the obligations, the more inhibition takes place, and the greater the chances for interpersonal conflict. In addition, potential opportunities for receiving praise, recognition, or attention are diminished (Marsella, et al., 1970). Larger numbers of people in households interfere with personal processes in a variety of ways which, in turn, affect the quality and quantity of stresses with which an individual must cope. Thus, a relationship develops between the amount of available physical space and physical and behavioral disorders. A lack of space results in physical or psychological withdrawal, drinking, remaining in bed, and general alienation.

Winsborough (1974) found that in Chicago, measures of health and mental disorder are associated with population density. That is, the higher the density, the higher the rates of infant deaths, tuberculosis, and public assistance. Thus, his findings suggest that increased density has a negative effect on the population. However, he suspects that there are at least three factors that need further examination: (1) socioeconomic status, (2) the quality of housing, and (3) the number of migrants. He believes that one or all of these may be confusing the relationship between density and pathology. As a result he controlled or removed the effects of socioeconomic status, the quality of housing, and migration. He then found that mortality and tuberculosis rates became negatively associated with density, as did one of the public assistance measures. However, the infant death rate remained virtually unchanged in its association with density. Thus, there is a relatively mixed set of findings in regards to density when other dimensions are controlled. Similar results were reported for rheumatic fever and density in Cincinnati (Wedum and Wedum, 1944).

In testing the hypothesis that high density of urban settlement is related to or generates pathologies, Choldin and Roncek (1975) suggest that most previous literature has examined larger areas in the metropolitan region, such as census tracts or even larger urban districts. They believe that this high level of aggregation may be clouding the relationship between density and social pathology. As a result they decided to use census blocks, a much smaller unit of analysis. In their analysis of Peoria, Illinois, they also added a number of other variables not generally examined. They chose a smaller unit at the block level because they believed that "an overwhelming fault of tracts and larger subareas is that the variation in environmental conditions and in the sociodemographic composition within tracts may be so great as to obscure the actual effect of the environmental factors on the population in regard to the generation of pathologies."

In examining the crude death rate, they found that density has a small and negative relationship to the crude death rate at the block level. Similarly, overcrowding had no relationship to the crude death rate. In examining age-specific death rates with children from birth to four years of age, they found that the percentage of units occupied at over 1.50 persons (overcrowding) per room was somewhat related to infant mortality. In further analysis, they found that density and overcrowding measures did not corollate with the general crime rate in Peoria. In fact, they found that density has a negative relationship to the crime rate which, of course, is completely contrary to general expectations. They do note, however, that the percentage of population overcrowded has a strong and positive relationship to the violent crime rate. Also, other measures of overcrowding, such as the percentage of units overcrowded at 1.01+ persons per room and the percent overcrowded at 1.50+ per persons per room, have a large positive relationship with the violent crime rate.

Overall, Choldin and Roncek believe that density and overcrowding are not very important dimensions in death rates, crimes, and so forth. This is true even though they did note that there was a relationship between overcrowding and violent crime. In explaining why they found a lack of relationship between density and social pathology, they offer two explanations. First, they used a much different and smaller unit of analysis (city blocks) whereas other studies used the census tract and larger areas such as city health districts. Second, they also note that there may be variation among the cities studied; for example, the sizes and densities of Chicago and New York as opposed to Peoria are in different orders of magnitude. The Schmitt study of Honolulu is the one most similar; but there, again, results were quite different. By adding additional variables into their analysis, they report that "a central finding of this study has been those blocks that are most familistic have the least pathology" (p. 37). They suggest that, perhaps, the percentage of husband-wife families is a surrogate for age and indicates a young or middle-aged population with low mortality, but that it also indicates areas with lower general crime rates. They note that perhaps these are the areas where housewives are home in the daytime, and so these areas are unattractive to thieves. In any case, they note that this kind of result has not been found in other studies and needs further exploration.

Others have suggested that measures of density, such as over-crowding and high density per acre, result in pathological results only when the seeds have already been sown in individuals earlier. Loring (1956) suggests that some people are more likely than others to react pathologically in a highly dense situation that may aggravate an already existing individual condition. In criticizing the use of arbitrary standards of density, Michelson (1970, p. 157) gives two reasons why they are not meaningful. First, density figures have only an indirect relation to the actual spatial situations that confront individuals. He argues that it is not the number of people per acre but rather the nature of separation of people from each other and from nonresidential land use that is important to health and pathology. Second, he accounts for the discrepancy in findings, for example, in Honolulu and Hong Kong, as suggesting the need to know how the relationship between space and pathology is mediated by the cultural context. Hall (1966) also believes that various cultures and ethnic populations have different spatial requirements; the issue of density in relationship to social pathology becomes quite complex when such factors are considered (also see Day and Day, 1973). A study of Hong Kong (Mitchell, 1971) suggests that within that culture and setting, where almost everyone lives in a dense environment, variations in density are not related to severe emotional strain but are related to lack of control over children.

Galle, et al., (1970) examined several different pathologies in Chicago and related them to one measure of population density—the number of persons per acre. They found substantial relationships between mortality, fertility, public assistance, juvenile delinquency, and admissions to mental hospitals and population density. However, when social class and ethnicity were controlled, the relationships between density and social pathologies were almost nonexistent. This shows that the relationship between density and pathologies may be spurious, because it appears that social class and ethnicity may account for the relationship between density and social pathology.

Galle, et al., note, however, that they used only one measure of density; there are several others. They mention four possible components of density: (1) the number of persons per room, (2) the number of rooms per housing unit, (3) the number of housing units per structure, and (4) the number of residential structures per acre. Thus, it may be possible for an individual to have privacy in a particular housing unit in which he lives or to be constantly in contact with others; so there may be interpersonal stress involved. According to them, two of these measures of density involve possible personal stress, (1) the number of persons per room and (2) the number of rooms per housing unit.

In their analysis using these different measures of density, they show that the results are strikingly different when the one original population density measure was used. They found density related to each of the pathologies. In each relationship, significance between components of density and pathologies remained when class and ethnicity were controlled, thus implying an important element attached to density. When carrying out several different kinds of statistical techniques, they still found that density appears to account for more variations in these pathologies than other factors. They conclude that their results are compatible with the hypothesis that density (albeit different components) are related to social pathologies.

There is some variation in how density is related to different pathologies. There are four ways in which overcrowding is related to mortality: (1) increasing contact with others increases one's chances of contacting infectious diseases; (2) individuals become tired and rundown from overcrowding and thus have increased susceptibility to disease; (3) sick persons in overcrowded situations are more likely to be disturbed by the activity of others and less likely to get the rest and relaxation that is important for treatments; and (4) overcrowding may be associated with irritability, withdrawal, and ineffectual behavior. Similarly, it appears the greater the density, the higher the fertility rate. This, it should be noted, is in contrast to animal studies, which show that overcrowding leads to decreased fertility.

Juvenile delinquency is related to density. Galle, et al., believe that this is because children are apt to find the home a relatively unattractive place under dense conditions—full of constant noise and irritation with no privacy, no place to study, and so on. Thus, they are less likely to spend much time at home under dense conditions. Spending time away from home probably leads to more delinquent behavior. At any rate, these data show that the housing units per structure measure of density has more impact upon delinquency than it does on other pathologies. Finally, for psychiatric disorders the density component with the strongest relationship to admission to mental hospitals is rooms per housing unit. This may be related to the number of people living alone, because isolation may be a contributing factor in the development of mental illness.

In conclusion, the Chicago study shows that the density component of persons per room is related to mortality, fertility, public assistance, and juvenile delinquency. The second most important measure of density for pathologies is the number of housing units per structure. On the other hand, rooms per housing unit and structures per acre are relatively unimportant. For admissions to mental hospitals, rooms per housing unit accounts for virtually all the variation in hospital admissions associated with density.

PROSPECTS

It is highly unlikely that the density of the cities in the United States will change markedly over the next several decades. It does appear that there is a relatively long-term, slow-moving trend of decreasing density in most cities. It should be particularly noted, however, that most cities designed by the futurists and utopians (See Chapter 12) are highly compact and dense. Thus, it is imperative that density be studied in much more detail than it has been to date, so that the results of such research can be incorporated in the planning of future cities.

In attempts to control density within cities and metropolitan regions, land zoning is one mechanism. Most master plans of cities not only indicate what kinds of housing units or other kinds of buildings may be built in particular areas within the cities, but they also specify the height of buildings, and the number of units that may be built within a complex—all factors that relate to population density. It should be noted that in the United States there has been great variability over time in what is considered the desired number of housing units per acre, the size of units, the desired number of rooms, and so on. One of the problems in systematically determining the relationship of density to social pathology is that most new housing constructed in the United States since World War II has been on the outskirts of formerly built-up areas. In these outskirt areas ample land is available at a reasonable cost, permitting lower population densities and presumably better living conditions than in the city. It is highly unlikely that the United States will be able to continue building housing stock in such areas at reasonable costs in the future.

We have noted a number of ways density has been measured. But there is still much to be done in relating density to social pathology. For example, Greenfield and Lewis (1969) argue that most measures of overcrowding do not take into consideration cultural values. They note that measures of per person per household, for example, ignore a measure of persons-per-sleeping-room that defines adequate sleeping arrangements. An excess of persons-per-sleeping-room, especially for children, is important, because the values of our society dictate that each child of each sex should have a separate bedroom. Most measures of overcrowding fail to take into account an individual's needs and his/her own milieu for private living space, and they also fail to differentiate between appropriate age and sex relationships in terms of culturally prescribed sleeping arrangements. Thus, more analysis may be needed to apply more sophisticated density measures, especially within housing units. (For a recent theoretical statement, see Manderscheid, 1975.)

Finally, it should be noted that some people argue that there are some advantages of high density living (for a summary and bibliography, see Freedman, 1975). It may be an economizing circumstance—density may minimize the time and cost of exchanging goods and information. Similarly, high densities permit economies in the physical and service structure of cities. In high density cities, workers can be close to places of employment, personal and household services can be located conveniently, neighbors are close at hand for mutual aid, and individuals can enjoy a stimulating environment composed of people from many different experiences and backgrounds. Other possible positive density effects are as follows:

1. Institutional support for goal attainment efforts;
2. Unparalleled opportunity for gratification;
3. Opportunity for selective association relative to compatibility of values and motives;
4. Overload of opportunity for stimulation;
5. Mutual assistance in achieving access to scarce facilities and rewards;
6. Easy availability of like-minded associates for support in norm-following behavior; and
7. Involuntary exposure to education, cosmopolitanism, and innovative ideas (Hawley, 1972, p. 526).

Future cities probably will be more dense; fortunately, it appears that density may not have as dire effects on human populations as first believed (Freedman, 1975). Recent research shows, at least tentatively, that the negative effects attributed to density are in reality effects of poverty, unemployment, and poor living conditions and not of density as such (Carnahan, et al., 1974).

REFERENCES

Carnahan, Douglas L., Avery M. Guest, and Omer R. Galle. "Congestion, Concentration, and Behavior: Research on the Study of Urban Population Density." *Sociological Quarterly* 15 (Autumn 1974):488–506.

Choldin, Harvey M., and Dennis W. Roncek. "Density and Pathology: The Issue Expanded." Paper presented at the Population Association of America, Seattle, Washington, April 1975.

Day, Alice T., and Lincoln H. Day. "Cross-National Comparison of Population Density." *Science* 181 (September 1973):1016–1023.

Freedman, Jonathan C. *Crowding and Behavior.* San Francisco: W. H. Freeman, 1975.

Galle, Omer R., Walter R. Gove, and J. Miller McPherson. "Population Density and Pathology: What Are the Relationships For Man?" *Science* 176 (April 1972):23–30.

Glaab, Charles N., and A. Theodore Brown. *A History of Urban America.* New York: Macmillan, 1967.

Greenfield, R. J., and June F. Lewis. "An Alternative to a Density Function Definition of Overcrowding." *Land Economics* 45 (May 1969):282–285.

Groh, George, W. *The Black Migration: The Journey to Urban America.* New York: Weybright and Talley, 1972.

Guest, Avery M. "Urban Growth and Population Densities." *Demography* 10 (February 1973):53–69.

Hall, Edward T. *The Hidden Dimension.* Garden City, N.Y. Doubleday, 1966.

Hamilton, C. Horace. "The Negro Leaves the South." *Demography* 1 (1964):273–295.

Hawley, Amos H. "Population Density and the City," *Demography* 9 (November 1972):521–529.

Loring, William C. "Housing and Social Organization." *Social Problems* 3 (January 1956):160–168.

Manderscheid, Ronald W. "A Theory of Spatial Effects." *Progress in Cybernetics and Systems Research* 1 (1975):75–83.

Marsella, Anthony J., Manuel Escudero, and Paul Gordon. "The Affects of Dwelling Density on Mental Disorders in Filipino Men." *Journal of Health and Social Behavior* 11 (December 1970):288–294.

Michelson, William. *Man and His Urban Environment: A Sociological Approach.* Reading, Mass.: Addison-Wesley, 1970.

Mitchell, Robert E. "Some Social Duplications of High Density Living." *American Sociological Review* 36 (February 1971):18–29.

Schmitt, Robert C. "Density, Health, and Social Disorganization." *Journal of the American Institute of Planners* 31 (January 1966):38–39.

_____. "Implications of Density in Hong Kong." *Journal of the American Institute of Planners* 29 (August 1963):210–217.

_____. "Density, Delinquency, and Crime in Honolulu." *Sociology and Social Research* 41 (March-April, 1957):274–276.

Schorr, Alvin. *Slums and Social Insecurity.* Washington, D.C.: Government Printing Office, 1963.

Taeuber, Conrad, and Irene B. Taeuber. *The Changing Population of The United States.* New York: Wiley, 1958.

Wedum, Arnold G., and Bernice G. Wedum. "Rheumatic Fever in Cincinnati in Relation to Rentals, Crowding, Density of Population, and Negroes." *American Journal of Public Health* 34 (October 1944):1065–1070.

Winsborough, Hal H. "The Social Consequences of High Population Density." In *Comparative Urban Structure,* edited by Kent P. Schwirian. Lexington, Mass.: D.C. Heath, 1974, pp. 193–198.

PART III
URBAN PROBLEMS AND PROSPECTS

6
POWER IN URBAN AMERICA

INTRODUCTION

Two of the most important organizational aspects of contemporary urban society are the notions of *power* and *power structures*. The power to make decisions in cities, and at other levels, is important in determining much of what is and is not accomplished in contemporary urban United States. At the individual level, power is defined as the capacity to command a particular behavior or performance by another individual.[1] From a social system point of view, power includes the belief that every unit of human organization, the family, voluntary organizations, and the community, has a system of power organized to facilitate the performance of activities (Hawley, 1971, p. 210). *Urban power structures* are defined as the characteristic patterns within a city or urban complex whereby resources are mobilized and sanctions employed in ways that affect the city as a whole (Walton, 1967). Thus, the urban complex is considered as an organization of units revolving around the notion of power. At the community system level an organization or *power group* may be able to command performance or behavior by other individuals or organizations. Power is in operation when one organization is controlling another. Power (Lasswell and Kaplan, 1950) is found in the control of that which is valued by people in a society. In the United States, this means that whoever controls economic institutions holds power, influences decisions, and thus is able to implement decisions (Goldberg and Linstromberg, 1966).

Power in urban America has changed as urbanization has taken place. As society became urbanized and industrialized, channels of communication changed and conflict between elitist adherents and democratic idealists became an important issue in the United States. This conflict over decision making has generated a substantial body of literature and research in political science and sociology. This two-pronged research literature begins with different assumptions about decision making and generally results in contrasting conclusions about the exercise of power in urban America.

Questions that have been asked and investigated by persons interested in power structures are as follows: (1) Is there a single, monolithic hierarchically structured power system in the United States, or are there different power structures, the number and nature depending on the characteristics of the local city or metropolitan region's institutional system? (2) Who are the power elite (where they exist), and how do they exercise power in decision making and control of institutional functions? (3) To what extent are there interlocking power positions that include power derived from economic, political, and social institutions? (4) In what way is a local community power structure interlaced with regional or national power systems or both? (5) What methods or approaches are most effective in the study of community power and with what results? So far not investigated is the relationship of potential versus actual power.

URBANIZATION AND POWER STRUCTURES
Virtually no studies exist of the impact of urbanization on power structures. However, studies of early cities suggest quite clearly that they contained elites and that most of the population did not have any voice in decisions that affected them. Subsequently it appears that there has been increased participation in decision making by larger population segments. The two major transfers of economic power since the feudal period were brought about by the changing technology that disrupted the feudal order and transferred power to the corporate structure and by a second change now in process that is transferring power from the corporate structure to government, especially the federal government (Goldberg and Linstromberg, 1966, p. 8).

TYPES OF POWER STRUCTURES
Most investigators tend to classify power structures as *monolithic* or *pluralistic*. However, some research has shown that this dichotomy may be too simple. The conflicting notions appear to focus on four possible types: (1) monolithic, (2) pluralistic, (3) countervailing elites, and (4) amorphous (for another approach, see Agger, et al., 1964).

In the monolithic or pyramidal model there are established repetitive and predictable patterns of decisions made by an elite group, which generally controls the economic sphere of the city. In other words, a single solitary group controls decisions that are of city-wide scope; this is an authoritarian model. Within the monolithic type, subtypes can be identified that involve the two major aspects of power as set forth by Weber (1957); these are (1) *personal attribute factors* and (2) power as part of *established authority*.

A *pluralistic* model (sometimes called coalitional) has been proposed by political scientists (Dahl, 1961). Their notion also includes established, repetitive, and predictable patterns of decision making, but decisions are made by legitimate authorities; leadership varies by issue and is made up of fluid and interested persons and groups (Walton, 1967). Groups involved in making decisions are assumed to represent the people and are responsible to them. While such groups may compete, they generally have assigned and accepted areas of decision making.

The *countervailing elite* and *amorphous* types have been relatively neglected by theorists (however, see Galbraith, 1952) and by researchers. The countervailing elite model consists of at least two, durable competing elites who are attempting to control decisions. The major difference between this view and the pluralistic one is the number of durable factions; the degree of conflict is much greater and presumably involves different value systems and resultant implications for decision making and issue outcomes. An amorphous power structure is one that has not solidified—there are a large number of competing interest and power centers without a persistent pattern of leadership being exercised.

Cross-cutting all types are *concealed* and *visible* leaders. Visible leaders have been more closely associated with the pluralistic model. Concealed leadership has more often been associated with monolithic systems, although some argue that they are not limited to one type of leadership system (Miller and Dirksen, 1963). *Symbolic leaders* do not have much power according to other leaders, but are perceived by nonleaders as being powerful persons in the community (Bonjean, 1963). There is some evidence that visibility of leadership is related to city characteristics (Bonjean and Carter, 1965; Preston, 1969, p. 46).

DETERMINATION OF POWER STRUCTURES

Early studies of community power structures dealt with reputations of power within one local community which emphasized perceptions of various *knowledgeables*. A list of prominent leaders was generated by knowledgeable persons in the community who were interviewed. Interviewed leaders listed other leaders which resulted in "snowballing" as more leaders were named. Focus was on the extent of social interaction among nominated leaders, and a voting system determined the most influential leaders. The person nominated most often by other named leaders was presumed to have more influence than those who received fewer votes (Hunter, 1953).

The reputational approach has been criticized because emphasis is placed on perception of individuals and not on behavior in community political systems (Dahl, 1961; Wolfinger, 1960; Sayre and Polsby, 1965, pp. 127–134). Critics have asked the following: (1) Are reputations for power an adequate index of the distribution of power? (2) Even if the respondent's perceptions of power relations are accurate, is it useful to describe (political) systems by presenting rankings of leader participants according to their power? Also, it has been charged that reputationalists expect a tight-knit, monolithic structure to emerge because their ideology influences their research. Thus, according to critics, reputationalists look for a monolithic structure, assume a static distribution of power, and ignore goals, strategies, power bases, decisional outcomes, and recruitment patterns. (For reasoned critiques, see Anton, 1963; Danzger, 1964.)

Political scientists have more often studied issues and decisions by focusing on the political system. Emphasis is on political processes and on persons who have political positions that were gained through elections or political appointment. The major criticism of this approach is that it is primarily concerned with decisions made by persons in elected or appointed governmental and corporate positions. There has not been an attempt to go behind the scenes to determine whether there are persons or groups that hold power over political office holders.

Both perspectives illustrate the consistency or pattern of positions that leaders hold, including company presidents, managers of absentee-owned corporations, bank presidents, head cashiers of banks, mayors or city managers, city attorneys, medical association chairmen, bar association chairmen, and judges. Sometimes included are people who hold such positions as school superintendent, school board chairman, president of an influential union, newspaper editor, television station manager, pastor of a prestige church, police chief, or United Fund executive director.

Researchers utilizing the reputational approach tend to report centralized decision-making structures while researchers using other methods report varied structures (Walton, 1966). This has been interpreted as a method that influences research results and, of course, the resultant description of the city or community under investigation. Also, it has been argued that researchers with different methodological orientations study communities with characteristics that match their predispositions—for example, monolithic or pluralistic power structures (Clark, et al., 1968). If this is so, then a city's structural characteristics could explain more variation in power structure type than the discipline of the researcher (Blankenship, 1964).

NATIONAL POWER STRUCTURE

Mills (1959) believed that a national power elite rules the country and makes decisions on issues salient to the elite. According to him, the power elite consists of top men in the institutional hierarchies of the economy, political order, and military establishment. There is a "circulation of the elite," according to Mills, with interchangeability among top leadership positions. Thus, a high ranking military officer might retire and become a high level corporate officer, or a high ranking banker might become an ambassador in government service. These men generally are wealthy, but their wealth is a result of power rather than a cause of it. Further, Mills believes they form a self-conscious social class because they view themselves as different from other people and because their behavior toward each other is distinctly different from their behavior toward others (1959, p. 11).

Hunter (1959) also argued that there is a power elite in the United States that controls decisions. Hunter believes that the membership lists of the National Industrial Conference, the Committee for Economic Development, and the Business Advisory Council provide good starting points for anyone interested in a quick rundown of national leadership (p. 33). His conclusion parallels that of Mills—Hunter argues that a single, monolithic, hierarchically structured power system makes most of the influential decisions in the United States. These decisions deal not only with local and national issues, but with international issues as well. Further, he demonstrated that the national leadership is systematically interrelated with local power structures— that is, a network exists.

From Hunter's point of view, government is only an instrument for the execution of policy, not for the formation of policy. Most top leaders, according to him, are not political representatives but are those who raise political money and confer with others about suitable candidates for public offices. Although political representatives listen to the public, their focus is on industrial policy-makers and their desires (p. 209). Hunter gives the actual names of leaders, and so his work can be utilized for various analyses, including examining personal characteristics of top leaders in the power elite (also see Lundberg, 1968).

Domhoff (1967) also has asked the question: "Is the American upper class a governing class?" He concludes that, by all generally acceptable definitions of social class, a national super social class exists in the United States. This upper class owns a disproportionate amount of wealth, receives a disproportionate amount of yearly income, and controls major banks and corporations that in turn control the United States economy. In addition, this upper class controls foundations, elite universities, the mass media, and important "opinion-molding associations" such as the Council on Foreign Relations, the Foreign Policy Association, the Business Advisory Council, National Advertising Council, and so on and on. Also, members of the super-upper class control the executive branch of the federal government, and through it influence regulatory agencies, the federal judiciary, the military, the CIA, and the FBI. Through its control of corporations, foundations, elite universities, the presidency, the federal judiciary, the military, and the CIA, it qualifies as a "governing class" (Domhoff, 1967, p. 11).

On the other hand, several social scientists believe that, while there may have once been a single hierarchal ruling class, it has been replaced by "veto groups" and dispersal of power (Riesman, et al., 1956). Others believe that the U.S. power structure should be viewed as highly complex and diversified (rather than unitary and monolithic). They believe that the political system is more or less democratic (with the glaring exception of the Negro's position until the 1960s) and that the political elite is ascendant over and not subordinate to the economic elite (Rose, 1967, p. 492).

The controversy over what kind of national power structure exists in the United States continues. Each researcher must examine data to determine whether they correspond to the point of view of a monolithic structure or a highly complex power structure (see Allen, 1974; Lundberg, 1968; *Report of the Federal Trade Commission*, 1951).

CITY CHARACTERISTICS AND LOCAL POWER STRUCTURES

Many social scientists assume that all local community power structures are alike—rural villages, commuter suburbs, central cities, and entire metropolitan regions all tend to be included under the general concept of community. Yet there are variations among cities in industrial makeup, location in metropolitan regions, age, national region, growth characteristics, size, density, and functional type, and some of these characteristics may be related to type of power structure (Rogers, 1962).

In some cities absentee-owned corporations influence decisions that are made locally through the role executives from these corporations play in civic affairs. One such study of absentee-owned corporations and their executives in Bigtown (Baton Rouge, Louisiana) suggests that executives generally are attempting to further their corporate careers by participating in local decisions; however, at least some participate because they are concerned with the sorry state of community services in Bigtown and want to contribute toward improvement (Pellegrin and Coates, 1956). Nevertheless, since the executive depends on career advancement by his superiors rather than on local individuals or institutions, if a conflict between the local community and corporation exists, executives invariably side with the corporation.

From another view, Duncan and Schnore (1959) hypothesize that cities of different size and functional type comprise significantly different areas for the struggle between contending power groups. It also has been suggested that dominance within a community ordinarily is associated with those functional units that control the flow of sustenance (economic resources) into it (Hawley, 1950). Wealth as a resource of influence can be turned into control over other resources—such as personnel, or institutions—that can be utilized in influencing decisions.

A plausible hypothesis is that the more heterogeneous the city the more likely there is to be a pluralistic or amorphous power structure, especially where there is a great deal of economic diversity. An amorphous system is expected to be found in a heterogeneous community undergoing extremely rapid growth and other types of change. Yet Walton (1967) argues that region, population size, composition, industrialization, economic diversity, and type of local government are not related to type of power structure. On the other hand, local ownership, lack of adequate economic resources, status as an independent city (not a satellite), and lack of party competition are associated with a community that has a pyramidal or monolithic power structure.

Gilbert (1967) argues that self-contained communities are becoming rarer, and as a result most local community power structures are becoming more pluralistic. However, her description of many cities suggests an amorphous structure—diffuse and fragmented. The only way things get accomplished in such cities is for a strong leader to rise who is capable of pulling together disparate interest groups. Gilbert concludes that cities increasingly are becoming reformed and more pluralistic in nature; that they are continuing to have the same kinds of conflicts; that officials have decreasing power in an increasingly large proportion of cities that now have economic dominants at the upper levels of power; and that there is no apparent trend in increased utilization of experts in shaping policy. It appears that it is extremely difficult for innovation to be developed by experts in government or by generally established pressure or interest groups. However, there is some trend for ad hoc groups to develop innovative programs. Overall, Gilbert concludes that decision making is "less and less in the hands of a privileged few and is increasingly dependent upon the broker, be he elected official or not, who can bring together (to the extent he can bring together) various elements in the *community*."

When community consensus is limited, leadership tends to be more competitive (Walton, 1967). Further, "to the extent that the local community becomes increasingly interdependent with respect to extra-community institutions (or develops along its vertical axis) the structure of local leadership becomes more competitive." Development along extra-local lines involves interdependence and the introduction of new interests and institutional relationships and thus introduces competitiveness into the power structure.

Invariably, researchers suggest that more general knowledge about characteristics of communities needs to be obtained before we will be able to understand how social structure affects leadership systems. Studies have shown that such city characteristics as type of community, partisan or nonpartisan elections, and median age of population may be related to power structure type.

LOCAL POWER STRUCTURES
Most studies of power structures in the United States have focused on a single local community. One of the first studies reported that the power structure of Middletown (Muncie, Indiana) essentially consisted of one family and that, from the 1920s through the 1930s, this community power structure was continued by family sons. This particular family dominated the manufacturing, banking, hospitals, department stores, milk depots, political parties, churches, and the newspaper in the city and controlled the local airport (Lynd and Lynd, 1929, 1937). This degree of concentration of power in one family does not exist in most other cities, but power concentrations are systematically reported by researchers.

Atlanta, Georgia
The one study that set off a whole spate of power structure studies was carried out by Hunter (1953) of Atlanta, Georgia (Regional City) right after the end of World War II. This study reported that there were two power structures in Atlanta at that time. One consisted entirely of whites; and another power structure identified in the black community was beholden to the white power structure (see also Burgess, 1962). Hunter found about forty persons who made up the power structure. They were primarily presidents of companies, chairmen of boards of corporations or institutions, professionals (primarily lawyers), or socially prominent through inherited wealth. Most leaders knew other leaders, belonged to interlocking directorates in business and corporations, and had overlapping club memberships. Also reported in this study were links to national leaders, and these led Hunter to carry out his national study of top leaders discussed earlier.

Top leaders of Atlanta did not hold offices in charitable, civic, or social organizations. They exerted influence through organizations, by holding positions on boards of corporations, as presidents of banks, and so on. Nevertheless, top leaders exercised power over those who did hold offices in charitable, civic, or social organizations and thus kept these organizations under their power. Hunter concluded that Atlanta was governed by a concealed economic elite.

Most leaders of Atlanta lived in the most desirable section of the city. Only one person considered as a leader or high level professional in Atlanta actually lived in an undesirable residential area.

A decade or so after Hunter studied Atlanta, another study of decision making in that city was carried out. This particular study was not specifically a replication of the earlier study but was influenced by it (Jennings, 1964, see especially Chapter 8). At this time, top level influentials were highly politicized and involved in a moderate range of issues; however, there were issues in which top level leaders were not involved. In addition, persons other than those considered top leaders were involved in decision making over some issues. Thus, viewed out of the context of a large range of issues, it appears that Atlanta also had a general elite at the time of this study. However, this is not true, according to the author, because the city was actually dominated by a "number of slightly to moderately competitive coalitions, *not dominated by economic notables,* exercising determinative influence in their own policy areas" (p. 161).

At this time, economic notables were important in the decision-making process but not as important as reported by Hunter. Economic dominants played significant roles in decision making in Atlanta but there is a rejection of the idea that they prevailed over others in the community. However, the author notes that "we cannot deny the importance some of them have for decision making in Atlanta" (p. 166).

Apparently there is some overlapping membership among coalitions and some persons link coalitions together by participating in several different decisions. One problem with this study is that no distinction is made by salience of issues to influentials. Thus, leaders may not actively participate in some decisions that are relatively unimportant to them. However, if the issue were salient to the leadership— for example, taxes—would they systematically influence the decision?

Three possible explanations exist as to why contrasting findings were found in the two Atlanta studies. First, changes in the structure could have occurred over time; second, the authors had different orientations to the decision-making process; and third, differences in research techniques were utilized. There is some support for the change in power structure argument, since federal programs may have increased the impact local governmental officials have in obtaining such programs. Similarly, race relations have changed dramatically in Atlanta. Since these studies, a black mayor has been elected in Atlanta. However, these arguments were rejected by Jennings. Instead he believed that Hunter emphasized decisions in regard to *fixing priorities* and thus overlooked other phases, such as initiation, planning, long-range conditioning of attitudes, persuasion, bargaining, promotion, and implementation (p. 163). One could argue, however, that fixing priorities is the most important area of concern and that other stages are not as important because they are dependent on previously fixed priorities.

Syracuse, New York
In Syracuse, one study showed that local industrialists made up the top of the power structure (Hodges, 1958), with government officials and politicians being subordinate. Subsequent studies reported that a number of persons, from a variety of institutions, have and wield power in Syracuse (Martin, Munger, et al., 1961; Freeman, et al., 1960).

In fact, the monolithic power structure that "many knowledgeables in local affairs" believe to exist is a myth (Martin, Munger, et al., 1961, p. 306). One person is quite consistently mentioned as having the key power, an individual without whose "consent, tacit or explicit, nothing of importance can be done." He is referred to as Mr. Syracuse. Nevertheless, "analyses of actual decisions taken with respect to public problems in the Syracuse metropolitan area do not support an interpretation based on the concept of monolithic power" (p. 306).

As a result of relationships among reputation, position, and participation, leaders in Syracuse were classified as (1) *institutional leaders,* (2) *effectors,* or (3) *activists.* Institutional leaders are "the heads of the largest and most actively participating business, industrial, governmental, political, professional, educational, labor, and religious organizations in Syracuse" (Freeman, et al., 1963, p. 797), and were uncovered by reputational, positional, or organizational participation. Institutional leaders are not active participants in community activities. Many effectors are employed by institutional leaders and "it seems likely that their activities are frequently guided by what they view as company policy" (p. 798). Finally, activists are people who lack an institutional power base but are active in voluntary organizations, clubs, and so on. Though their commitments of time and effort they help shape the future of the community. At one time, perhaps thirty years earlier, institutional leaders and effectors were the same people, but over recent decades there has been a broadening circle of participants in decision making.

Information on participation in decisions by "won" and "lost" suggests that the dominant winning factions in Syracuse are the Republican Party, the Manufacturers Association, real estate interests, town government officials, and to a lesser degree, the village weekly newspapers. The Democratic Party, CIO, and League of Women Voters seldom, if ever, won a decision (p. 309). Nevertheless, three conclusions are cited in this study: (1) a monolithic power structure does not exist in Syracuse; (2) there tend to be as many decision centers as there are decision areas, and decisions are fragmented in persons, agencies, and institutions; and (3) there are many different kinds of community power.

Battle Creek, Michigan

There have been several studies of Battle Creek, Michigan (Community A). The first study delineated a power structure much like that of Atlanta (Belknap and Smuckler, 1956). The city at that time was described as having a fairly concentrated manufacturing base, with a small proportion of minorities. It was conservative, used a nonpartisan ballot, and was much like other Michigan cities in the same size category (about fifty thousand population). Around fifteen individuals made up the power structure. Nevertheless, one person stood out in all of the different ways in which power was determined—a lawyer and former three-term mayor from a well-known family. In Battle Creek, *positions* held in the community—for example, in industry or business, in city government, and in organizations—are closely linked to community leadership. The major exception is that positions in organized labor were not important in leadership in this city. Leaders were instrumental in most city activities and their backing and approval was sought. At a second level, approximately sixty other persons were designated as second echelon leaders. Thus, overall, this study suggests a small core of leaders, a somewhat larger pool of secondary leaders, and a mass of nonparticipants or nonactives—a pyramidal model.

Seven years later, a replication of the power structure in Battle Creek was accomplished (Booth and Adrian, 1962). During these seven years, the economic environment in Battle Creek had deteriorated, and downtown was being vacated by businesses for more favorable locations even though there was more than adequate parking. The city had a 10 percent decline in population, although the black proportion of population had doubled, as had the working class. Some of the important changes that took place during the seven years between the two studies were population and environmental changes resulting from slum clearance, flood control, expressway development, and the flight to the suburbs. Another major change noted was that more *city* leaders now lived outside the city limits.

The 1961 study did not use the same methodology as the earlier study, but results were comparable. Nearly all top fifteen leaders held important community positions, and virtually all leaders who appeared in the earlier study also were still leaders. During the interim seven years, a split had grown in the leadership of Battle Creek. The mayor, a labor union official, and one city councilman claimed to be members of the working class and to represent those interests. "All three representatives of the labor point of view were avowed and outspoken opponents of the old city leadership" (p. 288). Was this city moving toward a countervailing elite model? Unfortunately, there have been no additional follow-up studies of this city's power structure, so this question remains unanswered.

Other Cities

A large number of studies of other cities suggest that there are variations in decision making—some are described as monolithic and others as pluralistic. A study of cities along the United States and Mexican border showed that the reputational technique provided a good indication of perceived general influence apart from specific influence, and that reputed leaders are deeply involved in general community decision making (D'Antonio and Erickson, 1962). "Our findings suggest that a group of general community influentials did in fact exist in El Paso and that its existence has had important consequences for the community during the 1950s."

A study of Lorain, Ohio, reported multiple coalitions of individuals and groups that form in that city depending on the issue at hand (McKee, 1958). Another variation was reported in a study of an industrial suburb in which major plants had been absorbed by absentee-owned corporations. This study showed that managers of these plants did not meddle in local decisions, thus leaving decisions to be made by others (Schulze, 1958). This left an apparent power vacuum. Abdication of power by the corporation may be a result of the feeling that the local community could have little effect on the corporation. If the local community made a decision that adversely affected the corporation, the corporation could probably respond by using its potential power and by threatening to leave the city.

The higher the appraisal of a leader by the community, the higher the evaluation that leader had of greater support from the community. In addition, highest rated leaders were those who were perceived or identified as influential in a number of issue-related areas: business and industry, education, religion, politics, municipal affairs, and personal matters. Thus, there was no relationship between the *content* of issues and community evaluation. At least in one city, there appears to be a conjunction between community appraisal, leadership self-evaluation, and influence (Abu-Laban, 1963).

POWER STRUCTURES, COMMUNITY DECISIONS, AND ISSUE OUTCOMES

It appears that in every community there are individuals who have considerable influence over community affairs, over what gets considered as an issue, how issues are decided, and how decisions are implemented. Communities confront numerous problems, some recognized by everyone, some by a few, and some generally unrecognized. In addition, there is variation in the extent to which different community problems are considered important issues—tax rates, fluoridation of water, crime and delinquency, industrial development, antipoverty programs, water, air, or soil pollution, and so on. Of those potential problems that become issues, a variety of outcomes can be specified: (1) discussion, no specifics; (2) actual proposals pending; (3) proposals rejected with opposition; (4) proposals dropped; (5) adopted, no opposition; and (6) adopted, over opposition.

An important question is, what issues are decided at what levels? "The initiation of issues and the decisions about them may occur at quite different levels in the power structure" (Schermerhorn, 1961, p. 100). In the initial stage, there are three major areas of controversial issues. First, conflicts may arise over economic issues such as taxes and industrialization; second, disputes may arise over form of government, representation in decision making, and so on; and third, conflict may arise over certain cultural beliefs and values, such as educational philosophy and school desegregation (Coleman, 1957). An important question is, "what issues are not allowed in the area of public discussion, and what problems are allowed to become part of the public realm?" "This problem is important because the selection of issues—at least public issues—precedes the making of decisions" (Schermerhorn, 1960, p. 101). Some grievances and conditions never become issues. This may be because individuals or groups effectively prevent them from becoming issues. This too, of course, is the exercise of power. While this may describe a *nondecision* or *nonevent*, in fact the process of nondecision making may be the same as decision making (Bachrach and Baratz, 1963, p. 1970). Thus, many outcomes of urban power structures may not be observable, for example, the decision *not* to have an antipoverty or urban renewal program.

Many outcomes in an urban place are influenced by decisions made external to the local unit. That is, "policies and procedures of state or national organizations, by state and federal law, and by developments in the national economy" (Warren, 1956, p. 338) all influence community decisions. Cities and other places in the United States "are simply points of geographical contact of crisscrossing networks of different organizations like the Presbyterian Church, the Grange, Rotary International, Standard Oil Company of New Jersey, Atlantic & Pacific, and so forth" (Warren, 1956, p. 338). These extra-local influences limit local autonomy by regulations, by charters defining operating conditions, and by administrative directives.

Issues vary in their relevancy for the leadership system. In many instances issues are perceived as salient only if social change may become manifest because of a decision. Because monolithic leadership structures control the number and shape of important decisions, a concentration of power results in substantial activity or little activity as a result of leadership consistently influencing decision making on various types of issues in one direction. Therefore, two possibilities exist, depending on the value system within the monolithic structure. A monolithic structure can *block* decisions or it can actively seek, influence, and direct programs in the community (Fowler, 1958). In monolithic communities, if the issue is salient to the leadership, it is assumed that the program will be shaped and resolved in a fashion suitable to the leadership structure. Cities with a pluralistic power system probably offer the most opportunity for innovation in solving problems. This occurs because power centers interlock with each other and have a greater state of knowledge about each other. "For many issues this will mean the creation of an organization whose specific task is the implementation of the decision to innovate" (Aiken and Alford, 1970, p. 663) such as housing authorities and welfare councils (see also Turk, 1970).

Both countervailing elites and amorphous types are assumed to be nearly incapable of reaching long-term decisions, or of sustaining decisions. In the countervailing elite system, this occurs because centers of power alternately control community affairs. At times, coalitions may be formed that will temporarily allow decisions to be implemented, but coalitions tend to be short term. Thus, the countervailing elite model suggests a great deal of variability in decisions, as the ebb and flow of power in the community fluctuates and as issues become differentially important to each of the countervailing elites. When there are approximately equal countervailing elites, alternating periods of dominance should result in programs undergoing changes in number, kind, and shape.

In the amorphous type, inaction occurs because no decisions are made, inasmuch as there are no major power centers and alternately there are many veto groups. The amorphous type consists of a large number of power centers that have not coalesced into an effective decision-making or controlling system for community affairs, and/or a high level of citizen participation that generates conflict and prevents effective decision making (Crain and Rosenthal, 1967).

While the above assumes a *patterned* relationship between leadership structures and community decision making and consequent number and shape of community programs, little research has been carried out to verify such hypotheses. Also, it should be noted that at least several other perspectives have been developed. For example, a more elaborate and complex formulation was advanced by D'Antonio and Erickson (1962, p. 375), who noted in their studies along the U.S. and Mexican border that few cities had monolithic power elites and also that these cities did not fit the pluralist model. These cities had a small group of persons whose influence was "general" and cut across many issues, although at times these persons were in contention with each other in regard to the outcomes of decisions. Whether this study is generalizable or simply characterizes border cities has not been determined; however, a study of eighteen New England communities showed some very strong similarities (Gamson, 1966).

A view contrary to all of these studies has been advanced by Long (1958). He believes that when cities and decision making are examined closely, there is *no* structured decision making. Rather, he sees issues as being resolved by the development of a system of unintended cooperation among interested groups and institutions. Unintentional coalitions deal with metropolitan problems from a limited point of view, for example ones confined to their particular interests or institutional bases. Thus, he argues that the debate in the power structure literature is misplaced because it may have obscured the possibility that *no one is systematically making decisions.*

This may appear to be the case, even though it may not be true, because few studies have examined the full range of issues that come before a community and an individual decision-maker. Most issues and outcomes examined have been dramatic or controversial, rather than everyday decisions that affect the local community. Similarly, few studies conducted so far have been comparative in nature; that is, few have compared a large number of cities in regard to a variety of dramatic and nondramatic issues, decisions made in regard to them, and their subsequent outcomes (Rossi, 1957).

While there is a relative lack of knowledge, the flow of power structure studies, especially as they have been interrelated with outcomes, has slowed over the past few years. Nevertheless, it is quite apparent to anyone who works in cities that power exists, that it is being utilized, and that it has impact on the lives of all citizens. It is, therefore, regrettable that such studies have declined in recent years.

NOTES

1. For a critique of this notion of power, see Bierstedt (1950) and Bachrach and Baratz (1963; 1970).

REFERENCES

Abu-Laban, Baha. "Self-Conception and Appraisal by Others: A Study of Community Leaders." *Sociology and Social Research* 48 (October 1963): 32–37.

Agger, Robert E., Daniel Goldrich, and Bert E. Swanson. *The Rulers and the Ruled.* New York: Wiley, 1964.

Aiken, Michael, and Robert R. Alford. "Community Structure and Innovation: The Case of Urban Renewal." *American Sociological Review* 35 (August 1970): 650–665.

Allen, Michael P. "The Structure of Interorganizational Elite Cooptation: Interlocking Corporate Directorates." *American Sociological Review* 39 (June 1974):393–406.

Anton, Thomas F. "Power, Pluralism, and Local Politics." *Administrative Science Quarterly* 7 (March 1963):425–457.

Bachrach, Peter, and Morton S. Baratz. *Power and Poverty: Theory and Practice.* London: Oxford University Press, 1970.

Bachrach, Peter, and Morton S. Baratz. "Decisions and Nondecisions: An Analytical Framework." *American Political Science Review* 57 (September 1963):632–642.

Belknap, George, and Ralph Smuckler. "Political Power Relations in a Midwest City." *Public Opinion Quarterly* 20 (Spring 1958):73–81.

Bierstedt, Robert. "An Analysis of Social Power." *American Sociological Review* 15 (December 1950):730–738.

Blankenship, L. Vaughn. "Community Power and Decision Making: A Comparative Evaluation of Measurement Techniques." *Social Forces* 43 (December 1964):207–216.

Bonjean, Charles M. "Community Leadership, A Case Study and Conceptual Refinement." *American Journal of Sociology* 68 (May 1963):672–681.

Bonjean, Charles M., and Lewis F. Carter. "Legitimacy and Visibility Leadership Structures Related to Four Community Systems." *Pacific Sociological Review* 8 (Spring 1965):16–20.

Booth, David A., and Charles R. Adrian. "Power Structure and Community Change: A Replication Study of Community A." *Midwest Journal of Political Science* 6 (August 1962):277–296.

Burgess, M. Elaine. *Negro Leadership in a Southern City.* Chapel Hill: University of North Carolina Press, 1962.

Clark, Terry N., William Kornblum, Harold Bloom, and Susan Tobias. "Discipline, Method, Community Structure, and Decision Making: The Role and Limitations of the Sociology of Knowledge." *The American Sociologist* 3 (August 1968):214–217.

Coleman, James S. *Community Conflict.* Glencoe: Free Press, 1957.

Crain, Robert L., and Donald B. Rosenthal. "Community Status as a Dimension of Local Decision Making." *American Sociological Review* 32 (December 1967):970–984.

Dahl, Robert A. *Who Governs?* New Haven: Yale University Press, 1961.

D'Antonio, William V., and Eugene C. Erickson. "The Reputational Technique as a Measure of Community Power: An Evaluation Based on Comparative and Longitudinal Studies." *American Sociological Review* 27 (June 1962):362–376.

Danzger, M. Herbert. "Community Power Structure: Problems and Continuities." *American Sociological Review* 29 (October 1964):707–717.

Domhoff, G. William. *Who Rules America?* Englewood Cliffs, N.J.: Prentice-Hall, 1967.

Duncan, Otis Dudley, and Leo F. Schnore. "Cultural, Behavioral, and Ecological Perspectives in the Study of Social Organizations." *American Journal of Sociology* 65 (September 1959):132–146.

Fowler, Irving A. "Local Industrial Structures, Economic Power, and Community Welfare." *Social Problems* 6 (Summer 1958):41–50.

Freeman, Linton, et al. *Local Community Leadership.* Syracuse: University College of Syracuse University, 1960.

Galbraith, John. *American Capitalism: The Concept of Countervailing Power.* Rev. ed. Boston: Houghton Mifflin, 1956.

Gamson, William A. "Reputation and Resources in Community Politics." *American Journal of Sociology* 72 (September 1966):121–131.

Gilbert, Claire W. "Some Trends in Community Politics: A Secondary Analysis of Power Structure Data from 166 Communities." *Social Science Quarterly* 48 (December 1967):373–381.

Goldberg, Kalman, and Robin Linstromberg. "A Revision of Some Theories of Economic Power." *Quarterly Review of Economics and Business* 6 (Spring 1966):7–17.

Hawley, Amos H. *Urban Society.* New York: Ronald Press, 1971.

_____. *Human Ecology.* New York: Ronald Press, 1950.

Hodges, Wayne. *Company and Community.* New York: Harper & Row, 1958.

Hunter, Floyd. *Top Leadership, U.S.A.* Chapel Hill: University of North Carolina Press, 1959.

_____. *Community Power Structure: A Study of Decision Makers.* Chapel Hill: University of North Carolina Press, 1953.

Jennings, M. Kent. *Community Influentials.* New York: Free Press, 1964.

Lasswell, Harold D., and Abraham Kaplan. *Power and Society.* New Haven: Yale University Press, 1950.

Long, Norton E. "The Local Community as an Ecology of Games." *American Journal of Sociology* 64 (November 1958):251–261.

Lundberg, Ferdinand. *The Rich and the Super-Rich.* New York: Lyle Stuart, 1968.

Lynd, Robert, and Helen Lynd. *Middletown in Transition.* New York: Harcourt, Brace, 1937.

_____. *Middletown.* New York: Harcourt, Brace, 1929.

Martin, Roscoe C., Frank J. Munger, and others. *Decisions in Syracuse.* Bloomington: Indiana University Press, 1961.

McKee, James B. "Status and Power in the Industrial Community: A Comment on Drucker's Thesis." *American Journal of Sociology* 58 (January 1953): 364–370.

Miller, Delbert C., and James L. Dirksen. "The Identification of Visible Leaders in a Small Indiana City: A Replication of the Bonjean-Noland Study of Burlington, North Carolina." *Social Forces* 43 (May 1965):548–555.

Mills, C. Wright. *The Power Elite.* New York: Oxford University Press, 1959.

Pelligrin, Roland J., and Charles H. Coates. "Absentee-Owned Corporations and Community Power Structure." *American Journal of Sociology* 61 (March 1956):413–419.

Preston, James D. "The Search for Community Leaders: A Reexamination of the Reputational Technique." *Sociological Inquiry* 39 (Winter 1969):39–47.

Report of the Federal Trade Commission on Interlocking Directorates. Washington, D.C.: Government Printing Office, 1951.

Riesman, David, Nathan Glazer, and Reuel Denney. *The Lonely Crowd: A Study of the Changing American Character*. Garden City, N.Y.: Doubleday, 1956.

Rogers, David. "Community Political Systems: A Framework and Hypothesis for Comparative Studies." In *Current Trends in Comparative Community Studies*, edited by Bert E. Swanson. Kansas City, Mo.: Community Studies, Inc., 1962, pp. 31–48.

Rose, Arnold M. *The Power Structure: Political Process in American Society*. New York: Oxford University Press, 1967.

Rossi, Peter H. "Community Decision-Making." *Administrative Science Quarterly* 1 (March 1957):438–439.

Sayre, Wallace S., and Nelson W. Polsby. "American Political Science and the Study of Urbanization." In *The Study of Urbanization*, edited by Philip M. Hauser and Leo F. Schnore. New York: Wiley, 1965, pp. 115–156.

Schermerhorn, Richard A. *Society and Power*. New York: Random House, 1961.

Schulze, Robert O. "Economic Dominants in Community Power Structure." *American Sociological Review* 23 (February 1958):3–9.

Turk, Herman. "Interorganizational Networks in Urban Society: Initial Perspectives and Comparative Research." *American Sociological Review* 35 (February 1970):1–19.

Walton, John. "The Vertical Axis of Community Organization and the Structure of Power." *Social Science Quarterly* 48 (December 1967):353–368.

———. "Research Note: Substance and Artifact: The Current Status of Research on Community Power Structure." *American Journal of Sociology* 71 (January 1966):430–438.

Warren, Roland L. "Toward a Typology of Extra-Community Controls Limiting Local Community Autonomy." *Social Forces* 34 (May 1956):338–341.

Weber, Max. *The Theory of Social and Economic Organization*. Translated by A.M. Henderson and Talcott Parsons. Glencoe: Free Press, 1957.

Wolfinger, Raymond E. "Reputation and Reality in the Study of Community Power." *American Sociological Review* 25 (October 1960):636–644.

7
GOVERNMENT
AND SERVICES

INTRODUCTION

In the United States, counties, municipalities, and townships were the original jurisdictions of the local governmental system. Counties and municipalities helped state governments carry out some of their obligations in the legal system, conducting elections and providing services. Generally, states were divided into counties to facilitate such activities at the local level. Municipalities were organized to be the suppliers of local services in more densely populated places. While counties covered the entire population, municipalities were concerned primarily with residents in concentrated urban areas and included only a small portion of the state. Later, school districts also became prominent. School districts originated "because of the strong conviction that public education was of such importance to the society as to warrant its own local financing and its freedom from the politics of other local governments" (Bollens and Schmandt, 1975, p. 48). Thus, while counties and municipalities were primarily administrative units, school districts came into being to serve a particular purpose. Subsequently, the proliferation of special districts, school districts, counties, cities, and so on created tremendous problems related to the adequate and effective delivery of services.

Nonschool special districts came into being to meet needs that were not being met by traditional forms of government. These special districts primarily are a twentieth century development, especially since the end of World War I. Many early municipalities that were geographically distinct units joined together as populations expanded and interstitial areas filled in. Municipalities have partially incorporated this population into the cities by annexing territory and population adjacent to their old boundaries, although this is less prominent now than formerly. Thus, municipality boundaries tended to expand over time as urban population growth occurred. Similarly, some states subdivided counties into more units as population increased.

Associated with population growth in cities and their surrounding areas was the proliferation of many special districts, especially school districts, created to meet the needs of this expanding urban and suburban population. As population grew in and around urban centers, the growing number of municipalities, school districts, special districts, and unincorporated areas all increased the complexity of metropolitan area government. Currently, there is little resemblance to the original state, county, and township or municipal government approach of early days. Many laws made it easier to incorporate places than to annex area and population to already established cities. Thus, the legal code had great impact on current metropolitan governmental structure. Also, it should be noted that many people in current urban complexes live outside of municipalities; they live in a distinctly urbanized metropolitan district but in unincorporated territory.

After World War II, the annexation process once again began in earnest, although more recently annexation has fallen into disfavor. In recent times the number of counties in most states has remained virtually the same. In some places county governments contract out services to smaller municipalities. There has been a consolidation of some cities. The development of metro-government that has appeared in Nashville and Miami-Dade County, Florida, may be indications of the future. Similarly, substantial unification has taken place in school districts—elementary school districts have merged with each other, and so have some junior high and high school districts. In some places, all these levels have been unified, and some unified school districts include junior colleges.

Special districts have proliferated in urban regions, and there appears to be no abatement in this process. While many special districts cover only a small portion of the urban complex, others cover the entire metropolitan area. And some extend beyond the metropolitan region—for example, mass transit districts, airport districts, and harbor districts. These larger special districts have some elements of metropolitan-wide government, and they may be indicative of the future as more and more consolidation and unification takes place.

MULTIPLE LOCAL GOVERNMENTS
In most metropolitan regions there is a complexity of governmental jurisdictions. As Table 7–1 illustrates, in 1972 there were 22,185 local governments in 264 Standard Metropolitan Statistical Areas in the

Table 7-1 Standard Metropolitan Statistical Areas By Total and Average Number of Local Governments, 1972

SMSA Size Group (1970 Population)	Number of SMSAs	Number of Local Governments	Average Number of Local Governments
All SMSAs	264	22,815	86.4
1,000,000 or more	33	8,847	268.1
500,000–1,000,000	36	3,307	100.2
300,000–500,000	51	3,213	89.3
200,000–300,000	84	2,784	54.6
100,000–200,000	27	3,505	41.7
50,000–100,000	33	529	19.6

Sources: *Census of Governments: 1972*, Vol. 1, *Governmental Organization*, Washington, D.C.: U.S. Bureau of the Census, 1973.

Unites States. This means that the average number of local governments was 86.4 per metropolitan area. These included independent units such as cities, school districts, and special districts, and did not include various agencies, departments, and other specialized units of these individual governmental units. Each local government has "its own corporate powers such as the right to sue and to be sued and to acquire and dispose of property, its own officials, and its own service delivery system, and its own ability to raise revenue through taxation or charges. Each thus wears the potent mantle of public authority, which embraces financial extraction from the citizenry and the means of affecting people's lives beneficially or detrimentally. Since each is a separate unit and legally independent, it may (and sometimes does) act unilaterally and without concern for the needs and wishes of or the effect on residents in neighboring localities" (Bollens and Schmandt, 1975, p. 42).

There is regional variation in the number of local governments. The south generally has fewer jurisdictions than metropolitan regions in the northeast and north central regions. Similarly, it appears that "the greater the population of the area, the more local units are likely to be found" (Bollens and Schmandt, 1975, p. 43). Generally, larger urban complexes have a greater number of local governments, with the largest metropolitan areas having the most governmental jurisdictions. There is some variation within metropolitan size ranges, with some larger places, such as Baltimore, having fewer jurisdictions than other cities of similar size. On the other hand, Portland, Oregon, and Madison, Wisconsin have many more local governmental jurisdictions than do other cities and metropolitan complexes of their size.

Special districts and municipalities make up more than 60 percent of local government units within metropolitan regions. School districts make up a substantial portion, about one in every five units. Many incorporated places in urban regions are relatively small, with populations under 2,500. Some have populations less than a 1,000, and many are small in overall land size.

OVERLAPPING LOCAL GOVERNMENTAL JURISDICTIONS

While many local governmental jurisdictions in urban regions cover separate geographical areas, many also have overlapping boundaries. The most obvious overlapping jurisdictions and boundaries occur in school districts and special districts. Thus, there may be several elementary school districts that send children to a junior high school district, while several junior high school districts may be overlapped by one or several high school districts. A junior college district may encompass all of them plus many other elementary, junior high, and high school districts. Overlapping all of these various school districts will be city boundaries, unincorporated areas, special district boundaries—sewage, fire, or disposal districts, with perhaps a regional airport or port commission thrown in, not to mention county governments.

A NOTE ON FINANCING SERVICES[1]

Services, of course, have to be paid for. Generally they are paid for by taxes or by direct charges for them, or both. In some cities, services such as garbage collection, water, and electricity are paid for by residents directly to the city or contractor. However, many other services are paid for by property taxes, privilege taxes (paid by those who work or live within municipal boundaries), income taxes, sales taxes, and so on.

Hawley (1951, p. 100) has pointed out that municipal expenditures benefit not only those who live within the city but also meet needs generated by various kinds of activities carried on within the city. He notes that substantial city activities are a result of the population residing outside city boundaries, and thus the city subsidizes those who live outside of its boundaries. He found that "municipal government costs of metropolitan centers vary with the sizes of their satellite populations" (p. 106). Factors most closely associated with operating costs of cities were population density and housing density within central cities, and, in surrounding areas, the size of population, number of white-collar workers, percent of the population incorporated into satellite cities, and housing density. Generally he reports that white-collar workers use central city facilities more intensively than do others. Clearly the size of metropolitan population not included within the limits of the principal city represent costs to residents of that city.

Funds for expenditures are obtained from extra-local federal sources, such as urban renewal or redevelopment, antipoverty programs that are available only on an applied-for basis, state aid for public welfare expenditures, and revenue sharing. Of course, some other services typically are funded by local taxes, and some services are paid for directly at the local level, for example, health and hospitals. Other services and activities may be funded from a variety of sources, including federal grants, state aid, and local taxes.

A recent development in financing services is revenue sharing, which is an attempt by the federal government to distribute funds to state and local government with few strings attached. Most funds that come to the local level from the federal or state government are for specific categorical expenditures. Revenue sharing, in its original conception, was based on the belief that people in local governments were more knowledgeable and more responsive to needs of their residents than people at the state or federal level.[2] Under revenue sharing, local officials determine the use of federal revenue sharing funds. Priority areas of expenditures are listed by the federal government, primarily in the social services sector, and a large number of other restrictions have been shown (Butler and Galper, 1974). But sanctions were not written into the law to force local units to use revenue sharing funds for such priority services. Rather it appears that revenue sharing funds in most jurisdictions (with several notable exceptions) have been used for capital investments, such as buildings and underpasses. One major unanticipated result of revenue sharing has been an increase in the number of citizen groups that take seriously the notion that such funds could be used for various projects for their local neighborhoods. Thus, many public officials have found irate citizen groups at their doorstep wanting some of these discretionary funds. For the most part, these citizen demands have been rebuffed. (For a good, quick illustration of the allocation process to the city level, see *The Minority Community*, 1973.)

On the face of it, municipal expenditures seem to have risen markedly over the past several decades. However, at least in one state public expenditures did not show any great increase when price factors, population, and prosperity were controlled in the analysis (Wright and Marker, 1964).

Finally, while it might be expected that levels of state and local government expenditures would be related to the adequacy of public services, it appears that such expenditure levels "do not exert pervasive influence upon the nature of public services" (Sharkansky, 1967, p. 1074). The relationship between expenditures and services shows that expenditure levels do not necessarily reflect service levels and that increases in spending probably will not alone produce improvements in services without additional effort and evaluation of the delivery of such services.

JURISDICTION OF SERVICES
One of the major distinctions made in meeting the service needs of city and urban residents is the extent to which service should be local or areawide. Currently, there is no satisfactory mechanism whereby services are allocated on a local or an area-wide basis. This, of course, suggests that the allocation of services is not based on a systematic approach to the delivery of services but rather on historical accident

in any given city or metropolitan area. An Advisory Commission on Intergovernmental Relations (*Performance,* 1963) suggested that air pollution control and water supply and sewage disposal (among others) should be area-wide services, whereas fire protection and public education should be locally administered. In between were, for example, parks and recreation and public welfare, which presumably could be administered either locally, area-wide, or in some other manner. In any case, the commission attempted to show how the delivery of important urban services could be optimized by utilizing different levels of governmental administration.

A very real problem in developing an optimal distribution of services within the metropolitan complex is the resistance of local governments and their adherents to developing area-wide services. This reluctance to give up control over services is based on the fear that area-wide jurisdiction will leave the local unit with little voice in the delivery of services. In addition, some people are unwilling to lose the power they have over local administrative units.

CITY AND URBAN VARIATION IN VARIOUS SERVICES

One of the major concentrations of current urban theory and research is in the attempt to show that systematic differences among cities and metropolitan areas have major consequences for people living in various types of places. The assumption tested in these studies is that various types of cities and metropolitan areas are systematically related to differences in public policy outcomes—such as the quality of life, expenditures for health, education and welfare, and fire and police protection. It would be fortunate indeed if we could interrelate city typologies to such differences. However, only a few such analyses have been carried out to date. As a substitute, we will review some studies that have investigated various outputs and relate them to specific variables—such as city size, density, age structure, income levels, and education—that characterize cities and have been used as key dimensions in typological studies.

Concern with public policy outcomes leads directly to ideologies related to who has social power, who should control the economy, how much economic concentration there should be, to what extent there should be a freely competitive market, and, most relevant for our discussion, how responsive the social environment should be to the needs of the people (Fowler, 1958). Most of the discussion in this section relates to city characteristics other than power. However, it should be recalled that in the last chapter we discussed how *community power structures* were related to community decisions.

Generalized models of public policy outcomes have been proposed by political scientists who rely primarily on the political character of the city (Dawson and Robinson, 1963; Dye, 1966) to explain social policy outcomes. Sociologists and others have viewed the process from a wider frame of reference and generally have included a greater range of dimensions.

Using some of the notions gleaned from these approaches, the generalized model shown in Table 7–2 presents a framework that serves as a guideline in which the research that has been carried out to date and reported in this section can be understood. The model assumes that there are forces external to the city and metropolitan area that influence social policy. External conditions might include availability of money for antipoverty programs, urban renewal or redevelopment, but also might include whether the United States is at war or peace and whether it is in a period of economic prosperity or depression. Thus, recognition of the possible importance of external conditions forces us to realize that these factors may be important at the local level. However, if they are uniformly applicable, no variation at the local city level can be attributed to these external conditions.

One major concern, of course, is the extent to which there are variations or differences in public policy and outcomes by city, urban, and metropolitan characteristics. We must also determine which external forces may be differentially important to cities and must be considered for some outputs. The basic assumption is that variation in city and metropolitan characteristics leads to different public policies and outcomes. Political systems and political processes can be considered as intervening factors, or they can be considered as outcomes of city characteristics—that is, dependent variables. Below we examine some of the major services that lead to different levels of community welfare.

Community Welfare

Investigations interrelating characteristics of cities and community welfare all have in common a reported variation in community welfare by selected characteristics of the city; they diverge in emphasis and variables that are considered as accounting for the variation. Fowler (1958) notes that many of these studies are ideologically based and that each investigator's ideology has influenced the findings of the study. Three hypotheses tend to dominate: (1) small-business industrial structures will produce higher levels of welfare than big-business structures, other relevant factors remaining relatively constant; (2) local pluralistic power structures will produce higher levels of welfare than local monolithic power structures; and (3) type of industry has effect equal to, if not greater than those of other industrial structure variables on welfare, other relevant factors remaining constant.

Fowler tested these hypotheses on thirty small New York state cities, ranging in size between 10,000 and 80,000, matched on population size and manufacturing ratio. Local welfare was measured by an index called the General Social Welfare (GSW) score made up of forty-eight rankings combined into the following eleven major welfare subcomposites: (1) income, (2) income security, (3) consumer purchasing

Table 7-2 A Model of the Consequences of Metropolitan and City Variations[a]

External Conditions	→	City and Metropolitan Characteristics	→	Political Systems	→	Political Process	→	Public Policy/ Outcomes
A. Physical Environment		A. Types 1. Functional 2. Multidimensional		A. Forms of Government		Articulation of Demand For Services		A. Performance 1. Effectiveness 2. Efficiency 3. Equity 4. Responsiveness
B. National and State Economics		B. Individual Characteristics 1. Size 2. Age of City 3. Demographic Composition 4. Economic Base		B. Social Stratification				B. Structure 1. Regulation 2. Ownership 3. Extensiveness 4. Functional Differentiation
C. State and Federal Political Policies and Structures				C. Legal Boundaries of Jurisdiction and Representation				

[a]This "model" was suggested by Dawson and Robinson (1963), Dye (1966) and Paulson, et al. (1969).

power, (4) home ownership, (5) housing adequacy, (6) health needs, (7) health facilities, (8) literacy, (9) adequacy of educational provision, (10) political expression, and (11) municipal wealth and service. He did not include some of the more traditional welfare measures, such as expenditures for public welfare assistance (see also Elgin et al., 1974).

In contrast to the hypotheses, Fowler (1958, 1964) reports that higher levels of community welfare are associated with concentration of employment in large-scale industry, heavier durable goods industry, absentee-ownership, and some industrial diversification. Monolithic power structures are associated with high welfare levels. Cities with big-business structures tend to have higher welfare levels because of their relationship to "the technically advanced nature of modern industry." Some of the reasons he posited are as follows: (1) big-business cities have more advanced technical modes of production that demand large numbers of highly skilled and thus higher paid personnel; (2) because these local establishments are part of large national organizations, the particular sites chosen by them were the result of careful site selection and long-term capital investment, thus making more tax revenue available for public services; and (3) the big-business plant draws ancillary industries with similar highly skilled and highly paid personnel. In addition, higher welfare levels are associated with the following gross socioeconomic and demographic variables: (1) occupational distributions, (2) large net population increase, (3) a low degree of industrial unionism, and (4) higher proportions of white, native-born, Protestants.

Fowler notes that even the largest industrial structures have extra-local pressures on them to make expenditures for community welfare. While he tends to discount local influence, his work supports the notion that city characteristics are systematically related to variations and differences in community welfare outputs. Fowler's work is in contrast to that of Mills and Ulmer (1946) and others in direction of findings but not in the fact that there is variation in community welfare outcomes by city characteristics.

In a study more specifically related to public welfare, Turk (1970) reported that, for the 130 incorporated cities in the United States that had a population of more than 100,000 inhabitants in 1960, those with a previous history of outside funding established antipoverty organizations more often than cities that did not. However, once established, there was little variation in extent of funding. In general, the greater the capacity for local organization in a city, the greater its capability for manpower organization. While he did not stress characteristics of cities in regard to antipoverty expenditures, his data show that density, democratic vote, welfare expenditures, and educational expenditures are positively associated with per capita antipoverty expenditures, and that age of city, migration, and educational level are negatively associated with antipoverty fund expenditures. The extent of need (his terms is "demand")—the poverty level in the city—was *unrelated to poverty fund expenditures.*

A virtually identical finding was reported by Paulson, et al. (1969). They analyzed antipoverty fund expenditures at a completely different level—the 100 counties of North Carolina, only six of which have cities large enough to be considered as a SMSA (central city of 50,000 or more). Both of these studies suggest that while some cities and counties that had antipoverty programs obviously needed them, cities and counties that needed them the most were the ones least likely to have them! In North Carolina counties, the major factor associated with antipoverty expenditures, as well as with local and state welfare expenditures, was the *percent of white unemployed* (Paulson, et al., 1969 p. 26).

Water Fluoridation

Pinard (1963) hypothesized that cities with certain kinds of characteristics were more likely than others to have forces that are apathetic to or opposed to the leadership of the city. The degrees and patterns of support, apathy, or opposition are largely influenced by the size of the city, rate of growth, racial and ethnic composition, occupational and power structure, and the level of unemployment. He reports that wherever there is a separation of the leadership and lower segments of the system, there is a body of unattached citizens who oscillate between apathy and systematic opposition to the leadership.

Indicators of weak attachments in cities are the extent of unemployment and rapidity of growth, and these characteristics are linked *negatively* to fluoridation. Thus, he suggests that cities that have a larger middle-class are more likely to oppose fluoridation of the water supply than are lower-class communities, and retail cities are more likely to oppose fluoridation than industrial cities. Similarly, the larger the proportion of native whites—that is, the more homogeneous the city—the more likely fluoridation referendums are to be approved by the voters.

Water Supply

"Urban areas require water for a variety of purposes including human consumption, waste disposal, manufacturing and recreation" (Bollens and Schmandt, 1975, p. 146). The need for water in urban areas has increased as a result of population growth, improved living conditions, and the needs of industry. There are regional differences in water. Quantity is ample in some places but of poor quality; other metropolitan areas have a deficit in water but the water they have is of adequate quality. Thus, while the United States as a whole has adequate water resources, distribution of water of high quality remains a crucial problem.

Currently the provision of water in metropolitan areas is extremely diversified, involving multiple tiers of government and in some instances private agencies. Municipal ownership is dominant in some metropolitan regions, such as Minneapolis–St. Paul; others have special districts or contractual relations between a larger city and its smaller suburban places. Over a thousand special water districts serve a variety of communities in the metropolitan complex. The Metropolitan Water District of Southern California is the largest of these districts. It services multiple SMSAs in southern California, cutting across a number of county lines from the Colorado River bordering on Arizona and flowing to Mexico. This district brings water from central and northern California through viaducts more than 500 miles long to serve the huge population of this multiple metropolitan area. The complexity of this water district is evident in its implications for interstate relations (e.g., between California and Arizona) and international relations (between the United States and Mexico). Similarly, the relationships among Chicago, bordering states, and Canada show how complex the supply of water can become in contemporary urban complexes.

Sewage Disposal

At least fifty million people in the United States are drinking water that does not meet Public Health Standards (U.S. Department of Health, Education, and Welfare, 1967, p. 13). Much of this water does not meet minimum standards because of improper sewage disposal, which contaminates what otherwise might be safe water. Legislation concerning sewage disposal occurred after World War II and in 1956; however, it was not until 1972 that amendments to earlier legislation allowed some of the basic problems to be attacked. Among these were the ability to regulate discharges at the points where they occur. Thus farmers, industries, and municipal treatment plants all had to obtain permits that in effect controlled the constituents of effluents and schedules for achieving compliance with the new, stiffer regulations.

A variety of mechanisms currently are used in sewage disposal administration. A majority of cities have joint operations that include both collection and treatment facilities. Contractual agreements between larger cities and their suburbs are rather common, although some metropolitan areas still have a large number of smaller, inefficient districts. A few metropolitan areas have split the responsibility between local units and a regional agency. To date, no metropolitan region has been able to integrate all of its units into one system (Bollens and Schmandt, 1975, pp. 150–151). Finally, some municipalities are beginning to handle the construction and operation of local sewage collection facilities. The major interceptor sewers and treatment plants are being furnished by the metropolitan level. And the state and national governments are establishing the policy framework, especially for minimum water purity standards, and are providing financial assistance.

Police and Law Enforcement

Crime in the United States over the past decade has been rising at a faster rate than the population. This may be partially a result of better reporting procedures and more willingness by citizens to report crimes; however, even after these factors are discounted, crime apparently still has risen faster than the population. Thus, it is no surprise that many people in the United States express fear about crime and report it as one of the major problems facing our society.

In the United States the protection of people and their property is a highly complex and specialized undertaking. Police departments are twenty-four-hour service agencies and have responsibility for maintaining law and order in all parts of their political jurisdictions. Yet, it is obvious that law enforcement officers are differentially perceived in different parts of the metropolis. In minority neighborhoods, police officers are typically viewed as an occupation force, while in at least some other neighborhoods they are viewed as protectors.

Most often police are viewed as concerned with maintaining law and order and initiating actions against lawbreakers—investigation and arrest. On the other hand, they also spend as much if not more time in other activities. These other activities include controlling traffic, providing information, resolving marital and other kinds of interpersonal conflicts, and participating in a variety of other kinds of activities not related to criminals. Yet, most police officers have been trained only in traditional law enforcement procedures and these other activities, which actually may take up more than half of their time, have been neglected in training programs.

Some police departments have become aware of this past neglect and have attempted to compensate for it (for an example, see Butler and Cummins, 1967). Nevertheless, many programs that on the surface appear to be community services programs are in reality public relations programs. Public relations programs as such probably will fail to convince skeptical citizens of the serious intent of the police department. More likely to be successful are programs that emphasize police as public servants who do in fact spend substantial parts of their everyday working hours on what should be broadly conceived of as community services, rather than on law enforcement.

Most police departments in the United States are localized units; there are few special police districts. As with fire protection, police departments are highly varied in size and competence. Some law enforcement is carried out on a contractual basis, with a larger central city or county contracting out service to a smaller political jurisdiction. Variability in police departments is much more serious than in fire departments, because law violators may quickly travel from one jurisdiction to another. Thus, communication among police units becomes necessary, and records need to be kept in such a manner that they can be quickly sent from one jurisdiction to another. "Inadequate law enforcement in one community can have important social costs for the remainder of the area" (Bollens and Schmandt, 1975, p. 160). As a result, there have been some changes in police work over the past few years. These changes have partially resulted from federal legislation that encouraged (by monetary rewards), more elaborate planning on a statewide basis, centralization of communications, records keeping, laboratory facilities, training standards and other improvements.

A problem of our society, of course, is how to have adequate law enforcement without losing our freedoms. This is not an easy issue to come to grips with, and no obvious panaceas now exist to resolve this dilemma.

Fire Fighting and Prevention

The range of fire fighting and prevention activities in cities and metropolitan areas apparently is highly varied. The range is from volunteer fire departments in smaller urban places to large-scale departments and highly specialized equipment in larger cities with tall office buildings, apartment houses, and many kinds of industrial plants. Fire prevention activities are carried out in some smaller places by volunteer fire departments. In larger places it is extremely difficult to enforce fire prevention codes.

Fire fighting is extremely hazardous, and the number of injuries and deaths is higher than for any other profession. Fire protection is generally a highly localized activity. That is, the local fire protection district is not likely to extend beyond the town or city limits. This is partly a result of the local nature of most fires; fires seldom go beyond a single political jurisdiction. There are few special districts for fire fighting. In some places, a smaller city may contract with a larger unit, such as the central city or county, for fire fighting services, but generally these services are located locally in the contracting place rather than in the larger political jurisdiction. In the future, it is highly likely that fire fighting and prevention will remain a localized activity with a wide range of effectiveness.

Transportation

Typical intellectual responses to the automobile are negative. Yet there can be no denial that the automobile is extremely popular with the U.S. population. The automobile, since its inception around 1900, has reshaped the urban landscape. As automobiles increased, so did roadways, parking lots, freeways, motels, and drive-in theatres, banks, and eating places. With the increase in automobiles and automobile-related activities and services, mass transit, except in a very few cities, declined markedly.

With the exception of perhaps Boston, Chicago, Cleveland, New York, Philadelphia, and San Francisco-Oakland, virtually no city in the United States has even adequate mass transit. Yet even today the vast majority of transportation money in these cities, as well as in virtually all others, continues to be poured into roadways and associated services rather than into the development of balanced metropolitan transit systems. Few people in the United States travel to work by mass transit; similarly, few people use it to go into the central city for shopping or other activities. This is partly because mass transit in many cities does not exist; where some semblance of mass transit does exist, the facilities typically are outdated, schedules are uncertain, and mass transit is used only by those who have no other option.

Recently, the responsibility for transportation in the United States has been increasingly transferred from the local level to broader regional levels, and in some instances to the federal level. An example of the latter is the development of the interstate highway system. Many metropolitan region transportation commissions and authorities are now in operation, and more are likely to be created in the near future. Some regional authorities have little power and most cannot raise funds except from fares or the contributions of local governmental units. Some funds are available from the federal level; however, these funds are minimal and are generally available only for demonstration projects that do not meet the basic transportation problem and needs of metropolitan regions. One recent development is federal legislation that allows up to 800 million dollars—of the some 5 billion dollars annually collected from federal gasoline taxes—to be used to develop mass transit. However, this legislation does not mandate expenditures, and will last only three years. It will be interesting to see if the strong automobile lobbyists will be able to halt these expenditures and prevent extension of this bill.

Some recent trends include minibuses that transport people around downtown areas (in Washington, D. C. and Los Angeles, for example); dial-a-bus systems for shopping and visiting hospitals and doctors; medi-trans systems that have specific routes to carry people to various medical facilities; and satellite transportation modalities organized by corporations, colleges, and universities to get people to work or downtown.[3]

Finally, transportation has increasingly been recognized as an areawide function. This does not necessarily mean that all transportation-related activities come under the jurisdiction of an area-wide commission or authority, but it does imply that local streets and highways need to be articulated into a broader-gauged approach to the metropolitan transportation network, to include freeways and mass transit systems where they exist. Regional planning is one mechanism that might overcome some transportation difficulties in the metropolitan region. Funds, of course, would help. Ultimately, however transportation networks within most urban complexes will remain as problems until it is recognized that efficient, well-balanced transportation systems benefit all metropolitan residents. This means recognizing that some elements in the system may not be self-supporting and will have to be subsidized. (For an analysis of free-fare transit, see Scheiner and Starling, 1974.)

Social Services
Social services usually are carried out at the county or state level, with substantial federal legislation and funding influencing their administration. Many lack coordination and some services, and evaluation of services is often inadequate or nonexistent. For example, a city may have multiple private and public agencies dealing with family planning. Yet, any single agency may not be aware of the others and their services, the extent to which there is overlapping clientele, or the unmet needs of the community. For example, no place in the United States has an adequate knowledge of the incidence or prevalence of drug abuse, the extent to which the need is being met, or the effectiveness of existing programs in meeting needs and solving problems. And this is true of every kind of social service in virtually every city and urban place in the United States, even though millions of dollars are spent each year on such services.

PUBLIC SERVICES: EXPANSION
As communities expanded, conflict was engendered between newcomers and longer-term residents. Newcomers tended to bring new ideas about schools, water systems, playgrounds, and other public services, all of which required increasing taxes. Similarly, the concentration of families with children in suburbs increased the demand for school facilities and teachers.

With expanding population and suburbanization, municipal services had to be greatly expanded or, in some instances, built in their entirety. Expansion of public water and sewage systems to replace private facilities and enlargement of police and fire protection services have been necessities. All of these services cost heavily. In residential suburbs where there is no industrial base, heavy taxes have had to be levied on housing and land. Thus, processes of raising and spending resources have engendered conflict between central city and suburban residents.

Cities first tried to overcome their financial difficulties by annexing surrounding territory. Until the 1920s, annexation at least doubled the size of the ten largest cities. Political opposition to this practice developed, and annexation has proceeded at a much slower pace since then. Recently stress has been placed on the abolition of political boundaries and on the need for consolidation, merger, and county-metropolitan government. Some public corporations that include central cities, residential and industrial suburbs, and unincorporated places have been formed to build bridges, tunnels, and airports; similarly, transit authorities have consolidated some metropolitan transportation networks.

PROSPECTS

Perhaps the most often proposed solution to the problems of delivering services in urban areas has been unification or consolidation of local governments into one jurisdiction. Friesema (1968) has made explicit at least four assumptions made by those in favor of consolidation (see also Greer, 1962; Sofen, 1963). These assumptions are as follows:

1. Intergovernmental relations between jurisdictions within metropolitan complexes are ad hoc and sporadic.

2. While other sectors of the metropolitan complex are becoming increasingly interdependent, the political integration of the metropolitan area is standing still.

3. "Political integration" is considered as a synonym for formal unification. It is a state to be achieved, rather than a continuing process.

4. Special districts, service agreements, and other contractual arrangements for solving individual metropolitan area problems are not satisfactory solutions to many problems in metropolitan complexes, at least in comparison to complete governmental unification.

To date there is scant evidence that unification will solve problems facing cities and urban places. While one may agree or disagree with this conclusion, Friesema's analysis is especially useful, because he makes explicit the implicit assumptions of a proposed solution to major urban problems. The approach he uses in making assumptions explicit and critically assessing them probably will be the first necessary step in solving urban service problems—if they are to be solved.

Arguments for the establishment of a single metropolitan government suggest that such a governmental unit could levy a single tax and have a single administrative agency, which could mean more equitable distribution of costs for services throughout the entire metropolitan complex (Hawley, 1951, p. 107). In addition, it has been argued that such a single governmental unit would facilitate and allow more systematic planning for the metropolitan complex.

Because there has been little effort to solve the financial dilemmas of cities, it appears that the financial plight of cities will continue well into the future.[4] In addition, it is apparent that few local governmental units have any idea of extent of the *need* for various kinds of services, little knowledge about overlaps and gaps in services, little awareness of what the public wants, and virtually no idea of how effective various programs are in meeting needs or their goals and objectives. The future appears to hold more of the same.

NOTES

1. For information on expenditures for a large range of services, see any issue of the *City and County Data Book.*

2. It should be noted that this may be an incorrect assumption.

3. Smith (1975) presents a variety of rapid bus options for cities and metropolitan areas.

4. For an up-to-date evaluation of the financial problems of major U.S. cities, see *Hearings.* . . ., (1975).

REFERENCES

Bollens, John C., and Henry J. Schmandt. *The Metropolis: Its People, Politics, and Economic Life.* 3rd ed. New York: Harper & Row, 1975.

Butler, Edgar W., and Harvey Galper. "Restrictions on Uses of Funds." In *Proceedings of the Conference on Revenue Sharing Research,* edited by Robert W. Rafues, Jr. Washington, D.C.: National Planning Association, 1974, pp. 26–30.

Butler, Edgar W., and Marvin Cummins. *Community Services Unit: First Report and Preliminary Evaluation.* Winston-Salem, N.C.: Winston-Salem Police Department, July 1967.

Census of Governments: 1972, Vol. 1, *Governmental Organization.* Washington, D.C.: U.S. Bureau of the Census, 1973.

Dawson, Richard E., and James A. Robinson. "Interparty Competition, Economic Variables, and Welfare Policies in the American States." *Journal of Politics* 25 (May 1963):265–289.

Dye, Thomas R. *Politics, Economics, and the Public: Policy Outcomes in the American States.* Chicago: Rand McNally, 1966.

Elgin, Duane, Tom Thomas, Tom Logothetti, and Sue Cox. *City Size and the Quality of Life.* Stanford: Stanford Research Institute, November 1974.

Fowler, Irving A. *Local Industrial Structures, Economic Power, and Community Welfare.* New York: Bedminster Press, 1964.

——. "Local Industrial Structures, Economic Power, and Community Welfare." *Social Problems* 6 (Summer 1958):41–51.

Friesema, H. Paul. "The Metropolis and the Maze of Local Governments." In *The New Urbanization,* edited by Scott Greer, Dennis McElrath, David W. Minar, and Peter Orleans. New York: St. Martin's Press, 1968, pp. 339–354.

Greer, Scott. *Governing the Metropolis.* New York: Wiley, 1962.

Hawley, Amos H. "Metropolitan Population and Municipal Government Expenditures in Central Cities." *The Journal of Social Issues* 7 (1951):100–108.

Hearings, "The Effect of Inflation and Recession on State and Local Governments." Washington, D.C.: U.S. Government Printing Office, 1975.

Mills, C. Wright, and Melville J. Ulmer. *Small Business and Civic Welfare.* Report of the Special Committee to Study Problems of American Small Business, U.S. Senate, 79th Congress, 2nd Session, No. 135, Washington, D.C.: Government Printing Office, 1946.

Paulson, Wayne, Edgar W. Butler, and Hallowell Pope. "Community Power and Public Welfare." *American Journal of Economics and Sociology* 28 (January 1969):17–27.

Performance of Urban Functions: Local and Areawide. Washington, D.C.: Advisory Commission on Intergovernmental Relations, 1963.

Pinard, Maurice. "Structural Attachments and Political Support in Urban Politics: The Case of Fluoridation Referendums." *American Journal of Sociology* 68 (March 1963): 513–526.

Scheiner, James I., and Grover Starling. "The Political Economy of Free-Fare Transit." *Urban Affairs Quarterly* 10 (December 1974):170–184.

Sharkansky, Ira. "Government Expenditures and Public Services in the American States." *American Political Science Review* 61 (December 1967):1066–1077.

Smith, Wilbur, and Associates. *Bus Rapid Transit Options for Densely Developed Areas.* Washington, D.C.: Government Printing Office, February 1975.

Sofen, Edward. *The Miami Metropolitan Experiment.* Bloomington: Indiana University Press, 1963.

The Minority Community and Revenue Sharing, 2nd edition. Washington, D.C.: Joint Center for Political Studies, June, 1973.

Turk, Herman. "Interorganizational Networks in Urban Society: Initial Perspectives and Comparative Research." *American Sociological Review* 35 (February 1970):1–19.

U.S. Department of Health, Education, and Welfare, Task Force on Environmental Health and Related Problems. *A Strategy for a Livable Environment*. Washington, D.C.: Government Printing Office, 1967.

Wright, Deil S., and Robert W. Marker. "A Half-Century of Local Finances: The Case of Iowa." *National Tax Journal* 17 (September 1964):274–291.

8
SLUMS, POVERTY, AND HOUSING

INTRODUCTION

A metropolitan complex is a mosaic of commercial, industrial, park, residential, and other kinds of areas. Perhaps the least understood, although perhaps the most extensively studied, are the slums. Slums are areas characterized by blight and obsolete housing and occupied by a poverty-stricken population. Slums typically are located in areas of transition from one type of land use to another—in former residential areas located near the central business districts (CBD) that are being converted to commercial or industrial use. In addition to transitional area slums, there are older areas, located elsewhere in the metropolitan complex, where housing is deteriorating because of age and other factors. Thus, while slums primarily are located in transitional areas near the CBD, there are pockets of slums elsewhere in the metropolitan complex.

A distinction has been made between low-rent areas and slums. A low-rent area is one that has a fully organized social life—for example, the West End, an Italian neighborhood in Boston—as opposed to a slum in which "social disorganization" exists (Gans, 1962). Hannerz (1969, p. 11) has noted that the term *ghetto* is used to label inner city areas that others call slums. These terms are used interchangeably in this chapter to convey the idea that the areas and the people living in them have some characteristics in common; the common characteristic may be poor housing and living conditions; it may be ethnicity or skin color. The slums and ghettos examined extensively in this chapter have prevailing poverty and blighted housing.

POVERTY

Poverty means not only low incomes but also despair and hopelessness. In the slums there are large numbers of unemployed or underemployed workers, large families with reduced or minimum resources, and, in some instances, missing males. The problems of meeting basic needs and their relative costs must be taken into account in any definition of who is and who is not poor. If today's poor are compared with the poor of 1960, they are relatively worse off because of the decreased buying power of their incomes (Haley, 1971). According to the U.S. Department of Labor, in June of 1974, any family of four with an income of less than $4,550 was living in poverty. (For an analysis of sixteen different measures of poverty, see Williamson and Hyer, 1975.) By-products of poverty include ignorance, disease, delinquency and crime, alienation, and indifference. The poor can be distinguished from the middle class by differing competence to manage change and their available resources (Schorr, 1963).

Who Are the Poor?

There probably is no one generally acceptable and uniform measure of who is poor. Nevertheless, "if it is not possible to state unequivocally 'how much is enough,' it should be possible to assert with confidence how much, on an average, is too little" (Orshansky, 1965, p. 3). In 1963, the Social Security Administration estimated that a total of 7.2 million families and 5 million individuals living alone or with nonrelatives "lacked the wherewithal to live at anywhere near a tolerable level." Thus, in 1963, these two groups of poor totaled some 37.5 million persons. One in seven of all families of two or more and almost half of all persons living alone or with nonrelatives had incomes too low in 1963 to enable them to have a minimal diet providing adequate nutrition and still have enough left over to pay for all other living essentials (Orshansky, 1965, p. 4). Thus, somewhere around one-fourth of all citizens in the United States were then living at or below the poverty level.

Populations most vulnerable to risk of poverty have long been identified and publicized, but they make up only a small part of all the poor. Families headed by a woman are subject to a risk of poverty three times that of families headed by a man, but they represent only one-fourth of all persons in families classed as poor. Children growing up without a father must get along on less than they need far more often than children living with both parents. In fact, two-thirds of children in fatherless families have inadequate incomes. Three-fourths of poor families have a man as head, and two-thirds of all poor children live in a home with a man at the head. While many aged persons have inadequate incomes, almost four-fifths of poor families have someone under age sixty-five as head. Even among persons who live alone, nearly half of all individuals classified as poor have not yet reached old age. Nonwhite families suffer a poverty risk three times as great as white families, but seven out of ten poor families are white.

In our work-oriented society, those who cannot or do not work are poorer than those who do. Yet in more than half of all poor families, the head is working. Moreover, half of the employed family heads, representing almost 30 percent of all the families called poor, have been working at full-time jobs for at least a year. Of the millions of poor families, one in every six had a white male who worked full time throughout the year. Yet, this is the kind of family that in our present society has the best chance of escaping poverty. Of the 15 million poor children under age eighteen, about 5.3 million were in families headed by a man or woman who was working at a full-time job all during 1963.

In addition, as reported by the Council of Economic Advisors 1971; the poor in the United States can be characterized as follows:

One-fifth of families of the total population are poor.

Of the total poor, 22 percent are nonwhite, and nearly one-half of all nonwhites live in poverty.

The heads of over 60 percent of poor families have grade school educations.

Even for those denied opportunity by discrimination, education significantly raises the chances of escape from poverty. Of all nonwhite families headed by a person with eight years or less of schooling, 57 percent are poor. This figure falls to 30 percent for high school graduates and to 18 percent for those with some college education.

But education does not completely remove the effects of discrimination: at the same level of education, when nonwhites are compared with whites, nonwhites are poor about twice as often.

One-third of poor families are headed by a person over sixty-five, and almost one-half of families headed by such a person are poor.

Of the poor, 54 percent live in cities, 16 percent on farms, 30 percent on rural nonfarms.

While over 40 percent of all farm families are poor, over 80 percent of nonwhite farmers live in poverty.

Less than half of the poor are in the South; yet a southerner's chance of being poor is roughly twice that of a person living in other regions.

One-fourth of poor families are headed by a woman; but nearly one-half of all families headed by a woman are poor.

When a family and its head have several characteristics frequently associated with poverty, the chances of being poor are particularly high; a family headed by a young woman who is nonwhite and has less than an eighth grade education is poor in ninety-four out of one hundred cases. If she is white, the chances are eighty-five out of one hundred that she and her children will be poor.

Thus, although most poor people are white, nonwhite families are more likely to be poor than are white families, and about half of all poor families are headed by women, an older person, or a disabled person.

Not only do the poor have less income, they have to pay more for the goods and services that they receive (Caplovitz, 1967). This includes professional services, some of which could be free to the poor. A prime example is that the poor pay higher rents for poorer housing; non-whites pay more for smaller places, in worse condition, occupied by more people, and thus are more likely to be overcrowded (Kerner Commission, 1968). Thus, differences between the poor and those better off are not only a matter of economics but also a matter of recognizing that a problem exists, that there are experts who can handle such problems, and that the poor person must feel secure in the company of service providers.

Similarly, it should be noted that there are other pressures that lead to the poor paying more than for comparable goods available elsewhere. Providers of goods and services in poor neighborhoods pay higher per unit costs, higher insurance rates, and have higher theft losses. Each of these higher costs are passed on to consumers in poor neighborhoods and the result is that the poor pay more.

Most poor people are ill-prepared to cope with consumer problems. This lack of preparedness has led to many illegal and quasi-legal consumer practices. There is a general lack of knowledge about where or to whom to go to in case of consumer fraud. Many who are aware of potential assistance believe that the helping agency or person would not intervene effectively if called on for help. This, perhaps incorrectly, has been called apathy. In fact it may be realistic expectation that the system will not operate in a favorable manner for the poor—an expectation based on previous experience.

Poverty and Employment

It is a basic value of our society that individuals should work and that the poor especially should have the desire to work (Sussman, 1964, p. 397). Not considered in this value is the increasing probability that even if a poor person is motivated, industrious, and ambitious, there are insufficient job openings for those who want them. Structural conditions may obviate these individual characteristics—regardless of whether there are jobs available and regardless of whether the individual is trained for the positions that are available.

Bluestone has said of the urban poor that "the uneducated and unskilled poor have been left behind in a rapidly advancing and automated technology and hence have failed to operate successfully in the newly emerging job market" (1968, p. 410). Another hypothesis is that many people with skills are not being provided with jobs. This last hypothesis is supported by data on *underemployment*. The underemployed are those who are working full time but are not making enough money to survive above the poverty level. Almost a third of all families living below the poverty level in 1964 were headed by a person who worked through the year at a full-time job. These working poor spent nearly half of their waking hours at arduous, numbingly repetitious jobs devoid of opportunity for occupational mobility (Blue-stone, 1968, p. 410). These underemployed represent nearly one-fifth of the employed labor force.

Approximately one-third of underemployed persons were black, although, because of their greater absolute number, more whites than blacks are underemployed. Over half of the working poor are in the prime work years between the ages of twenty-five and fifty-four. Many of the jobs these people could be working in—for example, in manufacturing, transportation, communication, and wholesaling—are outside of the ghetto and require expensive, time-consuming travel (Offner, 1972). Ninety percent of working poor families are male-headed households, although in one-fifth of these families the wife also worked at least part time. Even so, the two incomes were not enough to raise these families above the poverty line. The working poor (and many of the unemployed) have sufficient education and adequate skills so the problem is not a lack of preparation but rather lack of jobs. They cannot find jobs because the jobs do not exist.

What are the solutions to underemployment and unemployment? One perspective relies on training, retraining, and education that would send individuals into the labor force equipped to function in the highly specialized U.S. labor market. Yet, great as the problems of adequate education and training are, the larger problem is the failure of the economy to furnish an adequate number of jobs above the pov-erty level. Since there are several million families in poverty despite the fact that the head member is working, stress needs to be placed not only upon increasing the numbers of jobs for the poor but also to make sure that there are better paying jobs with increasing job ad-vancement opportunities so that a full-time worker and his family will not remain at a poverty level of living.

A number of specific measures have been suggested to eliminate low wages. Among them are the following: (1) firms should allow closed union shops; (2) unions should take on the task of organizing the unorganized who are now earning low wages; (3) the minimum wage should be increased and extended to more workers; (4) the gov-ernment should ensure that jobs at a guaranteed minimum income level are available, with the government acting as an employer if nec-essary; (5) a negative income tax should be implemented; and (6) jobs should be created that not only insure a minimum income level but also utilize individual creativity. This last suggestion may call for a re-creation of the values of work (Bluestone, 1968, p. 418–419).

Poverty and Education
A recent study of twelve larger cities in the United States showed that high school graduation for whites is worth about $25 per week, while for nonwhites the difference is only $8.33. Therefore, the payoff

from high school graduation is about three times greater for whites than for nonwhites (Harrison, 1972, p. 804). Nevertheless, education facilitates the entry of both white and nonwhites into new occupations and, at least for poor whites, greater occupational mobility. It is easier for poor whites to move out of poverty, to obtain higher paying jobs, and to be occupationally mobile than it is for nonwhites.

Education increases the expectations and standards of ghetto workers. When, because of discrimination or exploitation by employers, these expectations are not met, frustration results. This, in turn, may reduce job attachment by workers. The worker may display greater absenteeism, more frequent recalcitrance when given orders by foremen, or less patience with what is perceived as racist behavior on the part of co-workers. If the ghetto resident is not presently employed, then—although he is indeed searching for work—the change in standards or expectations may lead him to increase the wages expected before employment will be accepted. If offered positions do not meet certain standards, the job will be rejected and the individual will search further, or turn to other income-generating activities such as public welfare (Sternlieb and Indik, 1973) or the "hustle." In this way, he may remain unemployed for a relatively long period of time (Harrison, 1972, p. 808). Finally, it has been suggested that "unless a black high school student is certain of completing college, he may be better off (in terms of his lifetime income) by dropping out of the educational system before finishing high school" (Harrison, 1972, p. 810).

Poverty Areas Within Metropolitan Complexes

Nonwhite families are segregated to a much larger extent in poverty areas than are white poverty families. Similarly, the U.S. Bureau of the Census (1966, p. 1) reports that "nonwhite families comprised about 12 percent of all families in SMSAs of 250,000 or more but made up 42 percent of all families in poverty areas and only 6 percent of all families in nonpoverty areas."

Poverty and Children

In 1963 the 15 million poor children represented more than one in every five of all children in families. Of these 15 million, only 3.1 million needy children were receiving assistance in the form of aid to families with dependent children, the public program specifically designed for them (Orshansky, 1965, pp. 15–16).

There are cultural deprivations that lower-class black youths face in regard to work; among them are (1) irrelevant job models, (2) exclusion from the prevailing work ethic, and (3) alienation from the culture of the modern factory and office. Thus, lower-class black children are denied the experience of daily association with workers (Himes, 1964, pp. 448–449). These young children do not learn that there is a linkage between effort and advancement. And when they do begin work in the office or factory, they become alienated from the structured situation quickly because they have not been socialized into what to expect in the work situation.

There are a number of myths surrounding children in poor families (Herzog and Lewis, 1970). One is that the matriarchial family dominates; this represents some families but is not even the desired mode in poor families (Kriesberg, 1970). Similarly, to characterize poor parents as being apathetic about the futures of their children is fallacious. However, the most important myth is that poor children cannot and are not able to take advantage of opportunities if they are presented to them.

Conclusions

Many people in the United States lose out on their chances to rise above poverty because they have been denied basic needs and opportunities. The fact that millions of people live in poverty suggests that past social policies, such as the "war against poverty," have not been effective and that more creative and innovative approaches are necessary (Clark and Hopkins, 1968; Moynihan, 1969). "The poor have been counted many times. It remains now to count the ways by which to help them gain a new identity" (Orshansky, 1965, p. 26). If the cycle of poverty is to be eliminated, unemployment and underemployment must be eliminated, the welfare system that rewards the father for leaving the household must be changed, expanded opportunities for poor persons must be developed, and mechanisms must be developed to restore the strength and vigor of families that are not coping effectively with contemporary society.

Further, there is ample justification for those who conclude that education and training programs are not likely to have any major impact upon unemployment and poverty unless they are accompanied by jobs. Training and education are not likely to have an impact unless involuntary part-time employment and substandard wages are eliminated. New and better paying jobs must be created. These jobs should be geographically accessible, and information about the availability of jobs and the possibilities for promotion must be disseminated to potential applicants. Only then will training and education have an impact. Thus, the emphasis must be directed away from alleged individual and family defects and toward the social structure and how it might be altered to eliminate constraints on ghetto employment and job opportunities.

SLUMS AND HOUSING

Wilson (1965, p. 2) believes that housing in the United States, especially in big cities, has been getting better over the past twenty or thirty years. According to him, this improvement in housing "has been one of this country's most significant yet often unheralded achievements."

He argues that the United States does not have a housing problem but rather that there are only problems of people in cities—problems such as poverty, race, and culture. By culture he means the problems of establishing an educational basis for a sound, stable family life that prepares individuals to take advantage of available opportunities. Yet, hard-core slum areas continue to deteriorate. And the people who live in them have little opportunity to obtain adequate housing, because most housing construction since World War II has been for upper-middle and upper-income families. Little low-income housing has been built since the middle 1920s. Thus, during almost a half century of rapid change in cities—including the great black urban migration—hardly any housing construction for low-income families has taken place.

Currently, most poor in the United States live in deteriorated and dilapidated housing that has been rejected by those with adequate incomes. In some cities (for example, Pittsburgh, New Orleans, and Dallas) 50 percent of the nonwhites live in deteriorated or dilapidated buildings, while about a third of nonwhites in most cities live in such housing. Minorities live in poor housing for two basic reasons: (1) most have low incomes; and (2) personal and institutional racism operate to keep minorities, including those with adequate incomes, in the slums. Thus, there is a shortage even of inadequate housing. For several reasons, blacks have not taken advantage of the housing market that does exist. A lack of knowledge about potential housing is one inhibiting factor. Reluctance to leave friendship patterns and relationships established in the ghetto is another.

Barth and March (1962) interviewed white homeowners in Seattle, Washington, who had advertised their homes for sale, to determine if these homeowners would object to showing or selling their homes on a nondiscriminatory basis. They asked permission to make the homeowners' addresses and names available to agencies that service nonwhite home-seekers. Of the homeowners interviewed, 18 percent were willing to have their names and addresses placed on a file available to potential nonwhite purchasers, and 32 percent more showed a willingness to sell their house on an open market.

At the time of this Seattle study, realtors played a substantial role in producing major barriers to prevent blacks from purchasing homes on the open market. Many realtors publicly opposed open housing legislation at the local and state levels, and a majority of them refused to sell housing to blacks. Thus, on the one hand they attempted legally to block open housing legislation and on the other hand they refused to sell to blacks. Thus, blacks were effectively cut off from even those white home owners (at least 18 percent) who were willing to sell their homes on an open market. Several local organizations provided open housing listings. But blacks in general believed that these houses were inferior or they would not have been listed. Thus, one of the major barriers preventing blacks from finding adequate housing is the barrier in communication. This barrier is partially self-imposed but is primarily a result of discriminatory practices by some realtors and others involved in the housing market.

In the United States, paradoxically, land value decreases and family income tends to increase with distance from center of the city. Typically, the poor live on some of the most valuable land while those who are better off live on less expensive land. Newer housing is being built primarily in suburbs while the older, inner city housing and other older housing in the metropolitan complex is filtering down to the poor. That is, as housing becomes older or goes out of style and as neighborhoods become less desirable, housing is passed down to families with lower incomes. As desirable housing is built and made available for those who want and can afford it, they move out of older, less desirable homes.

Current housing problems are partially a result of the early growth of cities. The greatest proportion of poor-quality housing in the United States is located in central cities of metropolitan areas. Earlier this housing was filled by immigrants from other countries. More recently in most cities this same housing has been occupied by southern blacks, and in some cities by Puerto Ricans and chicanos. Housing in central cities is more likely to be rented than owned, in contrast to the suburbs where ownership dominates. Generally, owned housing is newer and in better condition than rental units. Of those persons living in the central city, minorities are more likely than anglos to be renters. Further, whether owned or rented, housing utilized by minorities in cities tends to be older and more dilapidated. Two factors in particular account for deteriorated and dilapidated housing in the central city: (1) age—the housing stock was built decades ago, and (2) lack of maintenance, especially by absentee landlords.

When housing of a whole neighborhood becomes deteriorated and dilapidated, the area is considered as a slum. "The housing in such an area is a detriment to physical well-being. Usually such areas lack sunlight and fresh air, adequate water supplies, and sewage control, and often there are fire and accident hazards, as well as severe overcrowding (Beyer, 1965, p. 338). The population of slums include older people with inadequate incomes and minorities. Rates of illiteracy, physical and mental abnormalities, and other impairments are higher in slums than elsewhere. Typically, neighborhood facilities and services are inadequate in the slums.

Some areas characterized by deterioration and dilapidation can be rehabilitated. Generally rehabilitation, renewal, or redevelopment of areas in cities has been done by governmental action rather than by individual families or private contractors. This probably is because rehabilitation is not economically feasible for individual families or private firms.

Two oversimplifications exist that hinder solving inner city housing problems. First, there is the erroneous belief that all slum dwellers are alike in their population characteristics—for example, unemployment and race—and in their attitudes and behavior. Thus, it should be specifically noted that slum dwellers have different characteristics. Some work full time in good jobs, some work full time but are underpaid—underemployed. Others are unemployed and looking for work. Others are not in the labor force—they have given up looking for work. Similarly, people of many races and nationalities live in slums. For example, in one Chicago slum Italians, blacks, chicanos, and Puerto Ricans live in close proximity to each other (Suttles, 1968). In a Washington, D.C. slum, a variety of family patterns were reported (Hannerz, 1969). And a variety of life styles also were reported in the black community in Houston (McCord, et al., 1969) and in a Near Northeast black community in Washington, D.C. (Chapin, et al., forthcoming).

Second, most remedial action oriented toward curing problems of slums has been concentrated upon a single condition. Any effective ghetto-improvement strategy must be concerned with jobs and employment, education, housing, health, personal safety, crime prevention, and income maintenance for dependent persons—rather than with just housing—if it is to be successful (Downs, 1970, p. 31).[1]

PUBLIC HOUSING AND URBAN RENEWAL

"A decent home and suitable living environment for every American family" has been a stated national objective since passage of the Housing Act of 1949. Subsequently, the Housing and Urban Development Act of 1968 authorized a variety of new programs and refinements in existing programs in an effort to come to grips with housing problems that continued to exist, particularly for lower-income families. The Housing Act provided incentives to help people become self-supporting and not dependent on government welfare. The Housing Act recognized that more is involved than providing housing for lower-income families. The act provides that, to the greatest extent feasible, opportunities for employment and contracts for work arising in connection with construction or rehabilitation of housing assisted under special programs should be given to lower-income persons and business concerns located in areas where such housing is to be built.

In most cities, separate agencies are concerned with redevelopment, zoning, subsidized housing programs, zoning enforcement, and so on. Some cities have established Housing Authorities, and some cities have been involved in The Model Cities Program (*The Model Cities Program*, 1973; July, 1973). Within general guidelines set by federal public housing laws and by the Housing Assistance Administration (HAA), which administers low-rent public housing programs, local housing authorities have much room for constructive action. Local housing authorities may plan projects, determine specific criteria for admission to leased housing, and issue other administrative regulations. Unfortunately, rents must cover maintenance, housing authority staff, and the creation of a reserve fund for major repairs expenditures. If the authority increases its services, it must pay for them out of current rent collections or it must raise rents. This regulation has created a tendency to defer maintenance and to favor admission of tenants in higher ranges of eligible income categories, because they generate more rental income and demand less in managerial costs and time. This institutional arrangement has produced controversy when local authorities resist admission of tenants with lower incomes.

A widely criticized feature of public housing is the upper limit on tenant income. When income rises above certain levels, tenants are required to move. They are often pushed into housing markets where they cannot find housing at the prices they were paying for public housing. Tenants are forced to choose between not increasing their incomes and staying in leased housing or increasing their incomes and moving into inadequate housing.

In the past, local housing authorities often have built and leased massive, unattractive, institutional projects that are clearly different in shape, size, and character from ordinary apartments and housing developments. As a result, in many cities such housing is referred to as "the project." (For a description of life in a project, see Rainwater, 1970.)

Local housing authorities also may lease new or existing houses and sublet them to tenants. The authority pays the owner the difference between the approved rent and the amount the tenant can pay. This program makes it possible for low-income families to live in neighborhoods where other residents are not receiving subsidies. In effect, it is a "rent supplement" program with the potential for making more housing available for low-income families.

Another way to deal with substandard housing is to strictly enforce housing codes and create ordinances that pertain to "good housekeeping." Code enforcement can prevent blight from spreading to areas with standard housing and can upgrade basically sound and restorable housing. However there are some problems with strict code enforcement:

1. landlords force tenants to move if they complain about substandard conditions (for an extensive analysis of landlord and tenant relations, see Rose, 1973);

2. many tenants and landlords do not understand the codes;

3. many lower-income owners are financially unable to rehabilitate;

4. code regulations restrict new building innovations and techniques; and

5. many owners and tenants do not know what financial assistance is available to them.

Section 117 of the Housing Act of 1949 authorizes federal grants to cities, counties, and municipalities to cover part of the cost of concentrated code enforcement programs in designated city areas. Grants can help pay for concentrated code enforcement administration, for relocation assistance, for administration of federal section 312 rehabilitation loans and section 115 grants, and for provision and repair of necessary streets, curbs, sidewalks, street lighting, tree planting, and similar improvements.

Section 312, added to the Housing and Urban Development Act of 1964, authorized direct federal loans at 3 percent interest rates to low- or moderate-income owners of residential and business property in urban renewal areas and code enforcement areas, and to low- or moderate-income owner-occupants of residential property in areas where such activities are planned within a reasonable time. These loans also are made to enable owners to bring structures up to code or to urban renewal requirements. Section 115 grants and 312 loans are made by local urban renewal agencies or through a private, nonprofit group designated by an agency. Urban renewal agencies also operate directly in rehabilitating housing in some urban renewal areas. While improving existing housing is a worthwhile endeavor, substantial portions of housing in most cities is beyond repair and needs to be replaced. In addition, there is vacant land suitable for housing developments, and isolated vacant residential lots are available for building sites.

Low- and low-middle income families need low-cost, publicly subsidized housing, including renovated older housing as well as new housing. Subsidized housing is a necessity, because many families are unable to obtain adequate housing in the privately financed housing market. The following alternatives have been suggested (Johnson, 1965, p. 7) as a solution to the slum housing problem:

providing rent supplements for families across a wide range of lower and moderate income brackets so they can afford decent housing;

providing rent supplement assistance to those forced out of their homes by code enforcement and all forms of federally assisted government action, from highways to urban renewal;

using both urban renewal funds and public housing funds to rehabilitate existing housing and make it available to low and moderate income families. There is no reason to tear down and rebuild if existing housing can be improved and made desirable;

emphasizing residential construction and rehabilitation on a neighborhood-wide scale in the urban renewal program.

Several arguments have been advanced for public housing: (1) newly constructed housing is financially out of reach of families with low incomes; (2) housing that low-income families can afford is being removed from the housing market faster than it is being replaced; (3) diseases and hazards are more difficult to control under poor housing conditions; and (4) all families should be able to live comfortably in adequate housing. In addition, one justification of slum clearance and construction of public housing has been that slums and social problems accompanying them will be eliminated by such programs.

"Unfortunately, the contention that slum clearance is a solution to a multitude of social problems may detract from more basic arguments for providing adequate housing for the less fortunate and their families" (Shannon, 1966, p. 1). Wilson (1965) contends that urban renewal is either irrelevant or disadvantageous for these kinds of problems—"urban renewal has bypassed the real problems, or, in some cases, made them worse."[2]

Public housing projects do not always involve large-scale housing removal. Some of them involve rehabilitation of individual residences and piecemeal removal dependent on individual housing unit condition. Similarly, there are a few scattered site housing programs. However, most urban renewal or redevelopment programs involve mass removal and clearance of housing, which means that residents must move out of the destroyed neighborhood. Similarly, the typical urban renewal project prevents original residents from returning to the old area of residence; and even if they are able to return, churches, schools, kin, and friends are no longer in the neighborhood. In addition, rent substantially increases for over two-thirds of those involved in urban renewal programs. Many residents of inner cities are not aided by urban renewal, because they are forced to move to large, factory-like skyscrapers of public housing. Most people who move because of urban renewal move into adjacent areas that probably will be cleared in subsequent projects, which once again will require them to move (Lichfield, 1961).

In an area of Akron, Ohio destined for subsequent urban renewal, residents generally had a favorable view of government and their neighborhood; however, they were divided about the desirability of urban renewal in the neighborhood. Residents who were middle-class—relatively well educated, mobile, well paid, and knowledgeable about the project—tended to be favorable, as were younger persons. On the other hand, older persons, the less well educated, home-owners, persons not knowledgeable about the project, and those currently less capable of independent action tended to be negative. In addition, negative residents tended to have more friends and relatives living in the neighborhood. However, those who were positive visited more with people both in and out of the neighborhood. Race was not a factor in appraisal of the urban renewal project. Residents were questioned about urban renewal in the abstract; once the project began, their attitudes and behavior may have changed drastically.

Public Housing and Quality of Life

A basic assumption of public housing projects is that the rehousing of families will improve the quality of their lives. One of the first tests of this hypothesis was a study of Sumner Field Homes in Minneapolis carried out in 1939 and 1940 (Chapin, 1940). This particular study had an experimental group—those who moved into the public housing project—and a control group. The control group was similar to the experimental group in race, employment of husband, occupational classification, number of persons in the family, and income, but they stayed in the slums. At the beginning of the study public housing project dwellers and slum residents were substantially similar in morale, general adjustment, and social participation. One year later they were still similar in morale and general adjustment. However, public housing residents were substantially more active in social participation than slum residents. Public housing residents had gained more in social status, had better furnishings in the living room, and were less crowded than they had been. Thus, this study shows that there are definite, positive, social effects of good housing.

Rumney (1951) compared a low-income population of former slum residents who were living in a public housing project, and another low-income population residing in a deteriorated area of Newark, New Jersey. Illnesses and accidents were lower among public housing families than among slum residents. The tuberculosis rate per 10,000 persons was 29 for public housing residents and 59 in the area of substandard housing. Similarly, the infant mortality rate in public housing projects in Pittsburgh was 42 while it was 71 in the area of substandard housing. In addition, juvenile delinquency rates per 10,000 population were 383 in public housing and 570 in the slums.

A somewhat similar study was carried out in Baltimore during the 1950s (Wilner, et al., 1962). Families living in a public housing project and a control sample residing in an unrehabilitated area of the city were matched on size of dwelling unit, age of female head of household, age of oldest child, presence of husband, number of children, and so on. Illness (morbidity) rates were lower for rehoused families than for slum families, for persons under thirty-five and especially for children. Disabilities from childhood communicable diseases were lower in the housing project than in the slums, and illnesses for males and females in the age range from thirty-five to fifty-nine were lower for rehoused families. Housing project residents were somewhat better psychologically adjusted than slum families. Rehoused families had a substantial increase in neighboring and mutual assistance activities, such as helping out with household tasks in times of illness. Rehoused families had fewer quarrels and arguments, and had more mutually shared activities in household tasks and leisure time activities than those living in substandard housing. The rehoused had more pride in the neighborhood, spent more time improving it, and expressed more satisfaction with their style of life, living conditions, and neighborhood. Rehoused women had improved morale, more favorable self-images, and reduced anxieties. Children in the housing project made a better showing in school than those who remained in the old neighborhood. However, little difference was noted on the results of intelligence and achievement scores of rehoused and slum dwellers.

In summary, the Baltimore study shows that rehoused families are better off psychologically, socially, and physiographically as a result of movement from substandard to standard housing. In addition, some effects of changed environment might not have been discernable until more time had passed, and presumably these changes would be in favor of those who were rehoused.

More recently, a study was conducted in New Haven, Connecticut, which examined the impact on family functioning of moving large, low-income black families into privately owned homes or apartments located on scattered sites in various parts of the city (Weller and Luchterhand, 1973). These homes, "vastly superior to the former residences," were made possible by an 80 percent subsidy paid by the city. The research included two sets of control families that were compared with relocated families to evaluate the impact of improved housing. Relocated families had more living space, more bedrooms, and a reduced number of housing deficiencies, and fewer families had to walk through bedrooms to get to bathrooms. In addition, subsidized relocated families moved to "better neighborhoods." The results of the New Haven study do not offer any clear-cut findings of impact on relocated families, other than the effects of improved housing. However, since change was measured over a very short period of time, lag effects may show up later. Also, relocated families were not given a choice of residence; thus, the element of not being able to select a house and neighborhood may have been detrimental and so may have attenuated positive impacts. Further, it may be that, given the economic situations of the families, other problems were so overwhelming that improved housing alone was not enough. Improved housing may have to be buttressed by larger incomes that allow families to live a life style similar to their new neighbors—if they so desire.

In a study of public housing needs in Des Moines, Shannon (1966, p. 26) notes that the city needed low-rent duplex or quadruplex units or town houses, rather than the high-rent large, multiple unit structures that were being built. He estimated that four or five thousand units would be needed to adequately house those in Des Moines who needed low-cost housing; however, he estimated that the city was going to construct only enough such housing to meet one-fourth the total need.

Most studies of slum clearance by urban renewal have been of "old-style ethnic" areas, not of low-income black neighborhoods in which most contemporary urban renewal is taking place (Wolf and Lebeaux, 1967). Only about one-fourth of the residents of a black area of Detroit, Michigan, had "predominantly positive feelings" about the neighborhood. Almost two-thirds were "thinking about moving" or would have liked to move away if they could. No strong emotional or symbolic attachment to the neighborhood was found; in fact, there was a great deal of fear of "rowdy, violent, and delinquent behavior on streets and playgrounds." While results of this study are in contrast to some other studies, urban renewal even in this area could destroy strong and meaningful social and kinship ties.

A Note on Public Policy and Housing[3]

Many forces for change in housing are beyond control of the local government, especially those socioeconomic forces that affect population trends, economic vitality, technology, and federal policies regarding the financing of new and used housing. Local governments, however, can directly influence the housing market through such mechanisms as passing open housing laws, discouraging private market discrimination practices, developing public housing programs, and providing financial aids to consumers in the form of rent subsidies or mortgage insurance. To a lesser degree, local public policy can affect the course of change in built-up neighborhoods by examining zoning laws, levels of services, and housing codes. By providing services, by protecting an area from incongruous uses, and by discouraging neglect, local government can encourage a higher environmental quality and thereby remove some of the cause for dissatisfactions and need for urban renewal. Further, much of the potential for high quality maintenance is incorporated in the quality of original planning and construction, which can be influenced at the local level.

Local government may have indirect impact on housing by influencing agents in the residential development process—predevelopment property owners, developers, and financiers. Zoning, availability of urban services, and financing are important factors in housing decisions. Especially important are developers' decisions regarding site-planning and the characteristics of dwelling units, because much of the household's housing choice is based on the dwelling unit and neighborhood, as opposed to accessibility and the larger environment.

Conclusions

Without question there are serious poverty, health, service, and housing problems in the slums. However, the assumption that rehousing the poor will automatically solve other problems is not supported by available evidence. If changes are to occur, they probably will happen only when rehousing is accompanied by reorganization of the social life and perspectives of slum dwellers. This requires altering societal conditions so that adequate job opportunities and incomes are available to all.

There is a need to reconcile what is done to the physical shells of cities with what is accomplished for and by people who live in them (Wilson, 1965, p. 7). One major problem associated with large-scale slum clearance is the destruction of established patterns of social interaction with relatives, neighbors, and friends as well as the relationship of residents with church, school, shopping centers, recreational facilities, and so on. A useful program must recognize such factors. It does appear that "when all is said and done, political factors, rather than need, probably have the greatest weight in determining whether or not public housing is constructed" (Shannon, 1966, p. 22).

PROSPECTS

Downs (1970, p. 40) suggests that alternative ghetto futures can best be accomplished by focusing on major choices relating to the following questions:

1. To what extent should future minority population growth be concentrated within central cities?

2. To what extent should minority and nonminority populations be residentially segregated from each other in the future?

3. To what extent should society redistribute income to relatively depressed urban areas of populations in society as a process of enrichment?

Downs summarized a number of different possibilities into five different strategies:

1. *Present Policies:* concentration, segregation, and nonenrichment.

2. *Enrichment Only:* concentration, segregation, enrichment.

3. *Integrated Core:* concentration, integration in the core only, enrichment.

4. *Segregated Dispersal:* dispersal throughout the metropolitan area, but in segregated districts, enrichment.

5. *Integrated Dispersal:* dispersal and integration throughout the metropolitan complex, enrichment.

Downs opts for *integrated dispersal* with the added feature of *enrichment*. He believes that future jobs will be available primarily in suburban areas and that there will be a need to bring workers and jobs closer together; there is a need to end the clustering in schools of lower-income children in order to improve their education. Development of an adequate housing supply and provision of free-choice for lower-income and black families requires the construction of housing for them in the suburbs. However, the future probably will have continuing concentration of the poor—especially blacks—in central cities; this continuing concentration of the poor and black in central cities will result in a highly segregated society.

Insofar as housing is concerned, 500,000 additional units of housing are needed each year for the poor. In the past, generally the yearly construction of housing for the poor has averaged around 30,000 units—a net deficit of 470,000 units per year (Harrington, 1968, p. 4). None of the proposals funded in the United States so far have come remotely near to meeting the problem. The notion that private enterprise will help is probably incorrect, because housing for the poor is a poor risk for private investors. Thus, if the housing deficit is to be overcome there must be an uneconomic investment of public funds motivated by considerations of social and aesthetic values rather than by a calculus of private profit (Harrington, 1968 p. 6). Prospects for either private or public funding seem remote indeed.

NOTES

1. For a recent review of policy and legislation related to housing in the United States, see *Housing* (1974).

2. For a manual to guide evaluation of local urban renewal projects, see *Evaluating* (1975). It should be noted that this manual for the most part ignores the costs and benefits to the people living in the urban renewal area.

3. This section is partially derived from Butler and Kaiser, (1971).

REFERENCES

Barth, Ernest A. T., and Susan March. "A Research Note on the Subject of Minority Housing." *Journal of Intergroup Relations* 3 (Autumn 1962):314–319.

Beyer, Glenn H. *Housing and Society.* New York: Macmillan, 1965.

Bluestone, Barry. "The Poor Who Have Jobs." *Dissent* 15 (September-October 1968): 410–419.

Butler, Edgar W., and Edward J. Kaiser. "Prediction of Residential Movement and Spatial Allocation." *Urban Affairs Quarterly* 6 (June 1971):477–494.

Caplovitz, David. *The Poor Pay More.* New York: Free Press, 1967.

Chapin, F. Stuart, Jr., Edgar W. Butler, and Frederick C. Patten. *Blackways in the Inner City.* Urbana: University of Illinois Press, forthcoming.

Chapin, F. Stuart. "An Experiment on the Social Effects of Good Housing." *American Sociological Review* 5 (December 1940):868–879.

Clark, Kenneth B., and Jeannette Hopkins. *A Relevant War Against Poverty.* New York: Harper & Row, 1968.

Council of Economic Advisors. "The Problem of Poverty in America." In *Perspectives on Poverty and Income Distribution,* edited by James G. Scoville. Lexington, Mass.: D.C. Heath, 1971, pp. 66–73.

Downs, Anthony. *Urban Problems and Prospects.* Chicago: Markham, 1970.

Evaluating Local Urban Renewal Projects. Washington, D.C.: Government Printing Office, 1975.

Gans, Herbert J. *The Urban Villagers.* New York: Free Press, 1962.

Haley, Bernard F. "Changes in the Distribution of Income in the United States." *Perspectives on Poverty and Income Distribution,* edited by James G. Scoville. Lexington, Mass.: D.C. Heath, 1971, pp. 17–40.

Hannerz, Ulf. *Soulside.* New York: Columbia University Press, 1969.

Harrington, Michael. "Can Private Industry Abolish Slums?" *Dissent* 15 (January-February 1968):4–6.

Harrison, Bennett. "Education and Underemployment in the Urban Ghetto." *American Economic Review* 62 (December 1972):796–812.

Herzog, Elizabeth, and Hylan Lewis. "Children in Poor Families: Myths and Realities." *American Journal of Orthopsychiatry* 40 (April 1970):375–387.

Himes, Joseph S. "Some Work-Related Cultural Deprivations of Lower-Class Negro Youths." *Marriage and the Family* 26 (November 1964):447–451.

Housing in the Seventies. Washington, D.C.: U.S. Department of Housing and Urban Development, 1974.

Johnson, Lyndon B. "Message on Cities." Washington, D.C.: The White House, March 2, 1965.

Kerner Commission. *Report of the National Advisory Commission on Civil Disorders*. Washington, D.C.: Government Printing Office, 1968.

Kriesberg, Louis. *Mothers in Poverty: A Study of Fatherless Families*. Chicago: Aldine, 1970.

Lichfield, Nathaniel. "Relocation: The Impact on Housing Welfare." *Journal of the American Institute of Planners* 27 (August 1961):199–203.

McCord, William, John Howard, Bernard Friedberg, and Edwin Harwood. *Life Styles in the Black Ghetto*. New York: Norton, 1969.

The Model Cities Program: A Comparative Analysis of City Response Patterns and Their Relation to Future Urban Policy. Washington, D.C.: U.S. Department of Housing and Urban Development, 1973.

The Model Cities Program: Ten Model Cities: A Comparative Analysis of Second Round Planning Years. Washington, D.C.: U.S. Department of Housing and Urban Development, July, 1973.

Moynihan, Daniel P. *Maximum Feasible Misunderstanding: Community Action in the War on Poverty*. New York: Free Press, 1969.

Offner, Paul. "Labor Force Participation in the Ghetto." *Journal of Human Resources* 7 (Fall 1972):460–481.

Orshansky, Mollie. "Counting the Poor: Another Look at the Poverty Profile." *Social Security Bulletin* January 1965.

Rainwater, Lee. *Behind Ghetto Walls*. Chicago: Aldine, 1970.

Rose, Jerome G. *Landlords and Tenants*. New Brunswick, N.J.: Transaction Books, 1973.

Rumney, Jay. "The Social Costs of Slums." *Journal of Social Issues* 7 (1951): 77–83.

Schorr, Alvin L. *Slums and Social Insecurity*. Washington, D.C.: Social Security Administration, 1963.

Shannon, Lyle W. *An Assessment of the Need for Public Housing in Des Moines*. Iowa City: University of Iowa, Iowa Urban Community Research Center, 1966.

Sternlieb, George S., and Bernard P. Indik. *The Ecology of Welfare*. New Brunswick, N.J.: Transaction Books, 1973.

Sussman, Marvin B. "Postscript." *Journal of Marriage and The Family* 26 (November 1964):395–398.

Suttles, Gerald. *The Social Order of the Slum*. Chicago: University of Chicago Press, 1968.

U. S. Bureau of the Census. "Characteristics of Families Residing in 'Poverty Areas,' March 1966." Series P-23, No. 19, August 24, 1966.

Weller, Leonard, and Elmer Luchterhand. "Effects of Improved Housing on the Family Functioning of Large, Low-Income, Black Families." *Social Problems* 20 (Winter 1973): 382–389.

Williamson, John B., and Kathryn M. Hyer. "The Measurement and Meaning of Poverty." *Social Problems* 22 (June 1975):652–663.

Wilner, Daniel M. et al. *The Housing Environment and Family Life*. Baltimore: John Hopkins Press, 1962.

Wilson, James Q. "Urban Renewal Does Not Always Renew." *Harvard Today* (January 1965):2–8.

Wolf, E.P., and Charles N. Lebeaux. "On the Destruction of Poor Neighborhoods by Urban Renewal." *Social Problems* 15 (Summer 1967):3–8.

9
MORTALITY, ILLNESS, AND IMPAIRED COMPETENCE

INTRODUCTION

Early cities were unhealthy places. Sanitation was primitive, and the incidences of disease and death probably were higher in cities than in rural areas. However, little historical data are available that indicate the extent of mortality and illnesses in early cities and urban regions in the United States. We do know that at times epidemics swept through the population of some cities.

Recently, the distinction between urban and rural areas in incidence of disease and death rates has become less clear. All contemporary metropolitan regions in the United States have sanitary facilities that include provision for the disposal of solid wastes. Foodstuffs and dairy products now are produced under much more sanitary conditions than previously. However, health care facilities tend to be much more extensive, of higher quality, and more accessible in urban than in rural areas.

Rigid inspection of milk and use of sterilized milk resulted in a decline in infant mortality rates. Reduction of the infant mortality rate in urban areas substantially decreased urban-rural differences in mortality, because it was primarily at the earlier ages that the differential in mortality was greatest. In other words, in early cities high mortality rates consisted primarily of high infant mortality rates. Currently, some of the highest incidences of illness and mortality are in rural areas.

Like so many other social phenomenon, most of what is reported in this chapter depends upon social definitions and case-finding techniques. For example, if the definition of mental disorder varies over time and by different political and geographic jurisdictions, obviously any differences observed may be explained by varying definitions and case-finding techniques rather than by changes attributable to urbanization, industrialization, population distributions, or whatever. There are three main methods in case-finding and each may result in varying levels of disorder (Mercer, et al., 1964). First, case registers include all persons identified and labeled by official agencies. Second, some studies survey public and private agencies and hospitals to develop a register similar to that developed in the first method; reported rates are higher than those reported by the first method. Both of these techniques result in systematic biases, because they only include persons who have official contact with public or private agencies or hospitals. The biases are such that the lower social classes and minority population categories are overrepresented. A third method is the field survey. The field survey method may include all of the population in a given area, or it may involve a representative sample of some specified universe, such as a city, county, or some region within a metropolitan complex—for example, a health district or a neighborhood. The main distinction between this approach and the first two is that the entire universe or representative sample comes under scrutiny. The results of studies conducted by these methodological approaches differ radically; typically, higher rates are found by field approaches. In any event, it is absolutely necessary that the approach used is specified, because the method influences results and, therefore, conclusions about causation and the nature of society.

MORTALITY

Throughout recorded history there have been high birth and death rates that have offset each other and have led to small population increases and decreases (Antonovsky, 1967). From at least Greco-Roman times through the eighteenth and nineteenth centuries, life expectancy was between twenty and thirty years.

In New England in 1892, the death rate was lowest in rural areas and steadily increased with the size of city. Mortality was higher in the city than in the country in every period of life—that is, by every age category (Weber, 1899, pp. 343–367). Part of the "excessive urban mortality" was related to city occupations being more dangerous than rural occupations. In addition, excessive urban mortality was due to a lack of pure air, water, and sunlight, "together with uncleanly habits of life induced thereby." "Part cause, part effect, poverty often accompanies uncleanliness: poverty, overcrowding, high rate of mortality, are usually found together in city tenements." However, it may not necessarily be poverty and density in the city that create higher mortality, but rather the reactions of different populations of varying cultural backgrounds to poverty and crowded conditions. For example, Russian and Polish Jews, who were among the poorest people in New York City in the middle 1890s, lived under extremely crowded conditions; yet their infant mortality rate was relatively low. The answer is that these particular people were extremely careful in observance of Mosaic laws regarding cleanliness, the cooking of food, habits of eating, drinking, and so on. Thus, there is no inherent reason that people should die faster in larger communities than in smaller places, "provided they are not too ignorant, too stupid, or too selfishly individualistic to cooperate in the securing of common benefits" (Weber, 1899).

Metropolitan Areas and Mortality
Altenderfer (1947) studied ninety-two United States cities with populations of 100,000 and found that low-income cities had higher death rates than middle- and high-income cities. Similarly, the mortality rate declined as size of city decreased. There were clear urban-rural differences—the rural mortality rate was only about two-thirds that of the urban. In addition, there was a reported association of rheumatic fever and rheumatic heart disease with urbanization, overcrowded housing, nutritional deficiency, and poverty.

Metropolitan Subareas and Mortality
Death rates in New Haven, from 1930 to 1934, varied inversely with social class of area (Sheps and Watkins, 1947). Similarly, in Buffalo death rates had an inverse gradient (Yeracaris, 1955). The difference in death rates between the lowest social class and the next lowest social class was greater than the difference between the highest and the next lowest social class. If the death rate of the highest income level area had prevailed throughout Buffalo, 19.1 percent of deaths would not have occurred. Death rates in Pittsburgh (Patno, 1960) and Baltimore (Tayback, 1957) show similar differentials by residential area economic level.

Ellis's (1958) study of death rates in Houston reported death rates similar to Pittsburgh and Baltimore, with the exception that males in lowest social rank areas had a lower death rate than those in the next highest level. This may be because of the availability of free medical treatment for the residents of lower social rank areas. This strongly suggests that if medical care is effectively utilized, death rates can be lowered. In analyzing mortality data for the seven leading diseases in Houston (1949–1951), Ellis found an inverse relationship between mortality and socioeconomic status for both infectious and chronic diseases, with that of infectious diseases most pronounced. He also reports that socioeconomic differentials in mortality were *increasing* insofar as chronic diseases were concerned. Stockwell's study (1963a and 1963b) of Providence and Hartford during the same time period as the Houston study showed similar results.

In summary, these studies suggest that death rates vary by ecological area of residence and that this relationship is inversely related to social class. However, death rates may be lowered by having adequate medical care readily available (also see Klebba, et al., 1975).

Social Factors and Mortality

With the emergence of modern sanitation and medical practice, the life expectancy of middle and upper stratum increased at a rapid rate. On the other hand, there is some evidence to suggest that the life expectancy of lower social classes may have declined somewhat with industrialization. The changes wrought by industrialization appeared in the upper strata of society, then slowly percolated downward, resulting in increasing life expectancy differentials and death rates. Occupational differences in death rates have been reported. But in general socioeconomic differentials rather than specific occupational hazards are crucial in the relationship between social class and mortality. Further, this relationship appears to hold in a variety of places, despite the multiplicity of methods used to obtain the data and different kinds of indexes used. In other words, evidence conclusively shows social class mortality differences, especially for young children.

The mortality gap between social classes had been closing as a result of the triumph over infectious diseases, especially through modern sanitation techniques and mass innoculations (Antonovsky, 1967). However, in the future, access to medical care, preventive medical action, health knowledge and practice, and the increasing relation of chronic disease to mortality will result in lower-class people again becoming increasingly disadvantaged, and this will increase class mortality differences. This is *not* to say that the life expectancy in the lower social classes is going to decrease or that the death rate of the lower class is going to increase; it is to suggest that the relative *difference* between social classes is going to become greater again in the future.

Several other factors may increase death rates of certain areas within the metropolitan complex and may explain variation in death rates between cities. The age structure of a city or some subdivision within it influences death rates. Obviously even a relatively affluent retirement community may have a higher death rate than a poorer city populated by younger persons, because the retirement community has a larger population at high risk of mortality. Metropolitan complexes, as well as areas within them, may have differing levels of environmental hazards—population segments are differentially exposed to these hazards. Similarly, physicians and medical care are not distributed equally in different cities (Marden, 1966) nor equally within a metropolitan region (Elesh and Schollaert, 1972).

PHYSICAL ILLNESSES

Until the advent of modern sanitation practices, cities were unhealthy places to live. Yet, little evidence exists that directly demonstrates that urban people are inherently more likely to become physically ill than rural people.

In the United States, low-income persons have less access to medical care and what they do have access to is a lower quality and narrower range of services. Few services exist in the immediate residential area of low-income persons, and the ratio of doctors (other than certain specialists) is lower in cities than in suburbs (Bauer 1972, pp. 1–2). Thus, low-income persons are multiply disadvantaged in health. Persons with incomes of less than $5,000 have more limitation of activity, more disability, and more hospital stays than the total population. They have fewer resources for obtaining medical care, they are less likely to have hospital insurance, and they have less cash to pay medical expenses on their own. Of those with low incomes, aid recipients have poorer health and have higher rates on all health measures than nonrecipients—in many cases, twice as high.

Kadushin (1964) accepted the position that earlier lower social classes had high rates of physical illness due to the character of their everyday lives; however, he argues that the relationship between class and illness has been eliminated by modern medical research and practice. Whatever difference currently exists, he believes, is a result of lower-class people being more likely than others to report symptoms of physical illness. Mechanic (1968, pp. 259–266) argues that social class differences continue, especially for chronic diseases.

Recently Conover (1971), using data gathered by the National Health Survey (84,000 families representing 268,000 individuals from a national sample interviewed between July 1965 and June 1967), reported that "for whites and nonwhites, with age adjusted or not, there is a strong relationship between income and measures of chronic disease." Further, there are more dramatically higher rates in the lower social class. In addition, families with lower incomes have 50 percent more problems than families with higher incomes, whether white or nonwhite. Chronic illness is so widespread that about half of all people in the United States have some chronic illness (85 percent for those over age 65), although only 11 percent claim any limitation of activity as a result of chronic illness. Race differences are rather minor. When the relationship between social class and specific diseases are analyzed, the relationship appears to hold for all illnesses except for diseases of the thyroid gland. Thus, the evidence shows that there are social class differences in chronic diseases and, in fact, suggests that the relationship between social class and the more severe measures of chronic diseases are substantial.

Generally, research shows that poor housing tends to go with poor health and adjustment, while better housing is associated with better health and adjustment. Wilner and Walkley (1963) conducted a study in Baltimore of families (1,341 persons who had originally lived in a slum area but had subsequently moved to a new public housing project) and a *control* sample of families who remained in the slum. Their study was an attempt to unravel the effects of housing and personal characteristics on morbidity. In virtually every comparison, families who moved into the new housing project were better off than those who remained behind. "Test rates were regularly lower than control rates in three categories: infective and parasitic conditions, mainly the communicable diseases of childhood; digestive conditions; and accidents." Accidents were one-third lower in the housing project than in the slum. However, during the first five-month resettlement period in the housing project, rates of illness and disability for almost everyone under age twenty, regardless of sex, were *higher* than control rates. A change of residence for children may at first lead to a higher incidence of the more common communicable diseases.

In Baltimore, test families were more satisfied with housing and available space, had more neighboring, more common family activities, showed more pride in their neighborhood, and regarded the neighborhood more favorably as a place to live and to raise children. Morale of the test sample was better than morale of the controls. Test children "were considerably more likely to be *promoted* at a normal pace, control children being held back more often for one or more semesters." Test sample children were more likely than controls to attend school daily, and so improved housing quality played an indirect role in school performance—more regular attendance was made possible by better health.

Because age and social class are important in chronic diseases, there are substantial differences in rates of illnesses by areas within metropolitan areas. Little evidence suggests that similar differences will be found by comparing metropolitan complexes. However, if there is substantial variation in social class and age structure of two cities, perhaps it is reasonable to expect these differences to carry over into rates for the larger complex.

MENTAL ILLNESS
Urban life has been assumed to lead to higher rates of mental disorder than rural life; and generally, admission rates to mental hospitals have been higher for urban than for rural people (Rose and Stub, 1955). However, studies comparing urban and rural hospital admissions are inconclusive because of varying definitions of mental disorders, differential accessibility to hospital facilities, and varying abilities of urban and rural families to care for the mentally ill at home. One study accomplished across time, using similar definitions of mental disorders, reports a relative consistency in accessibility to a mental hospital (Goldhamer and Marshall, 1953). Between 1840 and 1940 in

Massachusetts, rates of admission for psychoses rose from 41 per 100,000 in the period from 1840 to 1845 to 85 per 100,000 in 1941. As urbanization occurred, so did increases in mental disorders; however, admissions for those between twenty and fifty were the same in the later periods as earlier. Thus, older people accounted for the increase in hospitalization rates. This is probably a result of two factors. First, more people living to an older age, and second, more of the older mentally ill were cared for at home in rural areas than in urban areas.

Does urbanization constitute a threat to mental health? Is modern civilization responsible for the alleged increase of mental ill-health in the present world? Early studies concluded that primitive or underdeveloped societies had virtually no mental illness. Yet others claim that mental disorder does not vary greatly by time, culture, and society. The lack of variation is expressed primarily by those who believe in a physiological point of view, as contrasted with others who stress sociocultural influences. Lin (1959, p. 25) notes that "There is good evidence that certain types of mental disorder are related to certain environmental (sociocultural) factors, and this deserves careful attention in order to understand the effect of urbanization on mental health." Further, he argues that the rate of neuroses increases with urbanization and industrialization. In addition, it has been argued that rates of psychosomatic diseases, such as hypertension, nonarthritic rheumatism, gastritis, peptic ulcers, exophtalmic goiter, and diabetes increase with urbanization. Nevertheless, the data are conflicting, and no definitive answer can be given at this time as to whether or not urbanization of society influences the rates of serious mental disorders.

Schroeder (1942) reported differences in rates of mental disorders in St. Louis, Milwaukee, Omaha, Kansas City, and Peoria. He found that such variation "could be expected in communities of varying size and situation." Unfortunately, he did not report specific rates for these cities, so no specific comparisons can be made.

Virtually every study of mental disorders reports that they are differentially distributed throughout the metropolitan complex and are concentrated or clustered in certain areas. Also, there appears to be systematic variation in the distribution of different types of mental disorders. Manic-depressives are spread evenly throughout the metropolitan complex, while schizophrenia follows the clustering pattern shown by all other types of mental disorders. The highest rates cluster around the center of the city and progressively decline at greater distances from the center. Early studies of mental disorders in Chicago, Providence, St. Louis, Milwaukee, Omaha, Kansas City, and Peoria all reported this pattern (Faris and Dunham, 1939; Schroeder, 1942). The only consistent exception to the general pattern in each of the cities was that in older, outlying deteriorated areas of the metropolis, rates were high, much like those in the city center.

Major subclassifications of mental disorder appear to have their highest incidence in areas with specified characteristics. The concentration of paranoid schizophrenics Faris and Dunham found in Chicago roominghouse areas led them to suggest that communication with others is necessary for normal mental stability. Social isolation leads to mental breakdown with mental disorders appearing to be more prevalent in areas of high residential mobility and a heterogeneous population than in areas characterized by residential stability and homogeneity. Rates of psychoses varied by race, nationality, socioeconomic status, and occupation. (For more recent information on Chicago, see Levy and Rowitz, 1971.)

Belknap and Jaco (1953) studied mental illness in Austin, Texas, to determine if there were different distributions of the mentally disordered in a political type city as opposed to an industrial-commercial type city. Their findings show that Austin's first admission rates were substantially different from Chicago's, and that the incidence rate was less than that of the United States. Nevertheless, significantly higher rates of manic-depressive, psychoses, senile psychosis, general paresis, psychoses with organic change of the nervous system, and cases without psychosis were found in Austin than in the United States. Rates for schizophrenia, psychosis with cerebral arteriosclerosis, and involutional psychosis were significantly lower in Austin. No differences were found for psychoneurosis and mental deficiency.

No pattern of decreasing rates from the center to the periphery was found. They found high rates in the central business district as well as near the edge of the city (also see Jaco, 1959, and Queen, 1940). Somewhat similar departures were reported by Schroeder (1942) for six cities. These variations may be reconciled by further knowledge of the individual cities; that is, probably these were atypical, older areas located on the periphery. Their sociological character probably is similar to central city areas where high rates have been systematically found.

An unusual feature of the Austin study was that "actual church membership figures" were related to mental disorders. Baptist, Methodist, Lutheran, Christian, and Church of Christ church affiliates had higher incidence rates, Catholic and Episcopalian affiliates lower rates, and Presbyterian and Assembly of God church affiliates average rates (Belknap and Jaco, 1953, pp. 239–240).

Since they found varying ecological distributions and rates of several major mental disorders, and these results were somewhat different from those typically reported for commercial-industrial type cities, Belknap and Jaco conclude that cities with different ecological bases have different distributions of mental disorders. If this is true, research in the ecological distribution of mental disorders should take into consideration the ecological base of the city. Also, care should be taken to consider city size, since Austin is smaller than

Chicago. Further, other factors may lead to differential ecological patterns.

Building on the earlier study of Austin, Jaco (1959) classified areas by all first admissions of diagnosed functional psychoses to the local state hospital for a period of twelve years, to determine high and low rate areas. In the high and low rate areas he selected a representative sample of *all residents* to determine if characteristics of areas are associated with the onset as well as the incidence of mental disorders. Residents of high areas had less knowledge of neighbors' names, fewer personal friends and acquaintances, visited friends less often, visited outside of the neighborhood and town less often, were less likely to hold a membership in a voluntary organization, such as a lodge, fraternal organization, or occupational group, and were less likely to vote than residents of low rate areas. In addition, economic instability and downward social mobility were very important factors. Residents of high rate areas exhibited more economic instability and downward mobility than those of low rate areas. Further, he noted that high rate areas had *less* spatial mobility, which may throw some doubt on the "drift hypothesis."

Finally, Jaco reports that disruption of the family (divorce and female employment) was more prevalent in high than in low rate areas. He concludes that persons who live in areas with high rates of mental disorders encounter more stressful life conditions than those who reside in areas with low rates. He suggests that if *individual* factors are considered as relatively constant in these areas, "then those communities whose inhabitants possess a high degree of social isolation, downward social mobility, economic instability, and family dislocation should exhibit higher incidence rates of the functional psychoses than those communities where these conditions exist to a significantly lesser extent" (Jaco, 1959, p. 409).

In a survey of community agencies that dealt with "various types of mental-hygiene" problems in Baltimore's Eastern Health District, Lemkau, et al., (1941, 1942a, 1942b) report that both the incidence and prevalence of hospitalized psychosis were about 25 percent above national averages. They suggest that this is "not surprising considering the urban character of the district." In comparing the nonhospitalized with the hospitalized, the race distribution was similar, but older age and female psychotics were more likely to be kept at home than younger age and male psychotics. The number of psychotics in the community was estimated to be one-third the number in the hospital, and child neurotics showed a different demographic pattern than adult neurotics. Finally, supporting other studies, they reported that both psychoses and neuroses appear to be most prevalent among the lowest socioeconomic classes of the white population.

Most of these studies of urban mental disorders utilized hospitalized cases in calculating rates. However, household surveys show that a

Mortality, Illness, and Impaired Competence **149**

substantial number of psychotics never enter a mental hospital. Potentially, nonhospitalized psychotics may be distributed differently in the metropolitan complex than those who are hospitalized.

Kaplan et al. (1956) studied the incidence of hospitalized and nonhospitalized psychotics in Wellesley, an above average socioeconomic level suburban area of Boston, and the Whittier Street area of the city of Boston which was below average in socioeconomic status. They reported that the rate of hospitalized psychotics was higher in the Whittier Street area than in suburban Wellesley. They interpreted these findings as confirming other studies that suggested an inverse relation between socioeconomic level, social environment, and mental disorders. Further comparisons, adding hospitalized and nonhospitalized psychotics in each area, reduces the relationship between socioeconomic status and mental disorders somewhat but does not change the overall conclusion that mental disorder rates vary by socioeconomic level and area of residence. More nonhospitalized cases were discovered in Wellesley than in the Whittier Street area. As a result, they argue that there are more nonhospitalized cases in Wellesley because a greater proportion of people there than in Whittier Street hold a negative attitude toward state hospitals.

It should be noted that the findings from this study, using both hospitalized and nonhospitalized cases, continues to support the notion that there are areas within metropolitan complexes with substantially different rates of mental disorders (see also Srole et al., 1962).

Faris and Dunham (1939) hypothesized that social isolation may be a determining factor in some types of mental disorders. They particularly suggest a relationship between mental disorders and high residential turnover. One possible explanation for the concentration of the mentally ill is that conditions within certain areas of the metropolitan complex help cause mental disorders. This view emphasizes stress factors, such as living under dense, crowded conditions, deteriorated and dilapidated housing and neighborhoods, and anonymity and social isolation.

A second approach speculates that mentally ill individuals drift into certain parts of the urban complex and that this results in high rates of mental disorders in those areas. Thus, the character of the current neighborhood is not the causal factor as in the first case— other factors are more important. Thus, the mentally disordered are assumed to have drifted to these deteriorated neighborhoods because they are downwardly mobile. If this is so, Clausen and Kohn (1954) suggest that it is more appropriate to obtain "data on area of residence in early childhood or at the time of the first clear sign of overt disorder" rather than current place of residence. Both of these approaches make note of the clustering of the mentally disordered that apparently exists in most cities. Any explanation of the causes and consequences of mental disorders needs to consider this fact or be rejected.

Clausen and Kohn (1954, pp. 142–143) also point out that area of residence might affect the probability that persons with similar characteristics will be labeled as having a mental disorder. They also argue that there may be social class differences in the degree to which children and adults are vulnerable to potential stress, and variation in the degree to which they are exposed to actual stress that may lead to mental disorder. Anyone who has visited or lived in certain areas of the city is aware that some are more stressful than others; so, again, it is no surprise that rates of mental disorder vary by areas within the metropolitan complex. Finally, people who do not fit in an area may be more prone to mental illness than those who do (Wechsler and Pugh, 1967).

IMPAIRED COMPETENCE

Mental deficiency, mental retardation, and impaired social competence are terms used at different times in the United States to categorize individuals who do not function adequately under some definition of social adequacy. As Lemkau, et al., (1942b, p. 278) noted, the definition of mental deficiency was originally based upon social competency, but diagnosis became dependent on tests designed to evaluate intellectual functions. The use of intelligence tests, especially in education, tended to make mental deficiency an inability to take these tests rather than an inability to live adequately in society.

The use of intelligence tests is associated with mental retardation. More recently, a return to the notion of *social competency* has resulted in the use of the terms *impaired competence* or *maladaptive behavior*. These terms emphasize the ability of an individual to get along satisfactorily in the community, rather than performance on IQ tests.

Little evidence is available indicating that urbanization has or has not affected the rate of impaired competence. Urban-rural differences in impaired competence are confounded by varying definitions, services, and resources utilized in case finding (Farber, 1968, p. 74). In Maine, the rate was higher in urban than rural school systems. Rural school systems reported more doubtful cases and a higher excess of males than did urban school systems. Farber reports opposite findings in Illinois. There the trainable, severely retarded, and slow learners have higher rates in rural than urban areas. He argues that in smaller school systems, the impaired are more visible and there is less reliance on "formal case-finding procedures"—and both of these factors lead to more "doubtfuls" who are treated as impaired.

Others have suggested that those persons who migrate out of rural areas are more intelligent than the population left behind. Klineberg (1935) showed that the longer southern-born black children lived in New York City, the higher their IQ test scores were. Lee (1951) replicated Klineberg's study subsequently in Philadelphia and reported similar results: The younger southern black children were when they entered the Philadelphis schools, the greater was their increase in IQ. Farber (1968, pp. 77–79) also partially tested this selective migration hypothesis and concluded that intellectually retarded people tend to remain as a residual population.

Most studies then point toward the proposition that there are rural-urban differences in rates of mental retardation. The implication of these studies is that higher rates will be found in rural areas, because the more intelligent population has selectively migrated to urban areas. None of these studies shed any light on whether or not impaired competence has increased as a result of the urbanization of society.

Metropolitan Complexes and Impaired Competence

The first important investigation of mental retardation in the United States was accomplished in the 1930s in Baltimore, Maryland (Lemkau et al., 1942b). This study primarily used agency files and records and IQ scores to determine if a person was mentally retarded, although some untested persons with an official history of mental retardation also were included. A prevalence rate of 12.2 per thousand population was reported. A curvilinear relationship with age was shown, with an increasing prevalence through adolescence and a steady decline with age thereafter.

Farber 1968, pp. 55–56) reviewed a number of other prevalence studies that "took place in large cities, others in rural dominated countries and sparsely settled areas, still others in states with much industry and widely differentiated economic areas." He reports a "marked similarity in the prevalence rates produced by these investigations," and notes that this is remarkable because of the widely varying environmental conditions and also because of the wide variety of case-finding procedures and measurement techniques used in these studies.

Metropolitan Subareas and Impaired Competence

Lei, et al., (1974) reported different utilization rates of mental retardation services by type of agency in Riverside, California. They showed similar distributions and concentrations of labeled mental retardates for public school nominees and retardates labeled by other public agencies. A different distribution emerged for the users of private agencies. These different distributions illustrate quite clearly variations in utilization by mental retardates in this city. Areas with the highest rates of retardates labeled by public schools and other public agencies were characterized by concentrations of minority families (chicano and black), lower socioeconomic status, poorly educated households, poor housing quality, old and deteriorated housing, and *longer* duration of residence in the community. Users of private agencies tended to cluster in areas of predominantly anglo, middle-class status, better housing quality, and newly developed residential neighborhoods.

In another study in the same city, Butler, et al., (forthcoming) reported a household field survey study of intellectual and behavioral impairments. This study supports the notion of differential concentrations of the intellectually and behaviorally impaired in areas characterized by ethnic minority populations, poor housing, overcrowded conditions, and inadequate neighborhood services. Interestingly, while rates between this household survey study and the agency study of mental retardation used different methods and data bases, the clustering of impaired people identified by public agencies parallels almost exactly the patterns reported for intellectual and behavioral impairments.

Jenkins and Brown (1935) studied the incidence of mental deficiency in various areas of Chicago between 1925 and 1934. The incidence of mental deficiency among children in various areas of Chicago corresponded negatively with socioeconomic status and positively with community disorganization—for example, juvenile delinquency. Mental deficiency rates were highest in deteriorated areas where poverty and dependency were common. Thus, their findings were similar to those of Faris and Dunham in Chicago for mental illness. A study of Liverpool, England, revealed the existence of residential clusters in which feeble-mindedness was apparent to a decidedly greater extent than elsewhere in the city. These areas were concentrated in inner city residential areas bordering on the industrial and commercial core (Castle and Gittus, 1957). Rates at two different times in the same parts of the city were similar, with the highest incidence of social problems found in the same areas that at an earlier time had had the highest rates (see also Jackson, 1974).

In another study of Chicago, concentrations of candidates for "ungraded classrooms" (for example, the mentally retarded) were located in the underprivileged sections of the city (Mullen and Nie, 1952). The "excused from school" lived in other areas. The results showed that the excused persons as a whole represented a more serious degree of mental retardation than ungraded candidates. Excused persons were scattered throughout the city and were not located in any obvious concentrations.

In summary, there is a general concensus that those who are labeled and who use specialized services for mental retardation are disproportionately distributed among populations living in various sections of the metropolitan complex; high rate areas are characterized by lower socioeconomic status, poverty, and deteriorated and dilapidated housing and neighborhoods.

Social Factors and Impaired Competence

Consistently more males than females are reported as mentally deficient; and the rate of blacks is nearly four times that reported for whites. However, this difference appears primarily at the younger ages. Similarly, more chicanos than anglos are reported as being impaired. Lower socioeconomic classes contribute more than their share to mental deficiency rates. All of the studies cited in this chapter also have reported that mental deficiency is greater among children than adults. Adult rates are composed of the most severely retarded or incompetent, while rates for younger people are primarily composed of those who have been labeled by a school system. Evidently these incompetents disappear into the normal population when they become adults!

A follow-up study comparing persons of "normal and subnormal intelligence" in Baltimore reported that normal persons move more often than subnormals; however, another follow-up study of normals and retardates showed that mentally retarded persons moved often but within restricted areas of the city (Baller, 1936). Selective movement could influence rates of retardation, especially if the movement is within narrowly restricted neighborhoods. In other studies, however, there does not seem to be a great deal of support for an explanation that relies on the drift of impaired persons toward clustering areas. On the contrary, Mullen and Nie (1935, p. 777) suggest that the debilitating nature of "pauperism, slumism, and their concomitants" appear to be the main causal factors.

INTERRELATIONSHIP OF MORTALITY, ILLNESSES, AND IMPAIRMENTS
Faris and Dunham (1939) showed that urban areas characterized by high rates of social pathology were also characterized by high rates of mental disorders. Similarly, Schroeder (1942–1943) reported that the areas of concentration of pathologies in the six cities he studied were similar to those of mental disorders. As an example, he reports the correlations of mental disorders with other measures of social pathology in Peoria are .81 for adult crime, .74 for juvenile delinquency, and .65 for suicide. In addition, correlations are rather substantial among social pathologies, lower social status, and deteriorating neighborhoods. He argues that there are "insanity" areas in cities comparable to the delinquency areas that Shaw (1929) reported.

A mental illness is more likely to be discovered in a mentally deficient person than in one of normal intelligence, because the mentally deficient person is likely to come in contact with persons who are capable of recognizing the presence of the illness (Lemkau et al., 1942b, p. 279). This, of course, suggests a higher rate of mental illness should be reported among the mentally deficient than in the general population, although real levels may be similar.

PROSPECTS
Differences in mortality, illnesses, and impaired competence may be systematically related to variation in types of metropolitan com-

plexes. In addition, there are substantial variations in mortality and illnesses in various areas within the metropolitan complex. The two important social factors appear to be socioeconomic status (social class) and ethnicity. There is little likelihood that the relationship of various social factors to mortality, illnesses, and impaired competence will change in the future. Whatever changes do occur will probably work to the disadvantage of the poor, minorities, and the aged, because the gaps that had been closing now appear to be becoming wider.

REFERENCES

Altenderfer, Marion E. "Relationship Between Per Capita Income and Mortality, in The Cities of 100,000 or More Population." *Public Health Reports* 62 (November 1947): 1681–1691.

Antonovsky, Aaron. "Social Class, Life Expectancy, and Overall Mortality." *Milbank Memorial Fund Quarterly* 45 (April 1967):31–73; also in *Patients, Physicians, and Illness*, 2nd ed. edited by E. Gartley Jaco. New York: Free Press, 1972, pp. 5–30.

Baller, Warren R. "A Study of the Present Social Status of a Group of Adults, Who, When They Were in Elementary Schools, Were Classified as Mentally Deficient." *Genetic Psychology Monographs* 18 (June 1936):165–244.

Bauer, Mary Lou. *Health Characteristics of Low-Income Persons*. Rockville, Md.: U.S. Department of Health, Education, and Welfare, Vital and Health Statistics, Series 10, No. 74, July 1972.

Belknap, Ivan, and E. Gartley Jaco. "The Epidemiology of Mental Disorders in a Political-Type City, 1946–1952." in *Interrelations Between the Social Environment and Psychiatric Disorders*. New York: Milbank Memorial Fund, 1953, pp. 235–243.

Butler, Edgar W., Tzuen-jen Lei, and Ronald J. McAllister. "Impaired Competence in an Urban Community: An Ecological Analysis." *Urban Affairs Quarterly*, forthcoming.

Castle, I.M., and E. Gittus. "The Distribution of Social Defects in Liverpool." *Sociological Review* 5 (1957):43–64; also reprinted in *Studies in Human Ecology*, edited by George A. Theodorson New York: Harper & Row, 1961, pp. 415–429.

Clausen, John A., and Melvin L. Kohn. "The Ecological Approach in Social Psychiatry." *American Journal of Sociology* 60 (September 1954):140–151.

Conover, Patrick W. "Social Class and Chronic Illness." Paper presented to the Southern Sociological Society, 1971.

Elesh, David, and Paul T. Schollaert. "Race and Urban Medicine: Factors Affecting the Distribution of Physicians in Chicago." *Journal of Health and Social Behavior* 13 (September 1972):236–250.

Ellis, John M. "Socioeconomic Differentials in Mortality From Chronic Diseases." In *Patients, Physicians and Illness*, edited by E. Gartley Jaco. New York: Free Press, 1958, pp. 30–37.

Farber, Bernard. *Mental Retardation: Its Social Context and Social Consequences*. Boston: Houghton Mifflin, 1968.

Faris, Robert E.L., and H. Warren Dunham. *Mental Disorders in Urban Areas*. Chicago: University of Chicago Press, 1939.

Goldhamer, Herbert, and Andrew W. Marshall. *Psychosis and Civilization*. Glencoe: Free Press, 1949, 1953.

Jackson, Robin. "The Ecology of Educable Mental Handicap." *British Journal of Mental Subnormality* 20 (1, 1974):18–22.

Jaco, E. Gartley. "Social Stress and Mental Illness in the Community." In *Community Structure and Analysis*, edited by Marvin B. Sussman. New York: Thomas Y. Crowell, 1959, pp. 388–409.

———. "The Social Isolation Hypothesis and Schizophrenia." *American Sociological Review* 19 (October 1954):567–577.

Jenkins, R.L., and Andrew W. Brown. "The Geographical Distribution of Mental Deficiency in the Chicago Area." *Proceedings of the American Association on Mental Deficiency*. Chicago: 1935, pp. 291–307.

Kadushin, C. "Social Class and the Experience of Ill Health." *Sociological Inquiry* 34 (Winter 1964):67–80.

Kaplan, Bert, Robert B. Reed, and Wyman Richardson. "A Comparison of the Incidence of Hospitalized and Nonhospitalized Cases of Psychosis in Two Communities." *American Sociological Review* 21 (August 1956): 472–479.

Klebba, A. Joan, Jeffrey D. Maurer, and Evelyn J. Glass. *Mortality Trends For Leading Causes of Death: United States, 1950–1969*. Rockville, Md.: National Center For Health Statistics, DHEW Publication No. (HRA) 74-1853, March 1974.

Klineberg, Otto. *Negro Intelligence and Selective Migration*. New York: Columbia University Press, 1935.

Lee, Everett S. "Negro Intelligence and Selective Migration: A Philadelphia Test of the Klineberg Hypothesis." *American Sociological Review* 16 (April 1951):227–233.

Lei, Tzuen-jen, Louis Rowitz, Ronald J. McAllister, and Edgar W. Butler. "An Ecological Study of Agency Labeled Retardates." *American Journal of Mental Deficiency* 79 (July 1974):22–31.

Lemkau, Paul, Christopher Tietze, and Marcia Cooper. "Mental Hygiene Problems in an Urban District." *Mental Hygiene* 25 (October 1941):624–646.

Lemkau, Paul, Christopher Tietze, and Marcia Cooper. "Mental Hygiene Problems in An Urban District—second paper." *Mental Hygiene* 26 (January 1942a):100–119.

Lemkau, Paul, Christopher Tietze, and Marcia Cooper. "Mental Hygiene Problems in an Urban District—third paper." *Mental Hygiene* 26 (April 1942b):275–288.

Levy, Leo, and Louis Rowitz. "Ecological Attributes of High and Low Mental Hospital Utilization Areas in Chicago." *Social Psychiatry* 6 (No. 1, 1971):20–28.

Lin, Tsung-Yi. "Effects of Urbanization on Mental Health." *International Social Science Journal* 11 (1959):24–33.

Marden, Parker G. "A Demographic and Ecological Analysis of the Distribution of Physicians in Metropolitan America, 1960." *American Journal of Sociology* 72 (November 1966):290–300.

Mechanic, David. *Medical Sociology*. New York: Free Press, 1968.

Mercer, Jane R., Edgar W. Butler, and Harvey F. Dingman. "The Relationship Between Social Developmental Performance and Mental Ability." *American Journal of Mental Deficiency* 69 (September 1964): 195–205.

Mullen, Frances A., and Mary M. Nie. "Distribution of Mental Retardation in an Urban School Population." *American Journal of Mental Deficiency* 56 (April 1952): 777–790.

Patno, Mary E. "Mortality and Economic Level in an Urban Area." *Public Health Reports* 75 (September 1960):841–851.

Queen, Stuart A. "The Ecological Study of Mental Disorders." *American Sociological Review* 5 (April 1940):201–209.

Rose, Arnold M., and H.R. Stub. "Summary of Studies on the Incidence of Mental Disorders." In *Mental Health and Mental Disorder*, edited by Arnold M. Rose. New York: Norton, 1955, pp. 87–116.

Schroeder, Clarence W. "Mental Disorders in Cities." *American Journal of Sociology* 48 (July 1942):40–47.

Shaw, Clifford R. *Delinquency Areas*. Chicago: University of Chicago Press, 1919.

Sheps, Cecil, and J.H. Watkins. "Mortality in the Socioeconomic Districts of New Haven." *Yale Journal of Biology and Medicine* 20 (October 1947):51–80.

Srole, Leo, Thomas S. Langner, Stanley T. Michael, Marvin K. Opler, and Thomas A.C. Rennie. *Mental Health in the Metropolis: The Midtown Manhattan Study*. New York: McGraw-Hill, 1962.

Stockwell, Edward G. "A Critical Examination of the Relationship Between Socioeconomic Status and Mortality." *American Journal of Public Health* 53 (June 1963a):956–964.

Stockwell, Edward G. "Socioeconomic Status and Mortality." *Connecticut Health Bulletin* 77 (December 1963b):10–13.

Tayback, Matthew. "The Relationship of Socioeconomic Status and Expectation of Life." *Baltimore Health News* 34 (April 1957):139–144.

Weber, Adna Ferrin. *The Growth of Cities in the Nineteenth Century.* New York: Macmillan, 1899.

Wechsler, Henry, and Thomas F. Pugh. "Fit of Individual and Community Characteristics and Rates of Psychiatric Hospitalization." *American Journal of Sociology* 73 (November 1967):331–338.

Wilner, Daniel M., and Rosabelle Price Walkley. "Effects of Housing on Health and Performance." In *The Urban Condition,* edited by Leonard J. Duhl. New York: Simon and Schuster, 1963, pp. 215–228.

Yeracaris, Constantine A. "Differential Mortality, General and Cause-Specific, in Buffalo, 1939–1941." *Journal of the American Statistical Association* 50 (December 1955): 1235–1247.

10
CRIME,
RIOTS, AND
RACIAL VIOLENCE

CRIME AND DELINQUENCY

In examining crime as an urban problem, it is necessary to recognize that most studies rely on official crime statistics. However, each locale may have peculiarities in reporting that determine the quality of information. Thus, the following must be considered (Schmid, 1960b, p. 675):

(1) Some crimes are not reported at all; (2) reporting crime differs from one area to another, which may distort in varying degrees and direction the derived crime rates for different parts of the city; (3) there is differential reporting according to the type or nature of the crime; (4) sometimes the police, in order to make a good showing or to protect the name of a community, may suppress or alter official crime records; (5) the policies of the police in making arrests and assigning officers to certain areas may bias recorded statistics; (6) early studies focused on where violations *occurred* and neglected where violators *lived*. For some crimes these areas are the same and for other crimes the areas are distinctly different. High crime rates may represent greater opportunities and conditions favorable for committing certain kinds of crimes.

Two contrasting positions have been hypothesized as explaining criminal and delinquent behavior. *Differential association* suggests that if a criminal or delinquent subculture exists and predominates in a particular area or areas within the metropolitan complex, then there will be crimes committed by the members of the delinquent subcul-

ture. Others have argued that crime rates are high in areas characterized by isolation, anonymity, depersonalization, and anomie (Schmid,
1960b, p. 677). Both hypotheses may help explain high crime rates
but they obviously are different; further, they may help explain high
crime rates in different kinds of urban areas.

Urbanization and Crime

Of crimes known to police, historically, except for crimes of violence,
rates are higher in urban than in rural areas, and higher in metropolitan areas than in smaller urban areas (Uniform Crime Reports, 1973).
In a study of sixty-two cities, Ogburn (1935) found that cities with
slowing rates of growth had higher crime rates than cities with increasing rates of growth. This difference is reported to be a result of declining economic opportunities in slower growing cities, whereas
faster growing cities have more opportunities and less unemployment. Studies in Iowa and in Sweden also found that urban offenders
were more likely than rural offenders to perceive themselves as criminal and to belong to or accept a "criminal culture," (Clinard, 1942,
1960). In summarizing, Clinard made the following observations.

(1) There is a progressive rate of increase in property crimes, when
measured by residence types, that is indicative of urbanism, with rates
varying directly with urbanism.

(2) Rural offenders are more residentially mobile, not as well integrated in their communities, and more impersonal in their attitudes
toward others when compared with nonoffenders.

(3) Previously, but not now, rural offenders more often committed
their offenses outside of the home community, in areas where they
were unknown.

(4) Differential association with criminal norms, particularly those
of delinquent gangs, is not as important in the development of rural
and small town offenders as among more urban offenders; however,
delinquent gangs play a more significant role among rural offenders
as society becomes increasingly urbanized.

(5) There is a marked difference between offenders from areas of
varying degrees of urbanism in the age at which they began criminal
activities and in progression in seriousness of crimes committed, with
urban offenders beginning at younger ages.

Ogburn (1935) analyzed a whole array of dimensions that might
help explain crime rates. According to him, cities with immigrants of
higher economic status, and faster growing cities where wages and
rentals are increasing, are associated with lower crime rates. In addition, the greater the proportion of males, the higher the crime rate.
Statistically, using multiple correlational techniques, he found that
the dimensions indicated above accounted for about one-half of the
variation in crime rates among cities. Some factors not important in
explaining crime rates were size of city, percentage blacks (although

he excluded southern cities), ratio of police to general population, home ownership, percentage apartment dwellers, and age.

In a later study of all cities in the United States in 1950 of 100,000 population or more, many of the same variables were used as in the Ogburn study (Schuessler, 1962). This study described five different factors. One factor was tentatively identified as "degree of social frustration" and includes positive associations with percentage nonwhite, overcrowding, and murder and assault—crimes against the person, and negative relations with percentage native white and higher incomes. Thus, this study leads to the hypothesis that because of racial segregation and living in dense, overcrowded conditions, aspirations will be more frequently thwarted in cities with high proportions of nonwhites and there will be more criminal violence in such cities.

Another factor, which Schuessler described as "degree of institutional control," was characterized by ratio of police to population, percentage married males, percentage foreign born males, percentage owner occupied dwelling units, and average value of dwelling units. A third factor, labeled "degree of industrialization," included median school years completed, percentage families of two or three persons, percentage in manufacturing occupations, and average dwelling unit rental costs. This factor is *negatively* related to each of the specific offense rates he analyzed. "It would thus appear that massive industrial employment tends to create and reinforce a community environment which mitigates against those offenses which become part of the official police record."

Both the Ogburn and Schuessler studies show that cities with ample economic opportunities have low crime rates, reminding us that crime may not be solved on an individual basis alone but that the solution may require a larger social perspective. These studies also demonstrate that variation in city crime rates may be "resolved into general statistical factors which possibly correspond to basic social dimensions that are integral to crime causation" (Schuessler, 1962, p. 323).

Studies of crime rates in various areas of any particular city consistently show striking differences from one part of the city to another. In general, central areas have the highest crime rates while peripheral and suburban residential areas have lower rates. Shaw (1929) was one of the first to report a decline of delinquency rates from the central business district (CBD) to peripheral areas of the city. In this early study, rate declines were apparent whether residences of offenders, mile-square sections of the city, or radials or gradients outward from the CBD were used. Thus, the rate of delinquency tends to vary inversely with the distance from the CBD and reflects differences in types of communities (Shaw, 1929, p. 62). Similarly, he reported a strong relationship between juvenile delinquency and adult measures of crime. Recidivism rates also were highest in central areas of the city and declined toward peripheral areas. The highest crime rates occurred in areas characterized by physical deterioration and declining populations.

In a study of Baltimore (1939–1942) that replicated a great deal of the earlier research by Shaw and McKay, Lander (1954) reported that almost three-fourths of recorded delinquency takes place within a two-mile radius of the CBD. Juvenile delinquency did not gradually decline but had a precipitous drop after the first two zones. However, several areas with a high percent blacks beyond these first two zones had high rates. Lander carried out a factor analysis and reported two important factors in explaining high crime rates. (1) *Anomie:* This is defined as normlessness or the breakdown and weakening of the fabric of society. Dimensions indicative of anomie, according to him, are high delinquency rates, percentage nonwhites, and percentage nonhomeowners or renters. (2) *Economic:* This factor includes median years of education completed, median rentals, percentage overcrowding, and percentage substandard housing. Lander (p. 59) concludes that his factor analysis clearly demonstrates that delinquency in Baltimore is fundamentally related to the stability or anomie of areas, but it is not a function of the economic characteristics of areas. Thus, according to Lander, a stable community would have a low delinquency rate even if it were characterized by poverty, bad housing, and overcrowding.

Lander (p. 74) rejects the notion that distance from city center is significant in the prediction and understanding of delinquency rates, because there is wide variation—some areas near the CBD have low delinquency rates and others on the periphery have high rates. Again, he uses the notion of anomie, or a lack of social cohesion or stability, in an area as the key factor explaining high and low delinquency rates. In addition, he rejects the notion that a high percentage of blacks in an area necessarily means that there will be a high delinquency rate in the area. He argues that in areas with high proportions of lower socioeconomic level blacks who have resided there for a long period of time—stable areas—the delinquency rate will be low.

Schmid utilized several different methodological approaches to describe crime areas, all of which showed a rather close relationship to each other and a variety of criminal behavior. One approach he used to elicit the underlying social and demographic dimensions of crime areas was to utilize the statistical technique of factor analysis. Schmid (1960a) described eight major factors in Seattle:

Factor I: Low Social Cohesion—Low Family Status. A factor representing low social cohesion such as weak family life and older, declining, lower status neighborhoods. High rates of automobile theft, theft from automobile, indecent exposure, shoplifting, nonresidential robbery, and check fraud are associated with this factor.

Factor II: Low Social Cohesion—Low Occupational Status. Low occupational and education measures, a large percentage of laborers, blacks, unemployed, foreign-born whites, older housing constructed prior to 1920, and a high percentage of males make up this factor. High crime rates consist of fighting, robbery (highway and car), nonresidential burglary, and disorderly conduct-miscellaneous.

Factor III: Low Family and Economic Status. This factor contains a large proportion of males, unemployed, and a low proportion of married population. High crime rates are drunkenness, vagrancy, lewdness, petty larceny, fighting and robbery (highway and car). "In the light of the present data, this constellation represents the urban crime dimension *par excellence.*"

Factor IV: Population Mobility. High in and out residential mobility, with no other dimension added, describes this factor. High crime rates of shoplifting, check fraud, burglary of residence by night, attempted suicide, burglary of residence by day, automobile theft, and theft from automobile are found in these areas.

Factor V: Atypical Crime Pattern. This factor consists primarily of the crimes of bicycle theft, indecent exposure, and nonresidential burglary.

Factor VI: Low Mobility Groups. No crimes are associated within this factor. In addition to population stability, a high rate of population growth (natural), foreign-born white population, owner-occupied dwelling units, older population, and proprietors, managers, and officials are demographic dimensions describing stable areas.

Factor VII: Ambiguous. A factor difficult to interpret, discarded by Schmid.

Factor VIII: Race. This factor is characterized by blacks with high nonresidential robbery and nonresidential burglary crime rates.

In examining the CBD, skid row, and contiguous areas, Schmid found that these sections of the city had the highest crime rates, although each area was characterized by different crimes. Crime in the CBD consisted primarily of high rates of check fraud, shoplifting, residential burglary, automobile theft, theft from automobile, and attempted suicide (Factors III and IV). In contrast, areas contiguous to the CBD were described by Factors I and VII. These areas contained rooming and apartment houses, with some single family dwellings and business establishments. These areas had higher rates of automobile theft, theft from automobile, indecent exposure, shoplifting, nonresidential robbery, and check fraud. Separate from the above, skid row areas included a large number of cheap rooming houses and hotels, with high rates of fighting, robbery (highway and car), nonresidential burglary, and disorderly conduct-miscellaneous crime rates.

Another interesting cluster of areas were those representative of Factor V, Atypical Crime Pattern, located contiguous to Woodland Park and Green Lake. Extensive use of bicycles, especially on the bicycle path around Green Lake, and several parks and bathing beaches, may help account for the high rate of bicycle theft, indecent exposure, and nonresidential burglary.

In further analyses, Schmid (1960b, pp. 666–670) computed crime rates by one-mile zones radiating outward from the CBD. Most crimes decreased, more or less, in direct proportion to distance from the city center to the periphery. Embezzlement was the most pronounced, with shoplifting, theft from person, rape, sodomy, and burglary also showing marked change from inner to outer zones. Bicycle theft was the only crime that had a higher rate in the outer zones. "The differentials between inner and outer zones, however, for peeping toms, obscene telephone calls, indecent liberties, and carnal knowledge are relatively small." Since most crimes conform to the gradient pattern, the generalized "total index crimes" for Seattle during 1960–1970 shown in Figure 10–1 represents the spatial distribution of most crimes in Seattle (Schmid and Schmid, 1972) during this time period, as well as for earlier times.

Polk (1957–1958) studied juvenile delinquency in San Diego and reports that no one social class is more delinquent than another nor is juvenile delinquency an indication of a breakdown in family life. Noting discrepancies in the literature about the influence of social class, Clark and Wenninger (1962) hypothesized that "rates of illegal conduct among the social classes vary with the type of community in which they are found." Within a given community they expected crime rates to be similar for all social classes. They studied four populations in the "northern half of Illinois" (p. 827): (1) a *rural farm* population, (2) a *lower urban* sample drawn from a crowded, largely black area of Chicago, (3) *an industrial city* of about 35,000, relatively autonomous, outside of the Chicago metropolitan complex, and (4) an *upper urban* sample of a very wealthy suburb of Chicago. Their measure of offenses was *self-reported behavior.* They failed to detect significant differences in illegal behavior rates among social classes of rural and urban areas, although lower-class areas had higher serious crime offense rates. Differences within larger areas by social class were generally insignificant. They concluded that the pattern of illegal behavior within small communities or within "status areas" of a large metropolitan center is determined by the predominant class of that area; they hypothesized that there are area-wide norms to which juveniles adhere regardless of social class.

This study also suggests that a "delinquent subculture" emerges only in large metropolitan places with large, relatively homogeneous social class areas. Similarly, they hypothesize that in areas of social class heterogeneity, those in the social class minority will take on the prevailing norms of the area, whether this is a delinquent subculture or a middle-class orientation. That is, "those who are taught to occupy middle-class positions apparently take on lower-class illegal behavior patterns when residing in areas that are predominantly lower-class." They conclude that "area patterns of behaviors obviously exist and must be handled in some manner." Within the inner core, crime rates

Figure 10–1 Total Index of Criminal Offenses
Reported in Seattle, 1960 to 1970

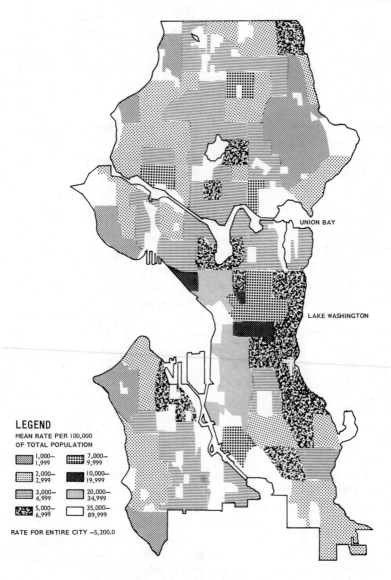

The data on this map represent cases reported to the police during the eleven-year period from 1960 to 1970. Cases have been allocated according to census tracts. There are certain areas in the city, such as Fort Lawton, Sand Point Naval Air Station, and the University of Washington, where normally the Seattle police do not have jurisdiction. Accordingly, no cases are recorded for such areas.

Solid lines delimit the census tracts of Seattle, Dot and dashed lines delimit parks, cemeteries, and other relatively large areas of public property, dashed lines delimit industrial, railroad, and vacant property.

The total number of cases represented on this map is 311,143.

Source: Adapted from Calvin F. Schmid and Stanton E. Schmid, *Crime in the State of Washington*. Olympia: Washington State Planning and Community Affairs Agency, 1972.

may vary. Rumney (1951) noted that the juvenile delinquency rate in a public housing project (383/10,000) was less than in nonpublic housing areas in the slums (570/10,000).

Less than one-quarter of the boys in the urban areas with high rates of delinquency are actually court charged as delinquents (Kobrin, 1951, p. 653). This could invalidate the notion that delinquency is primarily a cultural phenomenon rather than a result of personality or psychological processes. However, he shows that the official crime rate is only a minimum measure of crime. He demonstrates with more inclusive records that "not one-fifth but almost two-thirds of the boys in delinquency areas may be regarded as official delinquents" (p. 655). Most studies reported so far use relatively unrefined statistics and only show the minimum crime that takes place. More efficient record-keeping and reporting by victims would result in much higher crime rates than those now reported. This also has been demonstrated by Clark and Wenninger and others who have used questionnaires to measure reported hidden criminal or delinquent behavior.

Delinquent areas within metropolitan complexes can be thought of as those in which integration between the conventional and criminal value systems occurs (Kobrin, 1951, pp. 656–660). Areas range from those in which integration is well advanced to those in which it is minimal. In areas in which conventional and criminal cultures are well articulated, criminal and delinquent activity in these areas occurs when younger persons acquire skills such as the use of violence, concealment, evasion of detection, and purchase of immunity from punishment. On the other hand, Kobrin describes another criminal extreme in which there is little integration into conventional crime culture. Criminal behavior in these areas is characterized as being hoodlum in nature; violence and theft are forms of recreation. Kobrin is well aware that most delinquency areas fall somewhere in between these polar extremes, but they all express one form or another of these basic characteristics.

Urban crime areas, including areas where criminals reside *and* areas where crimes are committed, are generally characterized by low social cohesion, weak family life, low socioeconomic status, physical deterioration, high rate of population mobility, and personal demoralization as reflected by attempted and completed suicide, drunkenness, and narcotic violations (Schmid, 1960b, p. 678). Thus, to develop an adequate integrative theory of crime, it is necessary to examine individual behavior in specific areas of the city. A distinction must be made between areas where criminals reside and areas where crimes are committed. This separation leads to another approach to the study of crime patterns. Boggs (1965), in her study of St. Louis, showed that areas where offenders reside are not necessarily the same areas where most crimes occur. Typically, CBDs have the highest crime rates, while offenders are more likely to live in lower-class, nonwhite, anomic neighborhoods. Thus, there is a discrepancy between *crime offender* and *crime occurrence* rates. The standard crime rate is the number of crimes relative to the number of persons who live in the area of occurrence. A valid rate would be based on risks appropriate for each crime category. This notion leads to the need to consider, for example, the number of untended parked cars in auto theft rates, the number of occupied housing units in residential burglary rates, and so on, rather than only the population of the area (p. 900). From this approach, then, opportunities for crime vary from neighborhood to neighborhood, and these are reflected in different occurrence rates.

To determine whether a few general factors explain crime, Boggs carried out a factor analysis with twelve crimes and six offender variables. She related her analysis of crimes to the "social areas" of St. Louis to examine the question, "Do high rates of crime occur among residential populations characterized as lower-class, nonwhite, and anomic?" Note that this is different from asking if high rates of crime are committed by persons with these same characteristics. Her results show that burglary occurrence, homicide, and aggravated assault occurrence, and offenders of the above are directly associated with segregation (percentage black) regardless of an area's social rank or extent of urbanization. In addition, high occurrence rates in high offender neighborhoods indicate familiarity between offenders and victims. Bullock (1955) also noted that black homicides tend to occur in the block on which both the assailant and victim live.

Property crimes, auto theft, and grand larceny crimes occur in high-rank neighborhoods adjacent to offender areas (p. 907). Forcible rape and miscellaneous robbery are randomly distributed among social areas with no apparent distinguishable pattern. She notes that this factor is very similar to the one we described earlier, when we reviewed Schmid's study of bicycle theft, indecent exposure, and residential burglary in Seattle. The high occurrence of such crimes as forcible rape, larceny, and auto theft occur in neighborhoods with offenders, although the offenders may not reside in the same areas in which they commit their crimes.

Crime occurrence rates vary by the environmental opportunities specific to each crime category. From this approach, CBDs are not the most intensively exploited crime areas in the city. Further, crimes do not entirely take place within the area in which the offender lives; this varies extensively by type of crime and type of area. For some crimes, offenders and victims reside in the same area, even on the same block; yet other crimes illustrate that residence of offender and area of occurrence are widely separated.

Longitudinal Studies of Crime in Urban Areas

In the revised edition of Shaw and McKay (1969), several chapters are devoted to crime and delinquency rate differentials in cities other than Chicago. These include Philadelphia (1926–1938), Boston (1927–1930 and 1931–1934), Cincinnati (1927–1929), Cleveland (1919–1931 and 1928–1931), and a substantially different type of city outside of the manufacturing belt, the old, southern city of Richmond, Virginia (1927–1930). These cities showed patterns of crime and delinquency similar to that exhibited in Chicago and they experienced little change over time in crime rates and patterns.

Few current studies exist of changing crime patterns over time by specific areas within metropolitan complexes. Part of the reason, of course, is the paucity of reliable and comparable data over time for one city let alone for several cities. Aside from these problems, Shaw (1929, pp. 161–174) reported that the relationship between juvenile delinquency rates in the same areas of the city in 1900–1906 and 1917–1923 were extremely high (r=.84), as were recidivism rates between the two time periods. Given these high rates in the same areas for over a thirty year period, "it should be remembered that relatively high rates have persisted in certain areas notwithstanding the fact that the composition of population has changed markedly" (Shaw, 1929, p. 203).

In the revised edition of their earlier work, Shaw and McKay (1969, pp. 329–358) include rates for Chicago "for a period of sixty-five years, which is something more than one-half of the life of the city." The population of Chicago doubled between 1900 and 1930, while between 1930 and 1960 the increase was minimal—5 percent. However, suburban areas increased little before 1930 but very rapidly between 1930 and 1960. In comparing delinquency rates for 1934–1940, 1945–1951, 1954–1957, 1958–1961, and 1962–1965, Shaw and McKay report remarkably similar distributions. "The great suburban development, significant changes in the composition of the population, and the expansion of industry, together, seem not to have changed very significantly the number of different types of delinquency-producing areas in Chicago" (p. 345).

The few exceptions in which rapid increases and rapid decreases occurred in rates were in *both rapidly increasing and decreasing areas* with a predominantly black population. The *downward trend* occurred in areas in which blacks had been living for several decades. In addition, these data covering more than sixty years reveal that areas of high rates of delinquency typically also are those most disrupted by incoming populations. Similarly, Schmid (1960b, pp. 669–670) compared offenses in Seattle for two different periods, 1939–1941 and 1949–1951, and reported that they "manifest a substantial correspondence."

Finally, a study of crime in Boston between 1849 and 1951 showed that there was "an intermittent but persistent downward tendency in the rate of every major crime except forcible rape and manslaughter" (Ferdinand, 1967). As shown in Figure 10–2, rates in the 1950s are only about one-third those in the middle 1800s. As Ferdinand points out, this consistent downward trend in crime rates is in stark contrast to

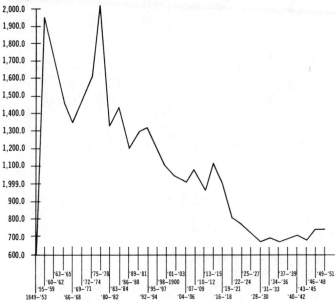

Figure 10–2 Rate of Major Crimes in Boston per 100,000 Population 1849–1951

Source: Theodore N. Ferdinand, "The Criminal Patterns of Boston Since 1849," *American Journal of Sociology* 73 (July 1967):84–99.

the popular belief that crime is growing each year. Unfortunately, comparable studies have not been carried out for other cities. Thus, the question of whether Boston is unusual or typical has not been answered. My guess is that it is rather typical.

Crime Victimization

All of the discussion about crime and delinquency so far has relied on official statistics. However, other studies have been concerned with the extent to which people have been victims of various kinds of crimes, whether or not the crime was reported. Surveys of hidden crimes thus consist of crimes that for a variety of reasons have not been brought to the attention of the police. The extent of hidden crimes has been surveyed by the National Crime Panel (United States, April, 1975 and June, 1975) in an effort to determine the extent of such crimes against persons, households, and commercial establishments. The results of one wave of the research examining victimization in thirteen cities are shown in Table 10–1. This table excludes so-called victimless crimes, such as drunkenness, drug abuse, and prostitution, as well as crimes against government entities involving income tax evasion, theft, and so on.

These data show that in 1973 there was substantial variability among these cities in personal crimes of violence and theft victimization. Interestingly, Washington, D.C., a city with a reputation for crime and

Table 10-1 Victimization Rates for Persons Age Twelve and Over by Type of Crime*

| City | All Personal Crimes of Violence | Personal Crimes of Violence | | | | | | | Personal Crimes of Theft | | |
| | | Rape | Robbery | | | Assault | | | All Crimes of Theft | Larceny With Contact | Larceny Without Contact |
			All	With Injury	Without Injury	All	Aggra-vated	Simple			
Boston	67	2	31	9	22	35	17	18	119	26	93
Buffalo	49	2	16	5	11	31	14	17	74	7	67
Cincinnati	63	2	15	6	9	47	22	25	111	7	104
Houston	53	3	17	4	13	33	17	16	122	6	116
Miami	22	1	10	3	6	12	7	5	44	5	39
Milwaukee	61	2	18	6	12	41	17	24	103	7	96
Minneapolis	70	4	21	7	14	46	18	28	120	6	113
New Orleans	46	3	18	5	13	26	13	13	94	14	80
Oakland	59	3	22	7	15	34	16	18	102	10	92
Pittsburgh	47	2	15	6	9	30	13	17	83	7	76
San Diego	53	2	11	4	7	39	16	24	141	5	136
San Francisco	71	3	29	9	20	39	14	25	129	23	106
Washington, D.C.	31	1	17	5	13	13	6	7	65	12	53

Source: United States, June, 1975.
*Rate per 1,000 resident population age 12 and over

violence, had one of the lowest victimization rates, especially for rape and assault. Minneapolis and San Francisco have some of the highest rates, especially for robbery with injury and assault. Cities with the lowest theft rates are Washington, D.C. and Miami, while San Diego and San Francisco have the highest rates among these thirteen cities. It should be noted that somewhere around 9 to 20 percent of these unreported crimes took place elsewhere than the city where the victim was living at the time of the interview. In any case, these surveys show that there is extensive crime taking place in U.S. cities that is not reported, and that the official crime statistics reflect only the minimum level of crime taking place.

Conclusions
Research following procedures set down by Shaw has confirmed the association of juvenile delinquency and crime with the physical structure and social organization of the metropolitan complex. Short (in the introduction to Shaw and McKay, 1969, p. xxvii) notes that "the association of delinquency with specific social conditions seems less important than the general pattern of association and the existence of areas within cities in which a variety of social ills are concentrated." Schmid (1960a, p. 542) stated that while "sweeping inferences are not warranted by a single study, it seems very likely on the basis of this investigation—as well as other research on the ecological structure of the urban community by the present author and his colleagues— that similar patterns are to be found in other American cities." As we have seen in this chapter in reviewing work accomplished by Schmid and his colleagues, and by others, his beliefs were well founded. (For a critical view, see Gordon, 1967.) Finally, Shaw and McKay (1969, pp. 101–107) report that in Chicago, delinquency rates are associated with infant mortality rates (1927–1933, $r=.75$), tuberculosis rates (1931– 1934, $r=93$), and mental disorder (1922–1934, $r=.72$). On the basis of these data, they hypothesize that delinquency and crime are not isolated phenomena but that they are closely associated, area by area, with rates of truancy, adult crime, infant mortality, tuberculosis, and mental disorder. They believe that if other problems had been examined, similar relationships would have been found.

RIOTS AND RACIAL VIOLENCE
Riots in U.S. cities in the early part of the twentieth century have been reviewed by Grimshaw (1960). He reports that in some of these early riots entire black areas were eliminated by white violence, arson, and looting. Since then there have been periods of relative calm. But in the late 1960s once again violence came to the fore and approximated that of previous times. The Commission on Civil Disorders reported that most deaths during these riots were a result of force used by the police and National Guard. In addition, of course, it will not be forgotten that student riots also occurred during the 1960s, although

they certainly were not as widespread as many people believe and did not involve violence to persons or major damage to property. Nevertheless, there continues to this day an extensive concern about what are called student rioters.

Ordinarily, riots are distinguished from other forms of violence. Riots are not thought of as attempts to seize state power nor are they planned and organized revolutionary activity. In other words, riots are thought of as spontaneous, unplanned, and disorganized activities not motivated by the thought of seizing the political power of the state (Bowen and Massoti, 1968, pp. 14–15), although riots may involve a politics of violence (Feagin and Hahn, 1973).

The school desegregation decision of 1954 and the Civil Rights Act of 1964 were made during a period when there were few large scale race riots; however, in August 1965, riots erupted in the Watts area of Los Angeles. Hundreds of people were injured, 34 deaths occurred (mainly blacks), and over 35 million dollars in property damage was reported. By the end of 1967, 8 major disturbances and 33 major and 119 minor disorders had been reported in the United States. These disturbances and disorders occurred in cities of all different sizes. Reports suggest that major grievances by blacks were police practices, unemployment, lack of housing, education, and recreational opportunities, and a political structure perceived as oppressive.

According to most reports, the typical rioter, in contrast to non-rioters, was better educated, better off economically, and a long-term resident of the area where riots occurred. Thus, the "criminal riff-raff and hoodlum theory of riot participation" receives little support from most research data. (For a review of one such riot—the Watts Riot of 1965—see Oberschall, 1968.) Further, the "outside-agitator, conspiracy notion" has been seriously questioned because of the lack of outsiders arrested during riots. In the 1965 Watts riot, poor police-black relations played a major part. Another major factor was the election during November of the previous year, when the white Southern California population voted by a two-to-one margin to repeal the fair housing act while virtually all black voters voted to retain it. The Watts riot was leaderless and, according to Oberschall, "was structurally and behaviorally similar to the Negro riots in other cities during the summers of 1964, 1965, and 1966."

Intermetropolitan Variation and Riots
Grimshaw (1960) has noted that we will not know why some cities have riots and other cities do not until data have been collected on at least four types of areas characterized by combinations of high or low social tensions with weak or strong external forces of constraint. However, it may be more realistic, given our current ignorance, to concentrate on broader types and characteristics of cities and to relate riots and lack of riots to types of cities.

Using a variety of data sources, Lieberson and Silverman (1965) examined precipitants and underlying conditions of seventy-six race riots between 1913 and 1963. As shown in Table 10–2, most immediate precipitants of riots involve interracial bodily injury and violations of interracial segregation taboos.

From another perspective, four major categories of conditions within cities have been assumed to be related to riot-proneness: (1) population growth and composition, (2) work situation, (3) housing, and (4) government. A frequently cited reason for riots is the rapid influx of blacks into cities. It has been assumed that such an influx disrupts the social order and creates problems that lead to race riots. However, in pairing cities of the same size, and in the same region of the country, one of which had a riot or riots and the other which did not (control cities), results clearly do not support this hypothesis, because no differences in racial composition are apparent between riot and control cities.

On the other hand, when the work situation is examined in riot and control cities, black male workers in riot cities are more likely to hold higher-level jobs than in nonriot cities. Thus, "encroachment of Negroes in the white occupational world evidently tends to increase the chances of a riot, although we must also consider the possibility that Negro militancy increases as Negroes move out of their traditional niche." This study suggests that low black incomes and relatively large differences between black incomes and white incomes are not necessarily associated with riot-proneness. Unemployment, whether white or black, does not increase the chances of a riot, and differences between store ownership by blacks in riot and control cities is rather slight. Further, housing quality is not associated with riots. Thus, housing and demographic characteristics of cities in general are not important underlying conditions associated with race riots. However, White (1968, p. 163) suggests that percentage black, total population size, density (unspecified as to which measure of density), and family income help predict (ex post facto) which cities will have riots (also, see Maloney, 1968).

Table 10-2 Immediate Precipitants of Race Riots, 1913–1963

Rape, murder, attack, or hold-up of white women by Negro men	10
Killings, arrest, interference, assault, or search of Negro men by white policemen	15
Other interracial murder or shooting	11
Interracial fight, no mention of lethal weapons	16
Civil liberties, public facilities, segregation, political events, and housing	14
Negro strikebreakers, upgrading, or other job-based conflicts	5
Burning of an American flag by Negroes	1
No information available	4
Total	76

From Lieberson and Silverman (1965, p. 889).

Lieberson and Silverman place most of their emphasis on conditions related to local government. For example, police force composition influences the likelihood of a riot—cities without riots had more black policemen per thousand blacks than did riot cities. The way in which the city council was elected also appeared to be important, because "the more direct the relation between voter and government, the less likely are riots to occur."

Spilerman (1970), however, argues that before the 1960s, city characteristics may have been important factors in riots, but since then conditions conducive to riots have been pervasive and city characteristics are no longer important factors in riots. Thus, in the 1960s "all cities shared an identical probability of experiencing a disorder." That is, he believes that local conditions do not differ significantly enough by city for them to overcome the exposure of blacks to various stimuli which lead them, as individuals, to develop black solidarity and to foster a consciousness of identity that transcends geographic and social class boundaries. He rejects the hypothesis that "cities which experienced racial disturbances in the 1960s are either structurally or demographically different from cities which did not have such disorders."

Nevertheless, Spilerman reports that "racial disorders are more likely to occur where the level of life for the Negro is least oppressive according to objective measures." That is, there are more disturbances where blacks, relative to whites, are better off educationally and economically than blacks living elsewhere. Also, disorder-prone cities tend to have more stable populations and better quality housing. Further, supporting Lieberson and Silverman's analysis, Spilerman reports that disturbances are more likely in high population per councilman cities and in cities where there is a mayor-council structure. In spite of this evidence, Spilerman states that "the *only* community variable related to the location of disorders" is the number of blacks (italics in original statement). This led him back to explain that blacks "in all cities have come to share in a riot ideology to mean that an individual's proclivity to riot is not influenced by community conditions, and we further assume that characteristics such as age and sex, which are known to affect participation, are distributed in substantially the same way in every community."[1]

Spilerman's conclusion, then, is that the racial disorders of the 1960s were *not* responses to local conditions in cities. He does vacillate in stating that disorder-prone cities do differ from their less traumatized neighbors in many significant respects. Racial violence is more likely where blacks are better situated in occupational status and in education and income, and where there is small population growth. However, he believes that these conditions have little to do with a community having racial disorder and are only incidental characteristics of cities with large black populations (p. 645).

In a critique of Spilerman's conclusion, Mazur (1972) argues that

In sum, one could assert the following about black urban riots in the 1960s without being grossly inconsistent with available evidence: National disorder-proneness increased from the early 1960s to the late 1960s and then decreased markedly by 1971. The location of riots within any one year may largely have been a matter of chance; however, there was an additional systematic tendency for cities with large Negro populations to have a high number of riots. This may be explained by the fact that these large cities are close to sources of riot contagion and/or by their large Negro population size per se. There is some evidence that the occurrence of rioting in a city increases (reinforces) the probability of a future riot there. Riots may be caused, in part, by underlying community conditions. In short, the causes of black riots are complex and not well understood.

Spilerman (1972, p. 499), however, remains unconvinced and believes that community characteristics and conditions are insignificant in the outbreak of protests and riots. The evidence to date, including his own, suggests otherwise.

In a recent study, Butler (1974) reports data that show the association between black residential segregation and both the number and intensity of race riots in the first nine months of 1968 to be inverse. Further, the degree of black political organization, interaction, and communication between blacks and whites working together in city welfare organizations had similar influence on the number and intensity of race riots. Examining 118 cities, Butler showed that cities with extended black and white relations—for example, in political organizations—riots were more likely to occur than where black political organization was more highly developed. The explanation offered was that "some degree of contact or interaction between two different groups is necessary in order for there to be conflict between them." Thus, in segregated cities there is less contact and less likelihood of conflict, and black political organization reduces possible conflict by disciplining individuals to work within organizations and to plan strategy.

Intrametropolitan Variation and Racial Violence

Two locations within metropolitan places appear to be the focal points of race riots (Grimshaw, 1960, pp. 116–118): transfer points of public transportation where members of one race pass through the territory of the other, and, government buildings. After 1960, racial conflict appeared in a previously unexperienced form which suggests that these ecological focal points are declining in importance.

East St. Louis, Washington, D.C., Chicago, Tulsa, and Detroit all had sharp increases in black population in the years immediately prior to major interracial disturbances, and there were accompanying strains in the accommodative structure (Grimshaw, 1960, p. 109). While there are sharp disagreements about most facets of urban race riots prior to the end of World War II, they converge in descriptions of their ecology. For example, Negro residential areas with no businesses, or a minimal number of business establishments had few racial incidents. These particular areas where no riots occurred contained populations in which income, years of education, and occupational status were above those of the larger black population. Similarly, white higher-class residential neighborhoods on the periphery of the city were virtually free of racial violence, although at times youths from these neighborhoods "prowled in automobiles in search of stray Negroes" to beat up.

The major race riots have been concentrated in black slums that were completely or partially destroyed during the riots. Violence typically began in the central business district and blacks then retreated to their own areas. Black victims accounted for the largest share of riot-related deaths in Springfield, Illinois (1908), East St. Louis (1917), and Tulsa (1921). Arson was widespread, and in Tulsa and East St. Louis black areas were almost totally destroyed. The Harlem, New York, (1935 and 1943) riots were limited to black areas and "physical clashes were usually between the resident population and the police" (Grimshaw, 1960, p. 112).

Discounting the existence of *stable mixed neighborhoods* (areas in which blacks and whites have lived amicably for long periods), Grimshaw believes that *contested areas*—areas previously dominated by whites and presently undergoing racial transition—and those in the line of movement of the black population are more typical sites of urban riots. Although it is not completely clear (see Grimshaw's comments on p. 114, and compare with his statement on p. 115), it appears that in transitional areas physical assaults take place on individuals, but there is a lack of major violence in contested areas. In white-dominated areas not contested by Negroes, only one major riot was reported. And this one riot probably took place as a direct result of peculiar circumstances not likely to occur again: black workers in a section of Chicago in 1919 had to pass through the all-white stockyards district to get home. Ordinarily they would have used public transportation to get through the area and home. However, because of a transportation strike, many blacks had to travel through this hostile territory on foot to get home. Those who attempted to get home through this district were assaulted and "many were beaten and several slain." In this riot, 34 percent of those hurt received injuries in black areas and 41 percent received injuries in the stockyards district.

Blacks, like other people, constitute different social groupings, and these different social groups tend to congregate in different areas within the ghetto. Schulman (1968, p. 267) concludes that the conditions that give rise to alienation are endemic throughout the different wards of Rochester. However, it remains to be determined whether the alienated also are those who participate in riots. In examining variation in riot behavior *within* Watts, Abudu et al. (1972) assumed that there was variability in riot behavior in different areas. As a result of their analysis, they conclude that the comparative incidence/nonincidence and frequency of riot-type events is highly variable within the ghetto. The number of fires correlated with blackness, lower level of education, and office and commercial enterprises; in such areas "there develops the sociodemographic fertile ground for massive, violent protest" (p. 423). Thus, while the proportion of blacks in a city may not be important in whether or not a riot develops, the extent of blackness within the ghetto is influential in determining where the most severe rioting behavior will occur. Evidently a critical mass is necessary for a riot to develop and this mass does not occur randomly in the ghetto.

"Neighborhood status modality" has an important influence on who does and who does not participate in riots (Warren, 1971). Persons with a higher status-modal position than their neighbors were more active in rioting than persons similar to or below their neighbors. In black neighborhoods with a great deal of social integration—for example, visiting with neighbors—rioting was less likely.

Lieberson and Silverman (1965, p. 898) stress that race riots are frequently misunderstood and attributed to "communists," "hoodlums," or "rabblerousers." But riots should be viewed in terms of how well the institutional structure is functioning or malfunctioning, and it should be realized that such conditions are influenced by social institutions. From this perspective, Abudu et al. (1972, p. 408) argue that the stoning of white-driven automobiles, the taunting of police and firemen, and the looting and burning of white-owned commercial establishments in the ghetto "may be considered more specific responses than either voting for, or writing to an office-holder who has little or no discernible or direct relationship to these ghetto experiences." Thus, black riots may be *politically* motivated and may represent attempts to demonstrate viability in the trade-offs of politics (see also Feagin and Hahn, 1973).

Wanderer (1969) developed an "index of riot severity" by using the following: killing, calling out the National Guard, calling out the state police, sniping, looting, interference with firemen, and vandalism. One city characteristic associated with this riot severity index was the percentage increase of blacks, although the percentage of blacks in the city was not. The greater the percentage increase in blacks, the greater the severity of the riot. However, the racial composition of the city was unrelated to the presence or absence and severity of riots. Housing appears to be unrelated to riot severity, as were median black rent, median value of black place of living, median percentage of black home owners, and population density. Similarly, no relationship between previous larceny and assault and severity of riots was found. Finally, no relationship between police preparation and riot severity was noted. The riot severity index research results suggests that riots are patterned and that severity of riots is linked to certain characteristics of cities.

Conclusions

Five general explanations of black protests have appeared in the literature (Geschwender, 1964). The "vulgar Marxist hypothesis" suggests that as blacks experienced a worsening of the conditions of life, they became increasingly dissatisfied until they rebelled. The "sophisticated Marxist hypothesis" or "relative deprivation hypothesis" assumes that as blacks experienced an improvement in their life conditions they simultaneously observed whites experiencing a more rapid rate of improvement and thus became dissatisfied and rebelled. A third, somewhat related hypothesis, which might be called the "rising expectations" hypothesis, notes that as blacks experienced an improvement in their life conditions, they also experienced a rise in desires. Desires rose more rapidly than life conditions, resulting in dissatisfaction and rebellion. The "rise and drop" hypothesis rests on the assumption that as blacks experienced an improvement in life conditions, a sharp reversal occurred and thus they became dissatisfied and rebelled. Finally, the fifth hypothesis is called the "status inconsistency hypothesis" and suggests that blacks possess a number of different status attributes which are differently ranked on the various status hierarchies that lead to dissatisfaction and rebellion.

In evaluating these hypotheses, Geschwander rejects immediately, on the basis of contrary evidence, the vulgar Marxist hypothesis. He writes "the position of the Negro is improving educationally, occupationally, and incomewise." It might be instructive, however, to ask black male ghetto residents whether or not they agree with the "fact" that their life conditions are improving, thus calling into question the vulgar Marxist hypothesis. Geschwender also rejects the rise and drop hypothesis, because he believes that blacks are steadily improving their levels of education, occupation, and income.

Geschwender believes that the three remaining hypotheses are closely related in that the sophisticated Marxist hypothesis and the status inconsistency hypothesis both have "relative deprivation" as the essence. He also notes that the rising expectations hypothesis sees blockages of legitimate aspirations as a key variable and again results in relative deprivation. Whatever explanation may ultimately be accepted, the fact remains that racial violence and riots in the past have been fairly consistently located in certain ecological areas of the metropolitan complex. Many observers expect a broader ecological base in the next series.

Flaming and Palen (1972 p. 275) analyzed the efficacy of the 1967 Watts and Milwaukee riots and report that whites continue to ignore the "message of the riots"; the problems of health, rat control, poor housing, underemployment and unemployment, and discriminatory law enforcement continue to exist in these areas. They further show that life conditions subsequently have deteriorated in riot-torn areas (also, see Berkowitz, 1974). If past experience is any guide, when race riots and violence again occur in the United States, they once again will be highly localized within specific areas of the metropolitan complex.

Finally, our description of riots in the United States more or less summarizes the state of current knowledge concerning riots. Thus, given that violence and riots have occurred extensively during the twentieth century in the United States, scientific knowledge about riots is still very meager and answers to some of the most basic and elementary questions still have not been found.

PROSPECTS

Given the concern of the U.S. population about crime, it may be surprising that such little scientific knowledge is available concerning variation in crime among different areas in the metropolitan complex. However, it is unlikely that in the near future research will be able to shed any more light on urban crime because minimal funds are available for such purposes. Up until now, most funds have been earmarked for such things as body armor and automobiles. However, as crime becomes more prominent in the suburbs, we can expect that pressure will be exerted to alleviate this growing suburban crime.

Similarly, the next impetus for obtaining information on riots will probably be after there is more rioting. Interest apparently flags when there are no riots.

With more attention being paid to protection against crime and riots than prevention of crime and riots, there is little likelihood that the future will be different from the present.

NOTES

1. It should be noted here that age and sex distributions do vary and that this can be determined by the use of U.S. Census data. Contrary to Spilerman's argument, it should *not* be assumed that there are no differences in this regard.

REFERENCES

Abudu, Margaret J.G., Walter J. Raine, Stephen L. Burbeck, and Keith K. Davison. "Black Ghetto Violence: A Case Study Inquiry into the Spatial Pattern of Four Los Angeles Riot Event-Types." *Social Problems* 19 (Winter 1972):408–426.

Berkowitz, William R. "Socioeconomic Indicator Changes in Ghetto Riot Tracts." *Urban Affairs Quarterly* 10 (September 1974):69–94.

Boggs, Sara L. "Urban Crime Patterns." *American Sociological Review* 30 (December 1965):899–908.

Bowen, Don R., and Louis H. Massoti. "Civil Violence: A Theoretical Overview." In *Riots and Rebellions,* edited by Louis H. Massoti and Don R. Bowen. Beverly Hills, Calif.: Sage, 1968, pp. 11–31.

Bullock, Henry A. "Urban Homicide in Theory and Fact." *Journal of Criminal Law, Criminology, and Police Science* 45 (January-February 1955):564–575.

Butler, Gerald E., *Residential Segregation and Race Riots in the 1960s*. Los Angeles: Laboratory for Organizational Research, University of Southern California, 1974.

Clark, John P., and Eugene P. Wenninger, "Socioeconomic Correlates of Illegal Behavior Among Juveniles." *American Sociological Review* 27 (December 1962):826–834.

Clinard, Marshall B. "The Process of Urbanization and Criminal Behavior." *American Journal of Sociology* 48 (September 1942):202–213.

_____ "A Cross-Cultural Replication of the Relation of Urbanism to Criminal Behavior." *American Sociological Review* 25 (April 1960):253–257.

Feagin, Joe R., and Harlan Hahn. *Ghetto Revolts*. New York: Macmillan, 1973.

Ferdinand, Theodore N. "The Criminal Patterns of Boston Since 1849." *American Journal of Sociology* 73 (July 1967):84–99. Copyright © 1967 by the University of Chicago Press.

Flaming, Karl H., and J. John Palen. "Urban Violence: A Question of Efficacy." In *Urban American Conflict and Change*, edited by J. John Palen and Karl H. Flaming. New York: Holt, Rinehart and Winston, 1972, pp. 270–276.

Geschwender, James A. "Social Structure and the Negro Revolt: An Examination of Some Hypotheses." *Social Forces* 43 (December 1964):248–256.

Gordon, Robert A. "Issues in the Ecological Study of Delinquency." *American Sociological Review* 32 (December 1967):927–944.

Grimshaw, Allen D. "Urban Racial Violence in the United States: Changing Ecological Considerations." *American Journal of Sociology* 66 (September 1960):109–119.

Kobrin, Solomon. "The Conflict of Values in Delinquency Areas." *American Sociological Review* 16 (October 1951):653–661.

Lander, Bernard. *Towards an Understanding of Juvenile Delinquency*. New York: Columbia University Press, 1954.

Lieberson, Stanley, and Arnold R. Silverman. "The Precipitants and Underlying Conditions of Race Riots." *American Sociological Review* 30 (December 1965):887–898.

Maloney, John. "Study Names Riot-Prone Cities." *Public Management* 50 (January 1968):12–14.

Mazur, Allan. "The Causes of Black Riots." *American Sociological Review* 37 (August 1972):490–493.

Oberschall, Anthony. "The Los Angeles Riot of August, 1965." *Social Problems* 15 (Winter 1968):322–341.

Ogburn, William F. "Factors in the Variation of Crime Among Cities." *Journal of the American Statistical Association* 30 (March 1935):12–34.

Polk, Kenneth. "Juvenile Delinquency and Social Areas." *Social Problems* 5 (Winter 1957–1958):214–217.

Rumney, Jay. "The Social Costs of Slums." *Journal of Social Issues* 7 (1951):77–83.

Schmid, Calvin F. "Urban Crime Areas: Part I." *American Sociological Review* 25 (August 1960a):527–542.

_____ "Urban Crime Areas: Part II." *American Sociological Review* 25 (October 1960b): 655–678.

Schmid, Calvin F., and Stanton E. Schmid. *Crime in the State of Washington*. Olympia: Washington State Planning and Community Affairs Agency, 1972.

Schuessler, Karl. "Components of Variation in City Crime Rates." *Social Problems* 9 (Spring 1962):314–323.

Schulman, Jay. "Ghetto Area Residence, Political Alienation, and Riot Orientation." In *Riots and Rebellion*, edited by Louis H. Massoti and Don R. Bowen. Beverly Hills, Calif.: Sage, 1968, pp. 261–284.

Shaw, Clifford. *Delinquency Areas*. Chicago: University of Chicago Press, 1929.

Shaw, Clifford R., and Henry D. McKay, *Juvenile Delinquency and Urban Areas*. Chicago: University of Chicago Press, 1942 (revised edition, 1969).

Spilerman, Seymour. "The Causes of Racial Disturbances: A Comparison of Alternative Explanations." *American Sociological Review* 35 (August 1970):627–649.

_____ "Strategic Considerations in Analyzing the Distribution of Racial Disturbances." *American Sociological Review* 37 (August 1972):493–499.

Uniform Crime Reports, U.S. Federal Bureau of Investigation. *Uniform Crime Reports for the United States,* 1973.

United States. *Criminal Victimization Surveys in the Nation's Five Largest Cities.* Washington, D.C.: U.S. Department of Justice, Law Enforcement Assistance Administration, April, 1975.

United States. *Criminal Victimization Surveys in 13 American Cities.* Washington, D.C.: U.S. Department of Justice, Law Enforcement Assistance Administration, June, 1975.

Wanderer, Jules J. "An Index of Riot Severity and Some Correlates." *American Journal of Sociology* 74 (March 1969):500–505.

Warren, Donald I. "Neighborhood Status Modality and Riot Behavior: An Analysis of the Detroit Disorders of 1967." *Sociological Quarterly* 12 (Summer 1971):350–368.

White, John, G. "Riots and Theory Building." In *Riots and Rebellions,* edited by Louis H. Massoti and Don R. Bowen. Beverly Hills, Calif.: Sage, 1968, pp. 155–165.

11
URBAN ENVIRONMENTAL HAZARDS

INTRODUCTION

Every metropolitan region has natural environmental features and man-made alterations of that natural environment. Technological developments have reduced substantially time required to alter the natural environment. The configuration of natural environment and man-made alterations of it produces hazards such as air and water pollution, noise, fires, floods, and earth slides (Van Arsdol et al., 1964, p. 145). Varying natural and man-made conditions result in metropolitan regions and areas within any given metropolitan complex having different environmental hazards. As noted previously, environmental hazards may be determined by objective measurements or subjectively determined by the degree of public awareness of hazards. Attitudes about environmental conditions may change over time, because only "a generation ago belching smokestacks were welcomed as indicators of full employment, whereas today they are more likely to be taken as symbols of technological obsolescence and management irresponsibility" (Ayres, 1969).

AIR POLLUTION

Air over a city serves both as a lifeline and a sewer (Rydell and Schwarz, 1968, p. 119). The quantity of unpolluted air in an urban complex changes over time; human alterations of the natural environment intensify the effects of temperature inversions and help generate air pollution and associated health problems. Metropolitan areas and cities generate substantial heat, which facilitates development of inversion layers that keep pollutants suspended above the city. In service center cities, air pollution is primarily an automobile by-product, whereas in manufacturing cities, industrial pollution is added to that produced by automobiles. Thus, type of city may affect the level of air pollution when severity of inversion layer is controlled.

Air pollution currently is not particularly severe in some locales such as the Granby Basin in Colorado and the Piedmont Region of North Carolina. However, with an increasing population base and man-made alterations of the natural environment, these locales, along with others, have a great potential problem because of extremely strong inversion layers (Leighton, 1966).

Generally, air quality criteria have been derived from (1) objective measures, (2) citizen awareness and complaints, (3) impact of air pollution on health, and (4) the economic analysis of how much air pollution and air pollution control measures cost in dollar terms (Rydell and Schwarz, 1968, p. 119).

Objective Distribution of Air Pollution

While air pollution is widely diffused in many metropolitan regions, there are certain areas within them that have heavier concentrations of air pollution for longer periods of time than other areas within the same metropolitan region. For example, in Los Angeles County, air pollution is widely diffused but tends to concentrate in more central sections and along the base of mountains to the east. In 1962, approximately 50 percent of the population in Los Angeles County lived in heavily polluted areas. Heaviest concentration levels of air pollution were in areas of older housing characterized by heavily traveled streets and freeways, concentrations of industrial and commercial activities, low rent, low status ethnics and minorities, and physical deterioration (Van Arsdol et al., 1964).

Air pollution problems may be increased in certain urban areas by the spatial and temporal arrangement of urban form (Rydell and Schwarz, 1968, p. 115). "Once pollutants are released into the atmosphere, their dispersion and transportation is caused by the urban microclimate, in particular the wind speed and the vertical temperature gradient" (p. 115). One control mechanism of air pollution in urban complexes is the city's form, which could be used to spread pollution to surrounding rural areas. This is not a long-term solution, because air pollution eventually would build up in suburban and rural regions. Nevertheless, man-made changes could help alleviate part of the urban pollution problem by proper design of buildings and streets to help spread pollution. Locating air pollution-producing industry downwind from the city would lessen urban air pollution, although that would increase suburban and rural pollution. New methods of transporting people and goods also could help in alleviating urban air pollution, as would more efficient allocations of open space and other land uses (Rydell and Schwarz, 1968).

Awareness of Air Pollution
The fact that air pollution exists but is perceived differently by individuals carries with it some important implications. First, to what degree is air pollution tolerable, and second, to what extent does toleration vary by different population categories. The perception of air pollution may be considered exclusive of its involuntary effects— illness and mortality. For example, air pollution has its most adverse effects on older persons, yet older persons are least perceptive of air pollution.

Only if air pollution is perceived as a problem is it an urban problem! Further, only those persons who believe that air pollution is a serious problem are likely to do anything about it! Studies of the perceptual awareness of air pollution have focused on the following (Medalia, 1964):

1. Awareness of the nature and extent of air pollution as a problem.
2. Where knowledge about air pollution is obtained.
3. Perceived causes of air pollution.
4. Attitudes about air pollution as a problem.
5. What, if anything, should be done about air pollution.
6. Programmatic elements persons would accept and support in efforts by local, state, and federal governments to overcome air pollution.
7. How accurately individuals perceive air pollution.
8. Whether or not awareness of air pollution resulted in individual behavioral responses.

Whether or not air pollution is perceived by populations and monitored by agencies depends primarily on the meaning given air pollution by people (Molotch and Follett, 1970). Air pollution is perceived by some people and not others even though they may both live in objectively measured air polluted neighborhoods (Van Arsdol et al., 1964). Similarly, some individuals live in areas objectively free of air pollution, yet they perceive and believe themselves to live in heavily polluted neighborhoods.

In a Los Angeles County sample in 1962, 28.1 percent believed that they lived in a neighborhood in which air pollution was a problem, compared to slightly over 50 percent who actually lived in heavily polluted areas by objective measurements. However, a subsequent Los Angeles study (Hohm, 1976) and a statewide California Poll by Mervin D. Field (1973) found that 64 percent of the population surveyed in Southern California reported that air pollution was a very serious problem. The general public, however, did not feel that air pollution was getting worse (between 1969 and 1973).

A national urban study conducted in 1966, and a follow-up of the same respondents in 1969, reports almost identical figures to the 1962

Los Angeles County study (Butler et al., 1972). In 1966, 30.2 percent reported air pollution as a serious problem in their neighborhoods; by 1969, the percentage of *the same persons* who reported air pollution as a serious problem in their neighborhood had increased only slightly to 31.2 percent. In the 1966 survey, 56.4 percent believed that air pollution was a problem at the metropolitan level! Apparently many people believe that air pollution is a serious metropolitan problem but not a problem in their particular neighborhood. Air pollution awareness may depend substantially on its perception—in some parts of the metropolis, tall buildings, signs, and other objects block long-range vision and thus make air pollution less noticeable.

Conventional sociological variables, such as age, sex, race, socioeconomic status, and education, were not related to concern about air pollution in Buffalo (De Groot et al., 1966, p. 246). The overriding factor, without exception, was actual air quality in areas of residence. Similarly, Rankin (1969) reported similar attitudes about air pollution in West Virginia as did Schusky (1966) for the St. Louis metropolitan area. On the other hand, only 13 percent thought that air pollution was a serious problem in Durham, North Carolina, although 74 percent said air pollution was a serious problem throughout the United States (Murch, 1971).

Van Arsdol et al., (1964, p. 152) report that "while nonwhites are concentrated in smog areas, the intrusion of social hazards in such areas and the concern of such populations with other social problems may have obscured their perception of environmental hazards." The entire social milieu of the ghetto or barrio makes it very unlikely that a rather remote societal problem such as air pollution would be near the top of one's priorities. The data suggest that poor lower-class anglos are considerably more likely than ethnic minorities to feel that air pollution is a salient problem. This reinforces the possibility that it is not status or class, but the overwhelming reality of being black or brown in a dominant anglo society that is the most important factor in their relative lack of concern about air pollution.

While air pollution is not highly salient to *any* population category, it is relatively more salient to anglos than to blacks or chicanos. Ethnicity effects on the saliency of air pollution do not disappear when SEI, income, and education are controlled. This is especially significant because much of the nonanglo population in Los Angeles lives in older residential areas where smog is most heavily concentrated, due to heavily traveled freeways and nearby industrial sources of air pollution (see also Hohm, 1976).

Reports show that most people perceive industry and automobiles as the principal contributors to air pollution. Nevertheless, there are people who believe that even without industry and automobiles, air pollution would exist, that is, it is a natural phenomenon. Little concensus exists in the public as to what should be done about air pollution; the range includes controlling industry and automobile exhausts, mandatory automobile inspections, gasoline rationing, money for research, and development of mass rapid transit. However, there is little agreement as to whether local, state, and federal government, universities, industry, or individuals should spearhead reduction in air pollution.

Air pollution may restrict the amount of physical exertion that is deemed desirable (for example, in schools, physical education may be terminated if air pollution reaches a specified level). Similarly, it may affect the individual so he or she cannot breathe properly or as eye or nose irritation, or so that the individual feels so poorly that he or she does not become involved in physical activities. Under severe air pollution conditions, visibility may be so reduced that normal community activities must be halted or altered. Air pollution may effect human behavior regardless of whether or not it is perceived. Under less severe conditions, visibility impairment may not be noted but, in fact, it may be reduced to such a degree that irritability, for example, can lead to automobile accidents. One obvious behavioral response to air pollution is to avoid it by moving to another pollution free location—if one can be found (Butler et al., 1972).

Persons in some occupations are likely to be exposed to severe polluted conditions for long periods of time and, accordingly, have an unusually high risk factor of morbidity and mortality. Occupations such as traffic policeman, automobile mechanic, and truck driver immediately come to mind. In addition, cigaret smoking, use of fireplaces, use of some methods of cooking, and of certain aerosal sprays all contribute to *individualized* air pollution. Such behavior by individuals contributes to the total air pollution problem as well as to their own specific likelihood of being affected.

Effects of Air Pollution On People

Some have hypothesized that air pollution might influence residential location, although the research so far suggests that the impact that air pollution has on population distribution is minimal (Butler et al., 1972). Air pollution may affect household activities—how often one washes the automobile, upkeep of the dwelling unit, and interior housecleaning—and leisure activities. Some effects may be more indirectly than directly attributable to air pollution.

Most concern with air pollution has focused on morbidity and mortality (Lewis, 1965). Goldsmith (1968) has pointed out that "a man can live for five weeks without food, for five days without water, but only five minutes without air." Before health effects of air pollution can be determined, the following requirements must be met: (1) pollution must be measured; (2) one or more effects must be measured; (3) a relationship between pollution and its effects must be shown.

While the street may be quiet, uncongested, and safe from crime and violence, life there may not be as safe as some believe, because of pollutants (Esposito, 1970, p. 8). Among major pollutants, carbon monoxide is the most lethal. Pollutants in large enough quantities can produce death; however, most exposure to pollutants is not sufficiently great so that death results. People who live in the northern part of Staten Island, New York, adjacent to industrial Bayonne-Elizabeth, New Jersey, have a high "excess death" rate (the number of deaths over and above the number normally expected). That is, for males over forty-five, respiratory cancer death rate is about 15 per 100,000 greater there than for males to the south where the air is not badly polluted. The respiratory cancer excess death rate for women is even larger, since twice as many women die from it in the polluted area as opposed to women living elsewhere on Staten Island (Auerbach, 1967). Similarly, an estimate of 100 to 2200 excess deaths occurred in New York City between 1960 and 1964 because of *episodic* high levels of sulfur dioxide (Esposito, 1970, p. 8).

Using sootfall as a measure, both Cincinnati and Pittsburgh had the highest air pollution in low-lying river bottom areas (Mills, 1943, p. 131). Both statistically and graphically this study showed a close relationship between high pneumonia and tuberculosis rates (white males only) and sootfall. "In the cleaner air of the higher suburban districts little difference exists between male and females' pneumonia or tuberculosis rates, but in the polluted air of the bottom districts, the increase in male rates is almost twice as great as that of the female" (p. 136). Thus, air pollution is a key factor in high pneumonia and tuberculosis rates and primarily affects males rather than females (Mills, 1954, p. 18).

In Chicago, "If the low pneumonia rates of the cleaner suburbs could be made to prevail over the whole city, Chicago would each year have over five hundred fewer deaths from this one cause alone" (Mills, 1954, p. 102). The Loop district is Chicago's dirtiest area; the measure of sootfall decreases in all directions outward from the Loop. Sootfall in the Loop is 150 tons per square mile per month, while it drops to 11 tons in the most northwesterly suburb. Variation in sootfall is matched by similar variations in deaths due to pneumonia (white males). Pneumonia death rates were highest in the Loop and progressively decreased toward the suburbs; Loop rates for white males were more than ten times higher than those in the suburbs. Similar contrasts between the dirtier Loop and cleaner suburbs were noted for pulmonary tuberculosis, with the Loop rate being 360 and the cleanest outlying districts being roughly 25. The death rate for cancer of the air passages and lungs was only one-third as high in the suburbs as in the Loop.

Because these rates might have been affected by social class of neighborhood, an analysis was carried out to determine if social class composition was a contributing variable. This hypothesis was discarded, because death rates by sex varied substantially in the Loop and suburban areas. The main effect was on white males, while females were relatively unaffected by dirtier air, much as in the Pittsburgh study. Male laborers who had the greatest outdoor exposure time to polluted air and inhaled greater amounts of it because of physical activity had the highest lung cancer and pneumonia rates in both dirty and clean parts of the city, although Loop laborers had much higher rates than suburb laborers (Mills, 1954, p. 113).

In another study of Chicago using sulfur dioxide as a measure of air pollution, acute respiratory illnesses coincided substantially with high daily levels of air pollution, especially among elderly persons with advanced bronchitis (Carnow et al., 1969, p. 776). Similarly, air pollution in Nashville was associated with several categories of infant deaths (Sprague and Hagstrom, 1969). Also, mortality from respiratory disease generally varied inversely with socioeconomic class, and in the middle class respiratory disease mortality was directly related to degree of exposure to sulfation (Zeidburg et al., 1967) and asthmatic attack rates for adults (Zeidburg et al., 1961).

One problem in measuring air pollution's effect on mortality is that a very large population is necessary so that excess deaths can be estimated—unless there is a disaster, such as the ones in Donora, Pennsylvania in 1948 (Roueche, 1953), London in 1948 and 1952 (Mills, 1954), New Orleans in 1955, and worldwide in 1962 (Goldsmith, 1968). The residential movement of people also hinders precise estimates of the effect of air pollution on mortality. In addition, mortality varies substantially by urban type and by areas within metropolitan complexes, because population age structure is highly variable.

The most susceptible to pollution mortality are the aged (Pond, 1950), infants, and those with a previous history of respiratory or heart problems. Low level air pollution may lead those who are susceptible to an earlier death than expected. Many others may have their health affected without immediate death or illness. As Esposito (1970, p. 10) points out, an individual may have gotten used to seeing air pollution, but that does not necessarily mean the body has adapted to it.

Substances floating in the air may cause ill health as well as affect the subsequent quality of future generations by mutagens, which damage genetic capabilities and cause mutations, and by teratogens, which interfere with normal fetal development and result in deformed babies. Ethyleneimines (from insecticides, solid rocket fuels, emissions from textile and printing industries, and other industrial processes), benzo-a-pyrene (primarily an automobile by-product), hydrocarbons (from incomplete engine combustion), carbon monoxide (from automobiles and other sources), and particulate matter (from burning coal, oil, and asbestos from automobile brake linings and clutch facings, and building materials) have been linked to birth deformities, cancer of the lung, stomach, esophagus, prostate, bladder, and to heart strain and aggravation of existing heart trouble. In addition, many automobile accidents routinely ascribed to drunkenness may actually be attributable to excess inhalation of carbon monoxide (Carr, 1965).

Goldsmith lists effects of air pollution other than those described above and argues that they are differentially distributed among persons of different ages and medical statuses: (1) acute sickness or death; (2) chronic diseases, shortening of life, or impairment of growth; (3) alteration of important physiological functions such as ventilation of the lung, transport of oxygen by hemoglobin, dark adaptation (ability to adjust eye mechanisms for vision in partial darkness), or other functions of the nervous system; (4) other symptoms, such as sensory irritation, which in the absence of an obvious cause might lead a person to seek medical attention and relief; (5) discomfort, odor, impairment of visibility, or other effects of air pollution sufficient to lead individuals to change behavior, residence, or place of employment.

Exposure to air pollution is a factor in chronic bronchitis and emphysema, although probably not the only causal agent. Cigaret smokers are more susceptible than nonsmokers in a common polluted environment. Furthermore, there is evidence suggesting a link between air pollution and asthma. Available studies are not definitive because they have not sorted out *individual* air pollution from *community* air pollution. One obvious solution is to study young children. When this has been done, studies indicate "a strong case for adverse effects of air pollution on lower respiratory tract conditions" (Goldsmith, 1968).

Finally, a series of studies conducted in California during the period from 1956 to 1961 indicate that perception of air pollution is associated with feelings of overall malaise, as well as with physical symptoms such as eye irritation, asthma, nose complaints, headaches, and chest pains. Further, these complaints were more prevalent during air pollution episodes than when more favorable weather conditions existed.

Goldsmith (1968) presents a cogent argument for the most sensitive measuring instruments possible, because an air pollution level which may have minimal effects upon some individuals will seriously affect others. Thus, there is the problem of ferreting out characteristics of persons with different thresholds of susceptibilities to air pollution. He concludes from his literature review that individual pollution— cigaret smoking and the like—is a major causal factor in lung cancer, whereas community-wide air pollution is, to date, only a "suspected" factor.

Costs of Air Pollution

Social values are inherent in the concept of *costs* (Teller, 1967). In estimating costs, reliable and valid measures of costs are necessary, yet costs vary according to the points of view of those who are calculating them (Collier, 1971). Trade-offs and alternative control management programs make sense only when one considers the values of the estimators. Emitors and receptors of air pollution have different views about the need for risks and about how much should be spent to avoid certain levels of risk..

Monetary costs of converting old plant equipment and transportation vehicles to acceptable levels (by whose standards?) and the building of new plants and vehicles can probably be estimated fairly accurately. However, social and health costs are virtually impossible to measure precisely. How does one measure the cost of a father or mother to their children? How much effect does pollution have on present and future earnings, average duration and severity of temporarily disabling and efficiency-reducing capabilities, permanent disabilities, increased probability of morbidity and mortality from other diseases, and absenteeism from work and school? Further, how can one estimate air pollutant costs in terms of the impact on the size, composition, distribution, and income of the population? Finally, how much would it cost to find and treat victims and what costs accrue to those who attempt to avoid air pollution altogether (Weisbord, 1961; Butler et al., 1972)?

How much does air pollution cost the homeowner (Nourse, 1967) who must paint the house more often? What are the added costs for routine cleaning, for the hours of use lost while garments are at the cleaners, for laundering supplies, for frequent car washes? How willing is the public to pay for amelioration of air pollution? These questions suggest that air pollution has many costs (Ridker, 1967).

Organization of the Human Population and Air Pollution

The environment, technology, and human population structure (spatial distribution, and so on) and organization are related to air pollution. Because of the ways that man uses the environment and because of the impact of technology on the environment, the human population is responsible for most air pollution. Man is the only species that can do anything about overcoming the air pollution problem.

People residing in large population concentrations ordinarily are organized around urban life forms. They use the environment in various ways and through their technology produce air pollution from automobiles, freeways, and factories. Air pollution may drift and be added to locally produced oxidants. The entire metropolitan complex, as well as the state and national governments must be involved in the study of air pollution problems. A study of the political impact and influence of various individuals, groups, organizations, and industries on decision-making at the local, state, and federal levels in regard to the control, management, and effects of air pollution is essential if we are to understand the organization of the human population and its impact upon the environment.

The communication and determinants of public information and consequent attitudes toward various alternative solutions to air pollution are substantially a product of the social organization of the population. One response to air pollution may be to organize and attempt to influence local, state, and federal officials in the use of power and management techniques to overcome air pollution. People may organize to study the problem of air pollution and how to effectively initiate local and extra-local public action; to discuss various alternative solutions; to evaluate monetary, health, and other costs of air pollution; to influence local, state, and federal officials in the use of social power in an attempt to overcome air pollution; and to study the impact regulatory measures have in controlling technology and energy use.

Currently, there are few organizations in metropolitan areas concerned with air pollution. There have been attempts by a few individuals to influence local, state, and federal officials in attempts to overcome air pollution. The forms that organizations may take are varied, and the impetus for organizations may be local or extra-local. With the aid of experts in air pollution, organizations may be formed that essentially utilize local, voluntary participation. Discussion groups and educational meetings should be helpful in educating local people about air pollution problems and what they can do about those problems.

Another community organization approach is to focus on conflict, stressing the external nature of enemies and ways that local residents can combat them. Hostility toward outsiders, including government and industry, is apparent in this approach. Organizations might be formed that would act as watch dogs over industry and public agencies that are charged with air pollution control and management.

Some argue that there is more to overcoming air pollution than organizing or acting as watch dogs. The solution to air pollution may be in determining who has vested interests in the continuation of air pollution and attacking the problem at that level. The controlling of air pollution from this perspective assumes that the use, control, and knowledge of *social power* is the only way that air pollution can be effectively managed and brought under control. A mobilized and organized public wielding its power would be a factor to be reckoned with and would make air pollution more than a symbolic issue.

Gilluly (1970a, p. 273) has pointed out that the Ninth Amendment to the Constitution states that "The enumeration in the Constitution of certain rights, shall not be construed to deny or disparage others retained by the people." And the Fourteenth Amendment to the Constitution, which states "Nor shall any state deprive any person of life, liberty, or property without due process of law," could be construed as protecting the public against environmental hazards. However, the courts have not been challenged to date to determine if these amendments apply to environmental polluters. If these and other laws were enforced, they would have a real impact on air pollution.[1]

Air pollutants vary among metropolitan complexes and by areas within any individual metropolitan region. The effects of air pollution are highly variable because such differential levels of exposure exist. In addition, *it is highly probable that only a fraction of the actual pollutants that have harmful effects on man have been identified to date!*

Technically, the control of air pollution is now possible. However, the extent of control desired greatly influences costs. Little meaningful effort is being made in most metropolitan areas to control air pollution. One major reason for ineffective efforts is related to the lack of cooperation among various cities and other governmental units within the metropolitan area. Most proposals for the correction of environmental pollution treat the problem as a matter of man's misbehavior. Environmental complexity is recognized, but there is insufficient awareness that the misbehavior in question is invariably embedded in a complex system of human relationships (Duncan, 1961). The relationship of man to the physical environment is maintained through an organizational structure. "If there is to be any hope of a lasting solution to environmental misuse, it will have to begin in the social structure of the community and society" (Hawley, 1971 p. 248). The recent experience of Pittsburgh suggests that it is possible, to some extent, to clean up the air. In 1945, the average amount of heavy dust collected in Pittsburgh was about 175 tons per square mile per month, whereas over the past six years, it has been 28 to 30 tons— an 85 percent reduction!

NOISE POLLUTION
Within metropolitan complexes, noise levels vary remarkably by neighborhood. Most noticeable is noise in areas near airports that accommodate large commercial jet aircraft. In addition, neighborhoods adjacent to freeways, thruways, industry, and heavily traveled streets have high noise levels. Some have made a distinction between noise and sound, with sound being music and children's voices, while noise is produced by machines, airplanes, and traffic. In addition, what is heard at work is generally considered noise. The major distinction between noise and sound is whether a person is annoyed by it (Cameron et al., 1972).

High noise levels attributed to automobiles and industry can be substantially reduced. Wider sidewalks and streets substantially reduce traffic noise (Knudsen and Plane, 1973). Reduction in noise can be made by using sound-absorbent street and sidewalk surfacing, and by the use of absorptive groundcover plants. These measures, in combination, could reduce current noise levels by three-fourths. In newer, developing areas, additional reductions in noise levels could be made by covering lower levels of buildings with acoustical tile. Also the tilting of lower floors of buildings would direct sound upward and reduce sound around ground-level noise sources.

The effect of noise on human beings has been studied by different approaches. Through in-depth interviews, it was ascertained that the major effect of aircraft noise near the Los Angeles International Airport is on communication, such as telephone conversations or television viewing. Other findings from this study indicate that a majority of respondents are not bothered or are only slightly disturbed by aircraft noise, that few persons made a formal complaint about the noise, and that there is limited awareness of noise abatement activity by community residents. Also, this study reports that a majority of residents were aware of the noise before they moved in, that their property value had not decreased as a result of noise, and that few persons were willing to make any personal expenditure to eliminate aircraft noise (Burrows and Zamarin, 1972)![2]

In contrast to the above study, an extensive survey (Miller, 1971) of the effects of noise on people reported the following results: (1) noise can permanently damage the inner ear, creating hearing losses that can range from slight impairment to nearly total deafness; (2) noise can result in temporary hearing losses, and repeated exposures to noise can lead to chronic hearing losses; (3) noise can interfere with speech communication and with the perception of other auditory signals; (4) noise can disturb sleep; (5) noise can be a source of annoyance; (6) noise can interfere with the performance of complicated tests and, of course, can especially disturb performance when speech communication or response to auditory signals is demanded; (7) noise can reduce the opportunity for privacy; and (8) noise can adversely influence mood and disturb relaxation. On the bright side, noise has not yet been successfully linked to excess deaths, shortened life span, or to days of incapacitating illness.

Another study (Farr, 1967) used sophisticated measuring instruments such as electroencephalographic (EEG) and behavioral measures and concluded that jet aircraft sounds created physiological effects that outlasted the physical presence of the auditory stimuli—for example, jet aircraft sound. In addition, "it was possible to note both behavioral and EEG changes during waking performances subsequent to nights disturbed by the jet aircraft flyovers which were not apparent during performances subsequent to undisturbed nights" (LeVere et al., 1972, p. 384). Thus, even limited exposure to nocturnal noise produces significant changes in an individual's pattern of sleeping and has a carryover in physiological disturbance, as measured by EEG devices. Several other studies have linked aircraft noise with acute and chronic illness (Cameron et al., 1972), with increased admission rates to psychiatric hospitals (Herridge, 1972; Abey-Wickrama et al., 1969), and with stress and lowered reading achievement (Glass et al., 1973). Generally, it appears that airports contribute substantially to noise pollution in some areas within the metropolitan complex, and residential areas located in low-level flight patterns especially are prone to noise pollution. Since the advent of jet powered aircraft in the late 1950s, noise from these jets has been a major cause of complaints from airport neighbors.

Relatively little research has been done exploring the effects that airplane noise has on the prevalence of health problems (Graeven, 1974). Borsky (1970) suggests that possible human responses to noise include an awareness of noise, disruption of normal everyday activities, annoyance reactions, and complaints about noise. In a study of areas in Foster City, part of which lies under the landing path to San Francisco International Airport, Greeven divided the city into four noise impact areas according to an objective level of exposure to airplane noise. Persons who lived in a high exposure area were more likely to report that they were exposed to airplane noise, more likely to feel like complaining about airplane noise, and more likely to report disruptions of normal everyday activities by noise, than were persons in less exposed areas. Persons who lived in high exposure areas spent less time at their place of residence than did persons who lived in low exposure areas. Finally, awareness of noise and annoyance reactions to it were systematically related to health problems, although the relationship between level of exposure to noise and health problems was minimal. In general, people who are aware of noise and annoyed by it are more likely than others to have health problems, even though the exposure to noise may be similar. Because noise pollution is differentially distributed within the metropolitan complex, area and individual perceptions of noise must interact to produce health problems.

Solutions to airplane noise pollution have included quieter engines and steeper glide patterns, but these remedies have not resulted in adequate reduction in noise level. Another solution has been land acquisition around airports. For example, when Los Angeles International Airport was to be expanded, almost 10 percent of the $500 million for costs were allocated to land acquisition (McClure, 1969, pp. 119–120). From the work of Van Arsdol and colleagues (1964: see especially the map on p. 147) it is apparent that it would be impossible to acquire all of the land near Los Angeles International Airport that is subject to severe noise pollution.

Proposed solutions to airplane noise include removing the airport facility from the metropolitan area to a rural area or to off-shore platforms (Miles, 1972). In both instances, problems of access to the airport would be intensified and would result in greater ground traffic. Dulles International Airport was built in the countryside, some distance from Washington, D.C., but the land around the airport and between the facility and the city is rapidly becoming filled with industry, office buildings, and residential subdivisions. This problem obviously would not apply to off-shore construction of airports. However, off-shore airport construction is expected to cost some 7 to 13 billion dollars, compared to an approximate 1 billion dollar cost for a similar land-based airport. In Los Angeles County in the early 1960s there were three airports for which noise data were available. Information gathered shows that there was no correspondence between areas of heavy aircraft noise pollution and heavy air pollution (Van Arsdol et al., 1964).

WATER POLLUTION

The movement of water is more predictable than the movement of air. Nevertheless, problems related to obtaining water and to disposing of it are substantial for most U.S. cities. Water supplies for cities are primarily lakes and streams. While these sources may contain abundant water, they may be reduced by pollution that occurs when they are used as waste disposal sites.

Major sources of water pollution are organic sewage, infectious agents (for example, typhoid), plant nutrients which come from sewage and fertilizer washoff, organic chemicals like pesticides and detergents, inorganic chemicals such as sludges and chemical residues, land sediments from soil erosion, radioactive substances, and waste heat from electric and nuclear power plants and industry (Revelle, 1968; Gilluly, 1970b).

In early cities, animals roamed the streets and served as garbage disposals. One of the first departments of sewers was created in New York City in 1849. Thus, it is not too surprising that early cities were characterized by periodic epidemics and high rates of illness related to inadequate sewage disposal. Similarly, water was polluted by disposal of sewage and trash into lakes and streams. Water used in early cities was taken from these polluted streams, lakes, and wells. "It is no longer the simple matter of a city's running a pipe out into a nearby lake or stream and taking in the water it needs with no more than elementary filtering and chlorination, or of dumping its sewage through an outfall line with no thought of treatment" (Fisher, 1971, p. 485). While at least 83 percent of the urban population in the United States is served by sewers, only 63 percent have sewage treatment facilities. Fortunately, virtually all U.S. cities and towns now have water purification plants.

One important aspect of water pollution in metropolitan complexes is the unwillingness of local governments to enforce conformity to water purification standards (Hawley, 1971, p. 246). Part of this reluctance to enforce purification standards is a fear that industry in the city will relocate elsewhere. Water also is used for recreational activities such as fishing, boating, and swimming. Millions of dollars have been allocated to make rivers once again useful for such purposes. For example 300 to 400 million dollars were spent to clean the Potomac

River in the Washington, D.C. area and the Hudson River in New York, so that they could again be used for swimming. Generally, the problems of obtaining water and disposing of it are too great for any city and probably require at least a regional authority.

OTHER ENVIRONMENTAL HAZARDS

Fires, earth slides, floods, tornadoes, and hurricanes are episodic environmental problems in some metropolitan complexes and especially for some areas within them (Widener, 1970). In Los Angeles County, fires (primarily brush fires) and earth slides occur in hilly sections, while floods take place in low areas devoid of adequate storm drains and elsewhere along bodies of water subject to storms. In contrast to air and noise pollution that affect large population segments, environmental hazards such as fires, earth slides, and floods affected only about 2 percent of the population in Los Angeles County (Van Arsdol et al., 1964). Technology has changed considerably since this study was conducted. Since then many hills that had not been considered suitable for housing have been flattened. These stairlike pads now have thousands of houses built on them, and the potential for earth slides has thus been increased. Also, thousands of houses have been built in low-lying ground which was extensively flooded during the late 1930s. Since that time, no large-scale floods have occurred because additional storm drains have been built *and because rainfalls have been below flood level.* The *potential* for earth slides and floods that would affect large segments of the population has increased markedly during the 1960s and the early 1970s.

In other regions, floods generally result from particularly high spring temperatures and rapidly melting winter snow or from extremely heavy rain over a brief period of time. Heavy rainfall may result in flash floods that develop quickly and take communities by surprise ("Mortality," 1974, p. 6). The two recent major flood disasters were the flash flood of June 9, 1972, in Rapid City, South Dakota, which took 237 lives (Farhar, 1976), and the "most extensive floods in United States history, unleashed by Hurricane Agnes, which caused at least 117 deaths on the eastern seaboard during June 1972" (p. 6). The North Atlantic and Missouri areas had the most deaths by floods during the years from 1965 to 1974.

Flood control involves a variety of measures such as reforestation of water sheds, construction of reservoirs and flood walls, diversion of rivers, and improved techniques for forecasting rising river levels (Burton and Kates, 1964). Recent legislation requires local governments to implement building codes aimed at reducing housing developments in flood plains. This should result in less flood damage and loss of life in future years ("Mortality," 1974, pp. 6–7). Mitigating against such positive appraisal is a study of residents of fifteen different sites along the East Coast, from North Carolina to New Hampshire. That study showed that a "high proportion of coastal dwellers take minimal steps to reduce their hazard," and many of them elect to live on the coast at considerable risk rather than reduce their seaward amenities by conservation measures (Kates, 1967, pp. 68–69). Further, many have opposed construction of seawalls and others have knowingly lowered sand dunes in order to improve views and accessibility to beaches (p. 69).

Other potential urban hazards are solid waste disposal, pesticides, lead, and disfigurement of the urban environment. To some extent, solid wastes have been useful as landfill. However, in larger cities discarding solid wastes is a large scale enterprise involving scores of trucks, men, and shifting landfill locations. Recent surveys have shown that there is substantial variability by cities in childhood lead poisoning and exposure to hazardous lead concentrations (*Childhood*, 1972). Pesticides "used in excess or applied sloppily not only can damage the countryside and the ponds, but also can be harmful to city people" (Fisher, 1971, p. 488).

Disfigurement of the environment results from poor planning, lack of architectural controls, poor construction, undisciplined city management, and undisciplined civic behavior. In addition, visual pollution is apparent in some places (McEvoy and Williams, 1970). These kinds of hazards have been little explored but appear in many cities.

PROSPECTS

Air pollution is the most frequently reported environmental hazard. Over one-fifth of persons residing in U.S. metropolitan areas believe that water pollution is a serious metropolitan problem, although only about half that many report it to be a problem in their immediate neighborhood. Around 7 percent cite airplane noise as a serious problem both at the metropolitan and neighborhood levels (Butler et al., 1972). The impact of noise on individuals has only recently become a subject of serious investigation. However, it appears that being subjected to high noise levels not only damages hearing capabilities but also is associated with a higher level of mental disorders and behavioral problems. Little scientific knowledge is available concerning the impact water pollution and other environmental hazards have on residents of metropolitan areas (*Environmental Quality*, 1970).

The effects of floods, fires, and earth slides on man are of a different magnitude than that of air pollution, water pollution, and noise, since they are mainly episodic rather than chronic. Each environmental hazard is related to the mental and physical health of the population. Little direct evidence exists which shows how much effect they have on health and mortality. But there is no doubt expressed by any knowledgeable authority about their impact, only the degree.

Since environmental hazards can be assumed to be related to health, and because all of them are amenable to some degree of correction, given contemporary technology, it is fair to ask why they continue to exist as urban problems. In part they continue to exist because not all of the solution lies within the direct influence of man (Kates, 1971). Nature's whim is an important factor. However, more important is the influence and power that has been exerted against those who attempt to solve environmental hazard problems.

Environmental hazards are differentially distributed both among and within metropolitan areas. Some population segments are more likely to be exposed to chronic hazards of air pollution and noise, while others are more likely to be exposed to episodic hazards such as fires, floods, and earth slides. It is highly unlikely that environmental hazards in metropolitan regions and in areas within them all will be alleviated during the next several decades.

NOTES

1. For a discussion of legal ways of combatting pollution and polluters, see Saltonsall (1970); Landau and Rheingold (1971); and Cox, (1970).
2. The authors of this article were employees of the Douglas Aircraft Company!

REFERENCES

Abey-Wickrama, M.F. a'Brook, F.E.G. Gattoni, and C.F. Herridge. "Mental-Hospital Admissions and Aircraft Noise." *The Lancet* (December 1969): 1275–1277.

Auerbach, Irwin. "The Pall Above, the Victims Below." *Medical World News* 8 (February 1976):60–69.

Ayres, Robert U. "Air Pollution in Cities." *Natural Resources Journal* 9 (January 1969):1–9.

Borsky, P.N. "The Use of Social Surveys for Measuring Community Responses to Noise Environments." *Transportation Noises: A Symposium on Acceptability Criteria*, edited by J. D. Chalupnik. Seattle: University of Washington Press, 1970, pp. 219–227.

Burrows, Alan A., and David M. Zamarin. "Aircraft Noise and the Community. Some Recent Survey Findings." *Aerospace Medicine* 43 (January 1972):27–33.

Burton, Ian, and Robert W. Kates. "The Floodplain and the Seashore: A Comparative Analysis of Hazard-Zone Occupance." *Geographical Review* 54 (July 1964):366–385.

Butler, Edgar W., Ronald J. McAllister, and Edward J. Kaiser. "Air Pollution and Metropolitan Population Redistribution." Paper presented at the American Sociological Association, New Orleans, Louisiana, August 1972.

Cameron, Paul, Donald Robertson, and Jeffrey Zaks, "Sound Pollution, Noise Pollution, and Health: Community Parameters." *Journal of Applied Psychology* 56 (February 1972):67–74.

Carnow, Bertram W., Mark H. Lepper, Richard B. Shekelle, and Jeremiah Stamler. "Chicago Air Pollution Study." *Archives Environmental Health* 18 (May 1969): 768–776.

Carr, Donald E. *The Breath of Life*. New York: Norton, 1965.

Childhood Lead Poisoning: A Summary Report of a Survey For Undue Lead Absorption and Lead-Based Paint Hazard in Twenty-Seven Cities. Cincinnati, Ohio: DHEW Publication No. (HSM) 73-10002, September, 1972.

Collier, Boyd. *Measurement and Environmental Deterioration*. Austin: University of Texas, Bureau of Business Research, 1971.

Cox, Jeff. "They Go to Court to Protect the Environment." *Organic Gardening and Farming* (September 1970):78–81.

De Groot, Ido, et al. "People and Air Pollution: A Study in Buffalo, New York." *Journal of Air Pollution Control* 16 (May 1966):245–247.

De Groot, Ido. "Trends in Public Attitudes Toward Air Pollution." *Journal of Air Pollution Control* 17 (October 1967):679–681.

Duncan, Otis Dudley. "From Social System to Ecosystem." *Sociological Inquiry* 31 (Spring 1961):140–149.

Environmental Quality. The First Annual Report of the Council on Environmental Quality, Washington, D.C.: U.S. Government Printing Office, August, 1970.

Esposito, John C. *Vanishing Air.* New York: Grossman, 1970.

Farhar, Barbara C. "The Impact of The Rapid City Flood on Public Opinion About Weather Modification." *Pacific Sociological Review* 19 (January 1976):117–144.

Farr, Lee E. "Medical Consequences of Environmental Home Noises." *Journal of the American Medical Association* 202 (October 1967):171–174.

Field, Marvin D. "The California Poll—Air Pollution." June 26, 1973.

Fisher, Joseph L. "Environmental Quality and Urban Living." In *Internal Structure of the City,* edited by Larry S. Bourne. New York: Oxford University Press, 1971, pp. 483–490.

Gilluly, Richard. "Taking Polluters to the Courts." *Science News* 98 (September 26, 1970a):273–274.

Gilluly, Richard H. "Finding a Place to Put the Heat." *Science News* 98 (August 1, 1970b):98–99.

Glass, David C., Sheldon Cohen, and Jerome E. Singer. "Urban Din Fogs the Brain." *Psychology Today* 6 (May 1973):93–99.

Goldsmith, J.R. "Effects of Air Pollution on Human Health." In *Air Pollution,* 2nd ed., edited by Arthur C. Stern. New York: Academic Press, 1968, pp. 547–615.

Graeven, David B. "The Effects of Airplane Noise on Health: An Examination of Three Hypotheses." *Journal of Health and Social Behavior* 15 (December 1974):336–343.

Hawley, Amos H. *Urban Society.* New York: Ronald, 1971.

Herridge, C.F. "Aircraft Noise and Mental Hospital Admission." *Sound* 6 (1972):32–36.

Hohm, Charles F. "A Human-Ecological Approach to the Reality and Perception of Air Pollution: The Los Angeles Case." *Pacific Sociological Review* 19 (January 1976):21–44.

Kates, Robert W. "Natural Hazard in Human Ecological Perspective: Hypotheses and Models." *Economic Geography* 47 (July 1971):438–451.

———. "The Perception of Storm Hazard on the Shores of Megalopolis." In *Environmental Perception and Behavior,* edited by David Lowenthal. Chicago: Department of Geography Research Paper No. 109, University of Chicago, 1967, pp. 60–74.

Knudsen, Vern O., and Vern C. Plane. "Model Studies of the Effects on Motor Vehicle Noise of Buildings and Other Boundaries Along Streets and Highways." Paper presented at the Acoustical Society of America, Boston, Massachusetts, April 1973.

Landau, Norman J., and Paul D. Rheingold. *The Environmental Law Handbook.* New York: Ballantine (Friends of the Earth), 1971.

Leighton, Phillip A. "Geographical Aspects of Air Pollution." *Geographical Review* 56 (1966, No. 2):151–174.

LeVere, T.E., Raymond T. Bartus, and F.D. Hart. "Electroencephalographic and Behavioral Effects of Nocturnally Occurring Jet Aircraft Sounds." *Aerospace Medicine* 43 (April 1972):384–389.

Lewis, Howard R. *With Every Breath You Take.* New York: Crown, 1965.

McClure, Paul T. *Some Projected Effects of Jet Noise on Residential Property Near Los Angeles International Airport by 1970.* Santa Monica, Calif.: Rand Corporation Report P-4083, April 1969.

McEvoy, James, and Sharon Williams. *Visual Pollution in the Lake Tahoe Basin.* Davis, Calif.: Tahoe Research Group, University of California, 1970.

Medalia, Nahum Z. "Air Pollution as a Socio-Environmental Health Problem: A Survey Report." *Journal of Health and Human Behavior* 5 (Winter 1964):154–165.

Miles, Marvin. "Floating Airport: Answer to L.A.'s Jet Noise Problem?" *Los Angeles Times,* June 4, 1972.

Miller, James D. *Effects of Noise on People.* Washington, D.C.: U.S. Environmental Protection Agency, 1971.

Mills, Clarence A. *Air Pollution and Community Health*. Boston: Christopher Publishing House, 1954.

_____ "Urban Air Pollution and Respiratory Diseases." *American Journal of Hygiene* 37 (January-May 1943):131–141.

Molotch, Harvey, and Ross C. Follett. "Air Pollution: A Sociological Perspective." *Project Clean Air Task Force Assessments.* Vol. 3. Riverside, Calif.: University of California, 1970.

"Mortality from Tornadoes, Hurricanes, and Floods." *Statistical Bulletin* 55 (December 1974):4–7.

Murch, Arvin W. "Public Concern for Environmental Pollution." *Public Opinion Quarterly* 35 (Spring 1971):100–106.

Nourse, Hugh O. "The Effect of Air Pollution on House Values." *Land Economics* (May 1967):181–189.

Pond, M. Allen "Environmental Health and the Aging Population." *American Journal of Public Health* 40 (January 1950):27–33.

Rankin, Robert E. "Air Pollution Control and Public Apathy." *Journal of Air Pollution Control* 19 (August 1969):575–579.

Revelle, Roger. "Pollution and Cities." In *Metropolitan Enigma*, edited by James Q. Wilson. Cambridge: Harvard University Press, 1968, pp. 107–120.

Ridker, Ronald G. *Economic Costs of Air Pollution*. New York: Praeger, 1967.

Roueche, Berton. *Eleven Blue Men*. Boston: Little, Brown, 1953.

Rydell, C. Peter, and Gretchen Schwarz. "Air Pollution and Urban Form: A Review of Current Literature." *Journal of the American Institute of Planners* 34 (March 1968):115–120.

Saltonsall, Richard, Jr. *Your Environment and What You Can Do About It*. New York: Walker, 1970.

Schusky, Jane. "Public Awareness and Concern with Air Pollution in the St. Louis Metropolitan Area." *Journal of Air Pollution Control* 16 (February 1966):72–76.

Sprague, Homer A., and Ruth Hagstrom. "The Nashville Air Pollution Study: Mortality Multiple Regression." *Archives of Environmental Health* 18 (April 1969):503–507.

Teller, Azriel. "Air-Pollution Abatement: Economic Rationality and Reality." *Daedalus* 96 (Fall 1967):1082–1098.

Van Arsdol, Maurice D., Jr., Georges Sabagh, and Francesca Alexander. "Reality and the Perceptions of Environmental Hazards." *Journal of Health and Human Behavior* 4 (Winter 1964):144–153.

Weisbord, Burton. *Economics of Public Health*. College Park: University of Pennsylvania Press, 1961.

Widener, Don. *Timetable for Disaster*. Los Angeles: Nash, 1970.

Zeidburg, Louis D., Robert J.M. Horton, and Emanuel Landau. "The Nashville Air Pollution Study: V. Mortality From Diseases of the Respiratory System in Relation to Air Pollution." *Archives of Environmental Health* 15 (August 1967):214–224.

Zeidburg, Louis D., Richard A. Prindle, and Emanuel Landau. "The Nashville Air Pollution Study: I. Sulfur-Dioxide and Bronchial Asthma. A Preliminary Report." *American Review of Respiratory Diseases* 84 (October 1961):489–503.

PART IV
URBAN PROBLEMS
AND THE FUTURE

12
PLANNING,
SOCIAL POLICY,
AND THE FUTURE

CONTEMPORARY URBAN PLANNING

City planning in the United States has emphasized the master plan, which sets forth the goals of a particular city. At first, plans typically evolved under the direction of a semi-independent planning commission; however, gradually planning began to be carried out by professionals under the direction of a mayor or city manager. A typical city plan contains statements and illustrations about land use and zoning, where open space and parks are or should be located, and generally presents requirements for future development and alteration of every neighborhood in the city. Recent developments in city planning have centered on *garden cities*. A garden city has a central business and civic center surrounded by residential areas, with industry located at the periphery. Surrounding the city is a greenbelt that delineates and separates the city from other cities and from rural areas. Generally these master plans have paid little attention to the social element and to the possibilities of overcoming or engendering problems.

"The planning of cities is regarded variously as an ivory-tower vision, a practical and necessary program for development, or an undesirable interference with the citizen's freedom to do as he wishes with his own property" (Thomlinson, 1969, p. 201). There are many definitions of planning but at the simplest level, *planning* is the thoughtful consideration of purposes and means to future changes. Because all planning involves value judgments, planning is political in nature. The question of whose values planners will seek to implement becomes crucial, especially if these plans either solve or engender urban problems.

Current criticism of planning questions whether the concepts and methods of civil engineering and city planning are suited to bringing about social change in a pluralistic and mobile society (Webber, 1968, p. 1093). "Our greatest potential, however, lies in our cities, which are collapsing not only because people who live in them have lost faith in their future but also because cities no longer evidence the realities of these times. Planning continues to be based on the assumption that the functions of production and transportation are the most important ones for a city to fulfill" (Theobald, 1968, p. 137).

There are three major types of planning organizations: (1) the semi-independent planning commission, (2) the executive staff agency, and (3) the legislative staff agency (Ranney, 1969, p. 49). First, planning was done by planning commissions organized to keep planning out of politics. Many cities continue to have planning commissions, but typically they are now advisory rather than decision-making bodies. The planning commission approach fell into disfavor, because it was unable to make effective plans and to carry them out. This failure led to the development of professional planning agencies and staffs. Proponents of the professional agency argue that only professionals know how to develop master plans and implement them. Along with change in orientation from semi-independent to professional staff agencies, the appointment of full-time planning directors passed from the planning commission to city manager or mayor (Ranney, 1969, p. 59).

Most planning has been carried out from a physical point of view. Some have called this *deductive planning* (Petersen, 1966). Many physical planners in staff agencies are single-purpose planners (Gilliam, 1967 p. 1142). They assume that whatever is physically planned, such as a freeway or industrial plant, affects only that part of the environment. However, if a freeway is to be built, broader concerns than moving traffic—such as disruption of neighborhoods, displacing homes, increasing air pollution, destruction of jobs, and scarring parks or scenic areas—also *could* be considered as important elements in planning. This latter perspective requires *multi-purpose planning.*

A multi-purpose orientation takes a broader view than a physical one of the process and requirements of planning. Multi-purpose planning expands the myopic world view of single-purpose planning and more realistically evaluates potential effects on the population and environment. Thus, in recent planning, there has been an attempt at coordinating public policies in a variety of spheres. This multi-purpose approach has come to be known as *inductive* or social planning. It appears to include the following (Petersen, 1966):

1. It is more concerned with process than state and it is concerned with moving from the present rather than only to some idealized future.

2. While the physical character of the city or region is important, it is only one element in a complex web of relationships in the "Social-Economic-Political City."

3. Relevant skills for planners are varied, as are problems planners must deal with; thus, demography, economics, architecture, and the full range of the social sciences are necessary in planning.

4. The choice of competing goals can be greatly facilitated by extending the principles of market and cost accounting to new uses. Thus, costs to human welfare, social welfare benefits, and so on need to be considered in decision making in regard to selection of plan goals.

Almost universally, planners desire to correct or avoid certain social and urban problems through organized, concerted, well-thought out programs. Physical planners believe that manipulation of the physical environment, along with provision of employment and recreation opportunities, will solve urban problems. Social planners and sociologists tend to stress the importance of the social milieu. Both orientations emphasize employment, but other aspects attached to physical planning remain questionable. In fact, physical design may only temporarily affect, or perhaps even hinder, social interaction. Social planners hold that citizens should be included in the planning process to assure that their needs and desires are taken into consideration. Thus, some planning involves collaborative relationships with citizens—planning *with* people rather than *for* them. From this perspective, the planner becomes a counselor-participant in community life, rather than a master planner (Goschalk and Mills, 1966).

The Planning Process[1]
Planning is a creative and conscious attempt to overcome perceived problems, rather than an immediate reaction to crisis and an effort to influence the future. As a creative, conscious effort to control future events, planning involves the following: (1) controlling events and delineating viable options (maximizing future options/alternatives); and (2) minimizing future uncertainty. It should be noted, however, that there are always unexpected or serendipitous results of planning decisions. Steps in establishing a plan include delineating the *purposes*, establishing *goals*, specifying measurable *objectives* for each goal, generating needed *information*, and determining how the plan can be *adopted* and *implemented*.

Purpose of the Plan. The purpose of the plan needs to be clearly delineated. What is to be the function of the plan? Is it a master plan for a city or a neighborhood or a program to overcome an urban problem? Many plans evolve without a clearly explicated purpose. Similar to a scientific research project, a plan will be more meaningful if its *purpose* is thought through and consistently carried out.

Goals of the Plan. Goals need to be established. That is, what are the general goals of the plan in (1) achievement, (2) performance, or (3) aspirational terms (Fitch, 1967, p. 33). Ordinarily, plans are more meaningful if goals are "doable" (Boyce, 1963 p. 250) and can be met within specified time frames. Similarly, goals need to be tested by reality.

While most changes in urban areas are related to improvements in transportation, building construction, and so on, a great deal of formal planning restricts change in the social sphere rather than facilitating it. As a result, city and urban planning may be too important to be left exclusively to planners. With their restricted world view, they have handicapped the development of the urban complex, hindered the application of new technology, virtually ignored the points of view of most citizens, and accomplished little in solving urban problems. Goals of the plan are important because they reflect value systems that set forth a possible future.

Objectives of the Plan. For each goal, specific measurable objectives need to be clearly stated and set within a specified time frame. Objectives are the mechanisms whereby goals are met and purpose of the plan fulfilled. Stating specific measurable objectives in a time frame allows a test of whether or not goals are being met and helps set priorities in the plan.

Information Collecting. Invariably, the planning process requires information. At the minimum, generation of data or information requires the following:

1. research plan preparation; formation of committees to determine data and/or surveys needed in land use, employment, education, transportation (public and private), health, and the physical, social and economic environment, and urban problems;

2. research (assessment of conditions by means of inventory, surveys, and compilation of existing data); physical environment, socioeconomic environment, public facilities, unique features, and assistance programs; and

3. analysis; review and consideration of findings.

Plan Adoption. Different mechanisms are necessary for plan adoption, depending on purposes, goals, and objectives of the plan. Obviously, the sponsoring unit will have influence over the plan adoption process. However, it needs to be noted that plan adoption does not necessarily mean that the plan will be implemented.

Plan Implementation. A plan, by virtue of its statements of goals and objectives suggests that, if in the future, specific actions are accomplished, certain events will be controlled through the exercise of viable options—that is, an urban problem will be solved, expectations of the future will be met. One major problem in all plans is that there are unanticipated factors that will mitigate every expectation of the plan being perfectly met. Indeed, occasionally there are instances of completely opposite results being accomplished. And a plan sometimes creates more problems than it has solved.

Participation in the Planning Process. Who should participate in the planning process? It should be noted that the participants in the planning process are important because planners, as opposed to citizens, may bring varying perspectives and values and may make different assumptions about the planning process and desired outcomes. Typically, planners and specialists oriented towards physical planning are primary participants in the planning process. Recently citizens have had some input in planning decisions.

Professional planners emphasize the *physical environment*. In doing so, they believe that their assumptions and values represent those of the public for whom they are doing planning. Standards and objectives similarly are assumed to be those desired and wanted by the general public, or at least by vested interests. All these assumptions are made on the basis of limited and sometimes contrary evidence.

Citizen participation in planning involves certain assumptions and values.[2] First, it assumes that citizens can make creative input into the planning process. It should be noted that citizens come to the planning process with fewer constraints than planners and thus are not as limited in what they believe may or may not be included in a plan. Citizen involvement almost invariably means a lessened focus on the physical environment and primary focus on the *social* and *economic environment* and the solution of urban problems.

An assumption of citizen involvement in planning is that primary attention must be given to the needs, desires, and goals of the people involved. In one plan, the following assumptions were paramount (Armstrong and Butler, 1974, p. 24–26):

1. People have the right to participate in decisions which affect their well-being.

2. Participatory democracy is a useful method of conducting community affairs.

3. People have the right to strive to create an environment which they desire.

4. People have the right to reject an externally imposed environment.

5. Maximizing human interaction in a community will increase the potential for humane community development.

6. Effective community planning assists human beings in meeting and dealing with their environment.

A corollary of these assumptions is that, if citizens have the right to participate in decisions that may have an effect on their well-being, then mechanisms must be prepared to facilitate participation. In a plan developed with citizen participation there may be a need for a facilitator. The major role of a facilitator is to motivate citizens to look at their total environment to see how it might be enhanced or improved. The facilitator encourages people to analyze their situation and set goals and objectives that provide a basis for future planning and for changing their physical and social environment and solving urban problems.

Planning with citizen participation, in accordance with realistic community goals and objectives, requires a common understanding among citizens and governmental agencies. One mechanism to assure the best possible recommendations for improvement is to form citizen advisory committees that represent various population elements.

A citizen advisory committee will, of necessity, spend many hours in meetings, gathering materials, making and evaluating recommendations, and carrying out the research inventory and planning effort. When citizens of different backgrounds, interests, and cultures come together, they bring to the total a wealth of variety. Although it may be difficult to achieve a situation where citizen participation in public decision-making is open to all interested persons, effort can be made to involve those people most concerned or directly affected by decisions. The belief that broadened representation and increased breadth of perspective are conducive to community planning can have a major impact on the outcome of a plan and may lead to more extensive community involvement.

It is important that mechanisms be instituted so that no viewpoint is excluded from the planning process. One mechanism for facilitating citizen participation is to hold community workshops *in the local neighborhood*. Workshops can help determine the main problems facing residents, develop suggestions for solving problems, determine the adequacy of services and facilities in the community, outline needed services and current needs, and evaluate how residents view public officials and their concern about the neighborhood. An important function of workshops would be to provide a forum for elected officials, the mayor, councilmen, assemblymen, agency personnel, and others living outside the neighborhood. These people could be asked to attend workshops and answer the same questions as do residents. Additional workshops might deal primarily with possible *solutions* to urban problems elicited in earlier workshops.

Data or Information. A variety of research reports, commission reports, and especially reports compiled by city planning departments, and population and housing data from the U.S. Census Bureau make possible both an analysis of the demographic composition of the community and some evaluation of the extent of some urban problems—for example, unemployment, underemployment, education deficiencies, and the extent of poverty. Such information can serve only as a guide, since planning is both value-laden and normative. The combination of values held by residents of a community will influence which kinds of information should be gathered. Laymen are often not aware of the existence of additional sources of data, such as government data books and reports. Such data can be distributed to citizens, so that the quality of citizen input is enhanced.

Data can be inserted into ongoing decision-making processes in a way that does not impair the process of search and discovery by citizens.

Future Planning

Future planning will involve many issues that some thought had been resolved in the past and others that are just now emerging. Among these issues are: (1) continuation of the physical versus social planning controversy; (2) optimum city-size and density of areas within cities and urban regions; (3) the question of whether cities should be compact or should be allowed to continue to sprawl; (4) boundary integrity and maintenance, especially as it affects solutions to urban problems; (5) the extent to which citizen participation should be encouraged and facilitated; (6) a revival of the controversy over where planning agencies and staff should be located—as staff agencies under the city manager or mayor, as semi-independent agencies, or as completely independent agencies; and (7) acquisition of funds for planning and implementation.

The struggle between physical and social planners is in its infancy; over the next several decades this struggle will become intensified. If problems facing cities and urban regions are to be solved, it will be necessary for social planners to win this struggle.

Discussion of optimum city-size began during the days of early Greek philosophers. The solution is no closer to being found now than it was then. Optimum city-size and density both rely on adherence to certain value systems and beliefs. As such, the perfect optimum city-size will depend on such factors as whether compact cities come into being or whether sprawl continues as it has in the recent past, on developing transportation technologies, and so forth. Thus, it should be apparent that this is a controversy that is expected to continue well into the future.

Arguments against urban sprawl center around increased costs of serving a more scattered population versus costs of serving a more compact population (Boyce, 1963, p. 245). However, sprawl also has advantages. It includes more open space, has lower population density, allows commercial and industrial development in outlying areas to be more accessible to a larger population, and has more development flexibility (Boyce, 1963). A corollary of a compact city is high density. Most people still opt for privacy and a place for children to play when given the opportunity, and thus they select relatively low dense suburban living as opposed to higher density apartment living (Michelson, 1970, p. 143). Future city designs now in development stress compact cities, and perhaps public antipathy for high density living will abate.

Local boundaries within larger metropolitan and urban regions have become more and more meaningless for human activities. Thus, attempts to deal with urban problems on a boundary basis will probably fail. As a result, more and more planning is being accomplished on a *regional* basis. There is substantial resistance to regional planning, because many smaller jurisdictions are wary of losing local control over planning.

Despite legal requirements of some legislation, citizen participation in planning activities to date has been rather slight. Many cities have had pseudo-citizen participation, forming committees or commissions and occasionally holding public hearings—generally at hours at which the general population is at work and unable to attend. Thus, to date citizen participation in planning endeavors has been minimal. This minimal participation may be a result of a lack of interest or it may be that the proper facilitating mechanisms have not been established for effective citizen participation. In many cities citizens are demanding and receiving the opportunity for input into planning. This pressure is expected to continue and to grow.

In the future, there will be pressures to remove planning functions from the executive of the city to a semi-independent agency or to a completely independent agency. Urban research shows that when effective, creative, innovative plans are successful, they are *not* originated by city officials but are a result of a coalition of individual citizens who band together to pressure city hall (*Citizens*, 1973). It may be assumed that if creative and innovative planning is to be accomplished, different mechanisms will have to be developed to remove planning from staff agencies and the city executive's office. Otherwise, static master plans that will not help solve the crisis of our cities will continue to be generated.

Ample funds are available in the United States for developing meaningful plans for and by citizens. However, it will be necessary to re-order priorities, to evaluate where current expenditures are fulfilling real needs, to evaluate all programs to determine if they are efficient *and* meeting real human needs, and to eliminate unneeded and ineffective services, if these funds are to be reallocated and efficiently used. In the future, it appears that programs at all levels will be required to demonstrate the basic *need* for the program, that the program is meeting needs effectively, and that some desirable outcomes are being generated. This means that planning agencies will be required to demonstrate the need for planning, that the planning has accomplished its goals and objectives, and that it has led to desired outcomes—as evaluated by power leaders, planners, or citizens, or some combination of these.

FUTURE CITIES

A number of perspectives have been developed that could influence the future city. Among them are the perspectives of Le Corbusier, who has already extensively influenced contemporary cities, and of Soleri, Jane Jacobs, Abrams, and compact city adherents.

Le Corbusier (1967) influenced the work of all serious contemporary architects and city planners (Anthony, 1966, p. 279). "With his elevated highways and stilted buildings, Le Corbusier was the first man to develop fully and defend the theme of complete separation of vehicular from pedestrian traffic, the first man to treat the pedestrian with the respect and honor we now accord only to the automobile" (p. 279). He advocated freeing the ground of cities for pedestrians by lifting buildings and roads above ground level with the whole ground level becoming large uninterrupted parks. His vision was of tall buildings within self-contained areas, with a proposed density of three hundred persons per acre and an optimum population of three million persons. All land in the city would be public property, in order to avoid land speculation and facilitate the city's organic and logical development (Anthony, 1966, p. 281). Le Corbusier's ideas have been utilized in such existing cities as Brasilia and Chandigarh (capital of Punjab, India) and in sections of other cities. Most models of future cities include Le Corbusier's ideas, ignoring, as he did, problems of *costs* and *individual preferences* (Le Corbusier, 1967).

A compact rearrangement of space is Soleri's (1969) means of bringing beauty, harmony, efficiency, and spaciousness to cities. He believes that *miniaturization* is the key to all life and that current cities violate this principle. Cities must become compact to reduce time and space obstacles to human activity. Following principles of miniaturization and utilization of the third dimension he calls *verticality*, once again homo sapiens will be in tune with nature and the natural evolutionary patterns of miniaturization that are being violated in today's cities.

One of the most ardent critics of most city planning practices is Jane Jacobs (1961). She criticizes current city planning practice on the basis of its uncritical acceptance of the open space concept and asks "more open space for what?" She feels that for open space to be useful, it must be used by ordinary people. One of the most important conditions for a lively, active, safe city, according to Jacobs, is the assurance of an intricate and close-grained utilization of streets, open spaces, and other public places that give each other constant mutual support, both economically and socially. City diversity is the keystone on which she believes lively neighborhoods are built. According to Jacobs, "diversity itself persists and stimulates more diversity." From this perspective, supermarkets, delicatessens, bakeries, foreign groceries, and so on, all make up a diverse neighborhood just as much as do movie houses, art museums, and so on. Diverse people and diverse elements in the city keep it from the "Great Blight of Dullness."

An attempt at bringing together the Le Corbusier, Jacobs, and Soleri perspectives was carried out by Dantzig and Saaty (1973). Space and time, they note, cut across all perspectives of city planning, of utopian communities, and of cities proposed by Le Corbusier, Jacobs, and Soleri. For example, Los Angeles currently utilizes approximately 35 percent of its land surface for transportation related use; if Los Angeles were "stacked" vertically, its land surface would correspondingly shrink, depending on the height of the stack. This vertical stress would make the city more compact. Similarly, they note that most, if not all, human activities take place within a time rhythm or cycle. Joining time and space dimensions should allow a more meaningful compact city to be contructed. This concept brings into play the views of Le Corbusier and Soleri, but also allows the diversity so dear to Jacobs.

The general plan for a compact city includes a population base of 250,000 residing in an area of 2.2 square miles. The city could have a radius of 3,000 feet with a population of 250,000 or 4,420 feet with a population of two million persons. "The shape chosen is circular with a radius eighteen times its height" (p. 37). Such a compact city would have five distinct rings: (1) core, (2) core edge, (3) inner residential area, (4) mid-plaza, and (5) outer residential area. The core contains shops, churches, hotels, and elements ordinarily thought of as being associated with the core of a city. The core edge would serve primarily as a parking area and would contain ramps for ascending and descending to various levels. Also, the core edge would have a promenade, with small parks and recreational areas. Beyond the inner residential area would be the mid-plaza, which would provide local facilities such as elementary schools, clinics, neighborhood shops, and play areas. Connecting the outer residential area, as well as all of the other areas, are two-way roadways that radiate from the core edge like spokes of a wheel; cross streets are alternating one-way roads. Automobiles would be electric-powered but probably would not be used very much because of the compactness of the city. Advantages of the compact city would be more available time and opportunity because of the increased accessibility to all parts of the city and because the city would fit the rhythm of the people who live there. Criticisms of the compact city approach revolve around the extensive crowding and increased density of population, lack of sunlight, sameness, and vulnerability. Each criticism, of course, involves a value judgment about how one should live. Dantzig and Saaty believe that the potential benefits make the negative consequences pale in comparison.

Another set of themes was proposed by Abrams (1965, pp. 287 ff). He enumerated a series of points that he believes would bring about more desirable future urban environments. Among them are the following:

1. Cities should set an example of better design and comfort in publicly assisted improvements.

2. Cities should utilize the natural features within the city and reclaim them wherever possible. Most cities in the United States were originally blessed with good landscapes and waterscapes that should be restored.

3. Cities should increase the number of trees, parks, and green

spaces. Street trees and small parks supply reprieve from the steel and cement facades that dominate cityscapes. It should be noted that trees serve not only aesthetic purposes but also provide ventilation and shade, absorb noise and dust. Recent evidence suggests that trees also can help reduce air pollution and help improve city weather.

4. Cities should be made more attractive for tourism, diversion, and leisure.

5. Cities must salvage the central business districts. Without the central business district there are only neighborhoods, and with only neighborhoods there is no contrast and no alternative, no easy escape and no real freedom of movement. Cities with pulsating downtowns are thought of as cities throughout the world. A downtown area lives or dies as a whole and not piecemeal, as many people and single-purpose planners prefer to believe.

6. Cities must build up existing neighborhoods rather than destroying them.

7. Cities should leave room for people to contribute to their own environment. Most current projects in the United States, because of their large size, impose strict limitations on citizen participation. Thus, people living in a neighborhood have not had the opportunity to add their creative parts to the environment. Abrams believes that the contributions of individuals and families to neighborhoods are as important as public additions.

8. Cities should give people a sense of belonging to their neighborhoods. This does not mean, of course, that all areas within the city should become neighborhoods; some people do not want to know their neighbors and this also should be allowed. Abrams argues that various public facilities in a neighborhood should be made available to the people living there; for example, the public school should serve multiple functions—not only as a place for educating children but also as a social meeting place, a theatre, a dance center, and a forum.

9. Cities should encourage "commercial clustration" and reinforce existing clusters. A cluster can be a wholesale or retail center, it can be an area where the focal point is the purchase of wares, entertainment, or services. It can be an area of antique shops, second-hand book shops, art/movie areas, and so forth. Whatever these clusters may be, Abrams believes that they should not only be allowed but encouraged to exist and to give variety to the city.

10. The city should be made a center for adult education. The reduction of working hours and availability of more free time, longer life span, increasing technology, and preparation of married women for tasks outside the home all imply a greater need for adult education opportunities.

11. Cities need to develop a *realistic* mass transportation program. As most city dwellers are aware, no city in the United States currently has developed an efficient, integrated mass transportation program.

12. Cities should enhance their walkability. One of the major elements of the cities that are thought of as cities—for example, Rome, London, and Paris—is that they have many walkable sections. Few U.S. cities are considered walkable cities.

13. Cities should be made more liveable for females. Current U.S. cities inhibit females and as a result the city has lost population because it has lost the confidence of the female—as one seeking love, as a wife, a career woman, and a mother.

14. Cities must improve public schools.

15. Cities should concentrate more effort on improving the environment for children. There are few playgrounds and few parks, and so pavements and sidewalks have become play spaces because they happen to be there. In the overall delineation of priorities, children's needs are forgotten and space left for them is minute. Abrams believes that one reason for this lack of concern with children is that most city planning deals with the housing environment while ignoring the neighborhood. If the city is to be a better place for children, it must be a better place for everyone.

According to Abrams, these factors "require a change in the nation's philosophy" (p. 361). The new philosophy must acknowledge that there are values worth preserving in cities, as there are in the suburbs. The new philosophy must acknowledge that the central city and suburb are entities that depend on each other for job opportunities, services, recreation, escape, variety and progress. The new philosophy needs to redefine state and federal functions in fulfilling the general welfare, which includes clear and definable lines of jurisdiction between federal government, state, and local governments. The new philosophy needs to assure to all citizens the right to live wherever they choose. Similarly, the new philosophy requires that low-income families be entitled to the opportunity to own homes and to own them without fear of losing them when unemployment, illness, or death intervene. Finally, this new philosophy should be concerned with poverty as a national problem. Obviously, Abram's philosophy requires substantial *value* changes. These changes are not likely to be acceptable to most people in the United States.

SOCIAL POLICY

The urban environment in the United States is greatly influenced by various policy decisions. However, it is quite clear that no goals and objectives have been set at the national level that are consistent with the development of blueprints for future U.S. cities and for solving urban problems. The 1949 housing act came closest to defining a goal for future cities when it promised a suitable living environment for every family in the United States, although no time frame was given. No other readily discernible goals and objectives are available, although in a variety of programs there are frequent references to community renewal and redevelopment and, of course, most communities have developed master plans. Nevertheless, few plans have specifically stated goals and objectives moving toward the future.

"The latent model in most planning and most considerations of the future city is curiously restricted to the traditional version of the multipurpose city—a static conglomeration of commercial enterprise, industrial production, and distribution points related to material transportation and warehousing" (McHale, 1968, p. 90). However, the future city may stop evolving as a multifunctional aggregate as it has in the past, and it might take many special forms for varied social purposes. Currently in urban society there is a proliferation of life styles that require an increasing number of different social environments. This increasing range and flexibility of urban life styles is a key issue in the development of future cities and the solution of future urban problems.

Another problem is that both wittingly and unwittingly some city rulers exploit the city and its inhabitants with public investments that are costly and wasteful (Long, 1972, pp. 159–160). Rather, they should be investing in making the local economy viable; a local economy that does not support itself is, in fact, living on welfare. Thus, cities need to "pursue a vigorous policy to restore the viability" of local economies, to rid themselves of economic dependence and become trading partners with equal stature.

To accomplish a goal of independence and economic viability, a city needs to undertake a "systematic inventory of its assets and its liabilities. A start can be made by inventorying the employed and employable population" (Long, 1972, p. 162). The state of employment is one of the most single important facts about a city. One of the most important tasks that can be undertaken in a city is to improve the rate of employment in that city. The rate of unemployment in a city is related to inadequate housing. Long (1972, p. 170) believes that a realistic approach to the housing problem in cities has only three real alternatives: (1) increase people's incomes, (2) decrease housing costs, and/or (3) review the standards of housing decency (in the United States it would be downward).

Long (1972, p. 162) says that "It seems scarcely credible that, after all the funds that have been spent on planning, the city should still lack an inventory of its human resources." Further, city expenditures in planning, health, education, and other services may not only prove unproductive but in some instances, counterproductive; thus, services, their costs, and their outcomes need to be seriously examined but rarely have been.

Few cities have examined the future in terms of realistic potential opportunity for utilizing their economic, manpower, and physical resources. For example, in some locations, one potential utilization is in health care. As Long (1972, pp. 180–181) has said:

The health industry also offers a major opportunity to utilize the city's unused and underutilized plant. Nursing homes, geriatric care, child care—all the health services that require nursing and some medical supervision can, in principle, make use of the city's stock of apartments and large older buildings. If the city would both promote the development and stringently supervise the quality of the services, it could command a growing, better met market for this kind of health care. As a health center with a rounded complement of capabilities, from multiphasic automated health-testing to produce economies of scale with medical parks and residence neighborhoods for doctors, nurses, technicians, and other employees to research and development efforts mounted by universities, hospitals, and industry to produce new bioelectronic and other technology, the city has a major interest in pushing health and the health industry as a major use of its people, plant, and location.[3]

Other opportunities exist, but without evaluating the need, without an inventory of its human resources, and an orientation toward effective social planning, these potential opportunities cannot be fulfilled.

While it is potentially possible to carry out some of the ideas advanced about the solution of urban problems, it is highly unlikely that such solutions will be made in your lifetime. Some elements, to be sure, may be changed, but the massive changes implied by all of the urban problems surveyed in this book require at least the following: (1) spending beyond imagination—much more than the 160 billion dollars of the Vietnam war; (2) overcoming the hold that traditional physical planning concepts have on planners, city officials, and the general public; (3) eliminating rigid value systems and attitudes; (4) developing economic incentives for individuals and cities to readjust their thinking about what cities can and should be like; (5) recognizing that all of the above are ingrained in the dominant value system of the population in the United States and appear highly resistant to change; and (6) recognizing that while the basic technological knowledge may exist to overcome problems, the ability to resolve the political conflicts of interest does not currently exist (Nelson, 1974).

The last two points are the most important ones. They stress that in the United States there has not been a substantial commitment to solving urban problems, constructing new cities, or altering the environment in a really meaningful manner, because funds are spent elsewhere, presumably for higher priority items. Overcoming the traditional emphasis on physical planning with a neglect of the social has made some progress. Nevertheless, the real test will come when it is necessary to commit economic resources to carry out social plans. Currently, for example, millions of dollars of revenue sharing allocations are spent on capital expenditures—for example, buildings; virtually no revenue sharing resources are spent on social planning or social services.[4] This is true even though revenue sharing funds are perhaps the only resources cities and counties receive that are available for both kinds of expenditures.

Finally, it should be noted that any realistic assessment of the next few decades cannot depend on or assume that there will be substantial changes in the composition of the central city, because it is highly unlikely that the minorities and the aged of cities will change drastically nor will the problems facing them in the future change remarkably. Thus, any discussion of solutions of urban problems is fruitless without recognizing the realities of future urban trends.

PROSPECTS

If present urban trends continue until the year 2000, water and air will be dangerously polluted. Such an increase of pollution at rates now characterizing larger cities will make relatively pure air and water among the most scarce and costly of all natural resources. In addition, traffic congestion will be horrendous. Similarly, open space close to where people live will become so scarce that the use of park and other recreational facilities will have to be rationed. If current trends continue, central cities will become more segregated than ever. Most of them will contain a majority of minorities and the aged, while suburban areas will be virtually all white. Slums in central cities will continue to expand and be the gathering ground for minorities, the aged, and other disadvantaged people.

Some larger cities will have the appearance of being "ungovernable" (Perloff, 1967). The gap between suburban communities and central cities with all their problems, including limited tax capacity, will be greater than ever. Some new towns will be built that will cluster around major metropolitan areas, providing an attractive environment for residents. But increasingly they will be beyond the reach of lower- and middle-income families. In addition, there will be impressive greenbelts to keep "undesirables" out of certain parts of the city. New superhighways, parking structures, and so forth, will cut cities to ribbons, and yet transportation will continue to be a major headache. This view of the future is based on the assumption that current trends will continue into the future. The grossest failures probably will be recognized as such and possibly some changes will be made, though it is relatively certain that some *conditions will get worse*.

Perloff (1967) believes that if urban problems are to be solved in the future city, certain kinds of questions are going to have to be asked. Among these questions are: How much do we believe in having unpolluted resources such as water and air? Should one-half to two-thirds of urban land be used for the movement and storage of cars and if so, where are streets to be placed—underground, on the surface, or above ground? The last consideration is a very important one: What is to happen to the space over urban land? That is, how high can buildings be built? Should highways and airways be allowed over the ground? And to what extent can polluted air be allowed? Similarly, questions are going to have to be asked about the degree to which water should be clean or unpolluted for consumption, recreation, and production purposes.

Perloff stresses that it will take tremendous resources, imaginative new solutions, and effective political in-fighting to reverse or to make a dent in the problem of ghettos and slums in cities. At this point, the necessary resources are not forthcoming, new solutions have not been thought of, and no one is willing to do the political in-fighting necessary to reverse present trends. The creation of new communities and new towns would broaden the alternatives that many people have to live in a diverse urban life style (Cook, 1968). Nevertheless, it also should be emphasized that new towns and new communities almost universally are beyond the economic resources of middle- and lower-class families.

Projections of future U.S. urban population growth suggest that by the year 2000 about 90 percent of the 350 to 400 million people in the United States will be living within existing metropolitan regions (Cook, 1968, p. 83). There will be two continuous urban conurbations along the East and West coasts and strip cities along the Gulf Coast, the Great Lakes, and possibly along the Rocky Mountains, with Denver as the nucleus (Pickard, 1967 and 1968).

One possibility for taking care of this expanding population, and a population increasingly living in urban complexes, is to develop planned and scattered metropolitan regions. One possibility focuses on the development of between 100 and 500 "metrocities" throughout the United States (Cook, 1968). These cities could be developed on federal public domain lands in the western states and the interstate highway system would be an effective link between them.

The cost of cities with an average population of one million would border at least around $1,000 billion—a large sum, yet not as much as the costs for a total urban renewal effort. According to Cook (p. 86), this program, if imaginatively executed, could do the following:

1. increase the efficiency of the economy by adapting production to market areas rather than tying it to natural resource deposits or cheap transportation areas;

2. create millions of new property owners, jobs, and entrepreneurial opportunities;

3. decentralize the concentrated pattern of decision-making now prevalent in our society;

4. compete with existing cities and metropolitan areas, thereby accelerating action for massive improvement in older major cities, as well as slowing their growth by attracting part of their population to new urban centers;

5. distribute minority groups more evenly throughout the United

States, and provide new ground-floor opportunities for the disadvantaged to participate in the economy.

It is highly unlikely that such innovative programs will be undertaken in the future. Thus, my conclusion is that most of the urban problems discussed in this book will be with us for the rest of our lifetimes.

NOTES

1. Much of this section is a revision of material presented in Armstrong and Butler (1974).

2. For a bibliography on citizen participation, see Hunt (1973).

3. From *The Unwalled City: Reconstructing The Urban Community* by Norton E. Long, © 1972 by Basic Books, Inc., Publishers, New York.

4. For most recent reports, see the 1975 volumes of *General Revenue Sharing* publications, Research Applied to National Needs, National Science Foundation.

REFERENCES

Abrams, Charles. *The City Is The Frontier*. New York: Harper & Row, 1965.

Anthony, Harry A. "LeCorbusier: His Ideas for Cities." *Journal of the American Institute of Planners* 32 (September 1966):279–288.

Armstrong, DeVonne W., and Edgar W. Butler, *Eastside Community Plan*. Riverside, California: City of Riverside, January, 1974.

Boyce, Ronald R. "Myth Versus Reality in Urban Planning." *Land Economics* 39 (August 1963):241–251.

Citizens Make the Difference: Case Studies of Environmental Action. Washington, D.C.: Citizen's Advisory Committee on Environmental Quality, 1973.

Cook, Daniel W. "Cosmopolis: A New Cities Proposal." *New Mexico Quarterly* 38 (Summer 1968):83–89.

Dantzig, George B., and Thomas L. Saaty. *Compact City: A Plan For a Liveable Urban Environment*. San Francisco: W.H. Freeman and Company, 1973.

Fitch, Lyle C. "Social Planning in the Urban Cosmos." In *Urban Research and Policy Planning*, edited by Leo F. Schnore and Henry Fagin. Beverly Hills, Calif.: Sage, 1967, pp. 329–358.

Gilliam, Harold. "The Fallacy of Single-Purpose Planning." *Daedalus* 96 (Summer 1967):1142–1157.

Goschalk, David R., and William E. Mills. "A Collaborative Approach to Planning Through Urban Activities." *Journal of the American Institute of Planners* 32 (March 1966): 86–95.

Hunt, Gerard J. *Citizen Participation in Health and Mental Health Programs: A Review of Selected Literature and State Community Mental Health Service Acts*. Arlington, Virginia: National Association of Mental Health, 1973.

Jacobs, Jane. *The Death and Life of Great American Cities*. New York: Random House, 1961.

Le Corbusier, *The Radiant City*. New York: Grossman-Orion Press, 1967 (English translation of the 1933 French version).

Long, Norton E. *The Unwalled City: Reconstituting the Urban Community*. New York: Basic Books, 1972.

McHale, John. "The Future City(s): Notes on a Typology." *New Mexico Quarterly* 38 (Summer 1968):90–97.

Michelson, William H. *Man and His Urban Environment: A Sociological Approach*. Reading, Mass.: Addison-Wesley, 1970.

Nelson, Richard R. "Intellectualizing About the Moon-Ghetto Metaphor: A Study of the Current Malaise of Rational Analysis of Social Problems." *Policy Sciences* 5 (1974): 375–414.

Perloff, Harvey S. "Modernizing Urban Development." *Daedalus* 96 (Summer 1967): 789–800.

Petersen, William. "On Some Meanings of 'Planning.' " *Journal of the American Institute of Planners* 32 (May 1966):130–142.

Pickard, Jerome P. *Dimensions of Metropolitanism.* Research Monograph 14 and 14A. Washington, D.C.: Urban Land Institute, 1967 and 1968.

Ranney, David C. *Planning and Politics in the Metropolis.* Columbus, Ohio: Charles E. Merrill, 1969.

Soleri, Paolo. *Arcology, The City in the Image of Man.* Cambridge, Mass.: MIT Press, 1969.

Spilhaus, Athelstan. "The Experimental City." *Daedalus* 96 (Winter 1967):1129–1141.

Theobald, Robert. *An Alternative Future for America.* Chicago: Swallow Press, 1968.

Thomlinson, Ralph. *Urban Structure.* New York: Random House, 1969.

Webber, Melvin M. "The Post-City Age." *Daedalus* 97 (Fall 1968):1091–1110.

NAME
INDEX

A

Abey-Wickrama, M., 194, 199
Abrams, C., 212, 214, 215, 216, 221
Abudu, M., 177, 179
Abu-Laban, B., 96, 99
Abu-Lughod, J., 48, 66
Adrian, C., 95, 99
Agger, R., 86, 99
Aiken, M., 97, 99
Aldrich, H., 56, 66
Alexander, F., 12, 201
Alford, R., 97, 99
Allen, M., 90, 99
Altenderfer, M., 143, 155
Anthony, H., 213, 221
Anton, T., 88, 99
Antonovsky, A., 142, 144, 155
Armstrong, D., 209, 221
Atelsek, F., 67
Auerbach, I., 188, 199
Axelrod, M., 19, 20, 24, 30
Ayres, R., 183, 199

B

Babchuk, N., 23, 30
Bachrach, P., 97, 99

Baller, W., 154, 155
Baratz, M., 97, 99
Barber, B., 23, 30
Barclay, W., 49, 66
Barth, E., 128, 138
Bartus, R., 200
Bauer, M., 145, 155
Becker, H., 11, 12
Belknap, G., 94
Belknap, I., 148, 155
Bell, R., 19, 30
Bell, W., 19, 23, 24, 28, 30, 47, 67
Berado, F., 21, 30
Berger, S., 65, 66
Berkowtiz, W. R., 179
Beyer, G., 129, 138
Bhak, A., 62, 66
Bierstedt, R., 99
Blankenship, L. V., 88, 99
Bloom, H., 99
Bluestone, B., 124, 125, 138
Blumberg, L., 19, 30
Boggs, S., 166, 167, 179
Bollens, J., 17, 30, 103, 105, 112, 113, 115, 119
Bonjean, C., 87, 99
Booth, A., 20, 21, 24, 30
Booth, D., 95, 99
Borsky, P., 199

Massoti, L., 172, 179
Maurer, J., 156
Mazur, A., 174, 180
McAllister, R., 30, 155, 156, 199
McClosky, H., 29, 31
McClure, P., 195, 200
McCord, W., 130, 139
McDonald, L., 67
McEvoy, J., 198, 200
McHale, J., 217, 221
McKay, H., 162, 167, 168, 171, 180
McKee, J., 96, 100
McPherson, I. M., 81
Meadow, K., 19, 22, 31
Mechanic, D., 145, 156
Medalia, N., 185, 200
Menzel, H., 11, 12
Mercer, J., 142, 156
Merton, R., 3, 12
Michael, S., 12, 156
Michelson, W., 77, 81, 211, 221
Miles, M., 195, 200
Miller, C., 27, 31
Miller, D. C., 87, 100
Miller, J., 194, 200
Mills, C. W., 88–89, 100, 111, 119
Mills, C. A., 188, 189, 201
Mills, W. E., 207, 221
Mitchell, G. D., 30
Mitchell, R. E., 77, 81
Mizruchi, E., 26, 31
Molotch, H., 185, 201
Moore, J., 45, 66
"Mortality . . ." 197, 201
Moynihan, D. P., 127, 139
Mullen, F., 153, 154, 156
Mumford, L., 41, 45
Munger, F., 93–94, 100
Murch, A., 186, 201
Myers, R., 11, 12
Myrdal, G., 23, 31

N

National Academy of Sciences, 44, 45
Neal, A., 29, 31
Nelsen, H., 26, 31
Nelson, J., 26, 31
Nelson, R. R., 218, 221

Nettler, G., 29, 31
Nie, M., 153, 154, 156
Nisbet, R., 3, 12, 14, 16, 31
Nohara, S., 21, 31
Nourse, H., 191, 201
Novak, E., 30

O

Obserschall, A., 172, 180
Offner, P., 125, 139
Ogburn, W., 160, 161
Opler, M., 12, 156, 180
Orshansky, M., 122, 126, 127, 139

P

Palen, J., 178, 180
Palisi, B., 21, 32
Passonneau, J., 36, 45
Patno, M., 143, 156
Patten, F., 30, 138
Paulson, W., 110, 112, 119
Pellegrin, R., 90, 100
Performance of Urban Functions: Local and Areawide, 108, 119
Perloff, H., 219, 222
Petersen, W., 206, 222
Pickard, J., 220, 222
Pinard, M., 112, 119
Plane, V., 193, 200
Polk, K., 180
Polsby, N., 88, 101
Pond, M. A., 201
Pope, H., 119
Preston, J., 87, 100
Prindle, R., 201
Pugh, T., 151, 157

Q

Queen, S. A., 148, 156
Quinn, J., 47, 67

R

Raine, W., 179
Rainwater, L., 131, 139

SUBJECT
INDEX

General Social Welfare (GSW), 109
Geographical mobility, 25
Ghetto, 19, 21, 39, 71, 72, 121, 176.
    See also Segregation, Slums
"Governing class," 90
Government-insured jobs, 125
Green spaces, 214–215

H

Health industry, 217
Home owners, 128
Hoover-Vernon model, 48
Housing Act of 1949, 130, 131, 216
Housing, 3, 4, 73, 127–137, 217. *See
    also* Urban renewal, Segregation
Housing and Urban Development
    Act of 1968, 130
Housing Assistance Administration,
    130
Housing authorities, 130–131

I

Illnesses, 3, 145–151, 183, 189
Immigrants, 24, 129. *See also*
    Segregation
Immigrant populations, 38–39
Immigration, 70–71
Independent units, 105
Index of dissimilarity, 156
"Index of riot severity," 177
Inductive planning, 206–207
Industrialization, 14, 17, 144, 161
Industrial Revolution, 16, 35
Industrial site selection, 111
Infant deaths, 74, 75–76. *See also*
    Mortality
Infant mortality rates, 134, 141
Inner city, 4, 19, 23–24, 40, 41, 90,
    121, 129, 133. *See also* Central
    business district
Institutional control, 161
Institutional leaders, 94
Institutional racism, 51
Instrumental organizations, 22
Interest groups, 91
Interlocking directorates, 92

Interstate highway system, 116
Isolation, 14, 78
Issues, selection of, 96–97

J

Job models, 126
Job training, 125, 127
Jurisdiction, 107–108
Juvenile delinquency, 134, 162, 164

K

Kinship networks, 18–20

L

Land use, 39, 41, 121
Land zoning, 78
Law enforcement, 114–115. *See also*
    Police
Legal codes, 64, 104
Life styles, 18, 23, 217
Living environment, 216
Local community, and conflict with
    corporations, 90
Local economy, 217
Local government, 103, 104–106
Locally conducted survey of
    agencies, as sources of data, 10
Longitudinal studies, 10, 167
Low-income families, 132, 135

M

Manufacturing base, 94
Mass culture, 15
Mass society, 3, 14–17, 25
Medical care, 143, 145
Medical practice, 144
Medical services, 145
Megalopolis, 16
Mental illness, 146–151
Mental retardation, 151
Metropolitanism, 40
Metropolitan regions, 90

Metropolitan Water District of
Southern California, 113
Mexican-Americans 41, 59–61
Middle class, 19, 122
Middletown Study of Mental Health
in the Metropolis (1962), 9
Migration
from abroad, 38–39
rural to urban, 36, 38, 72
of southern blacks to northern
urban centers, 26, 51, 72
to suburbs, 39
Miniaturization, 213
Minorities, 128
Model Cities Program, 130
Monolithic power, 109, 111
Monolithic power elites, 98
Morbidity, 187
Morbidity rate, 134
Mortality, 3, 36, 142–144, 183, 187
Mortality rate, 35
Multiple nuclei theory, 47
Multi-purpose city, 217
Multi-purpose orientation, 206
Municipal governments, 38
Municipal services, 37, 71
Municipalities, 103, 105
as geographic units, 104
Mutual aid assistance, 19

N

Native Americans, 50
Neighborhood, 17–18, 176, 210, 215
Neighboring, 20–22, 134. See also
Friendship patterns
Noise pollution, 193–196
Nonwhites, 122–123. See also Blacks,
Mexican-Americans, Native
Americans
Normlessness, 25

O

Occupational discrimination, 50
Occupational mobility, 125, 126
Operating costs, factors of, 106
"Opinion-molding associations," 89

Optimum city size, 211
Organization participation, 22–24
Organizations, types of, 22
Overcrowding, 71, 74. See also
Population density
and individual milieu, 80
and juvenile delinquency, 72
and mortality, 36, 77
and psychiatric disorders, 75, 78
and slum development, 171
Owner-occupied housing, 49

P

Participant observations, as a
research method, 9
Party competition, 91
Patterned relationship, 98
Personal attribute factor, 87
Peer groups, as integrating
mechanisms, 21
Planning, 3, 211
Planning organizations, 206
Planning process, 207
Plaza, 59
Pluralisitc power, 91, 97, 109
Police, 37–38, 161, 171
population view of, 114
Police departments, 114
Police systems, 71
Policy decisions, 216
Political activities, 22
Population, 39, 70, 129
Population density, 70–79, 142, 191,
211
advantages of, 80
and land use, 3
and social pathology, 69
Population, future in U. S., 42
Population growth, 3, 104
in U. S. (1790–1970), 40
checks on, 36
urban, 37–38
Population movement, 42, 163. See
also Migration
Population policy, 43
Population structure, 191
Poverty, 3, 16, 36, 37, 112, 122–127,
142

5270